WORKSHOP TO OFFICE

Workshop to Office

Two Generations of Italian Women

in New York City, 1900–1950

MIRIAM COHEN

Cornell University Press

ITHACA AND LONDON

First published 1993 by Cornell University Press

Library of Congress Cataloging-in-Publication Data

Cohen, Miriam, 1950–
  Workshop to office : two generations of Italian women in New York
City, 1900–1950 / Miriam Cohen.
      p.   cm.
  Includes bibliographical references and index.
  ISBN 0-8014-2722-3 (alk. paper). — ISBN 0-8014-8005-1 (pbk. :
alk. paper)
    1. Italian American women—New York (N.Y.)—History—20th century.
2. Italian American Families—New York (N.Y.)—History—20th
century.   3. New York (N.Y.)—Social conditions.   I. Title.
F128.9.I8C64   1992
305.48′85107471—dc20   92-52746

Library of Congress Catalog Card Number 92-52746
Printed in the United States of America

FOR MICHAEL

CONTENTS

ILLUSTRATIONS

TABLES

ACKNOWLEDGMENTS

Many people have assisted throughout the course of this project. The original work, begun when I was a graduate student at the University of Michigan, was supported by grants from the History Department, the Graduate School, and the Woodrow Wilson National Fellowship Foundation. As an undergraduate and graduate student in American social and urban history, twentieth-century history and women's history, I profited from the extraordinary teaching of scholars such as the late Herbert Gutman, Robert Sklar, Charles Tilly, Louise Tilly, and Sam Bass Warner, Jr.

During the research stage of this project I had help from Joseph Hipius and his staff at the New York County Clerk's office, and the librarians and administrative staff at Julia Richman High School. Thanks are also due Henrietta Dabney of the Education Department of the Amalgamated Clothing Workers–Textile Workers of America and Sheila Herstein of the Russell Sage Collection for their kind assistance in locating materials. Virginia Yans-McLaughlin was very helpful in pointing the way to useful sources and records in New York City. The Vassar College librarians provided invaluable assistance in checking citations and tracking down all sorts of information. I had help coding data, assembling bibliography, photocopying, typing, and proofreading from Michael Perlman, Jason Ralston, Jeanne Schock, and Gabrielle Tenaglia. Paul Killy and Cathy Whitaker assisted with computer programming. In addition to friendship and encouragement when I needed it most, Meryl Silver and her family provided excellent accommodations during several extended stays in New York City.

A number of scholars have taken time to read this manuscript in its various forms over the years. I thank Anne Bobroff, Mary Jo Buhle, Tom Dublin, Clyde Griffen, Jacquelyn Hall, Alice Kessler-Harris, Robin Jacoby, Elizabeth Pleck, Anne Scott, Molly Shanley, Judith Smith, Mark Stern, Charles Tilly, Carole Turbin, Adelaide Villmoare, Virginia Yans-McLaughlin, as well as anonymous readers, for their advice. I am especially grateful to Louise Tilly for her wisdom, her friendship, and for the countless hours spent on this book from its inception to its completion.

At Vassar College a group of friends and colleagues in women's studies have met regularly over the past decade to read, talk, and help each other think about the ever-changing issues in feminist scholarship. Thanks to Judith Goldstein, Eileen Leonard, Deborah Moore, Molly Shanley, and Patricia Wallace for the many stimulating hours arguing about and discussing our mutual concerns, and for their faith in my work. I feel especially lucky to teach in the History Department at Vassar College. My faculty colleagues, the administrative assistant Norma Torney, and our students have made Vassar an intellectually exciting place to work, and a most humane one as well. The department and Dean of the Faculty Nancy Schrom Dye have always supported my scholarship and my teaching interests, and have been generous about leave time. Nothing has meant more to me than the continuing support of my work by Vassar's senior Americanist, Clyde Griffen; now taking early retirement, he will be greatly missed.

Peter Agree, my editor at Cornell University Press, has an outstanding reputation among scholars for his capabilities and his integrity. Now I know why. At Cornell, Risa Mednick and managing editor Kay Scheuer have also been extremely helpful. My copy editor, Barbara Reitt, has done extraordinary work to improve the text and the tables.

I am grateful for permission to make use of materials that have appeared in two previously published articles: "Italian-American Women in New York City, 1900–1950: Work and School," reprinted by permission of Greenwood Publishing Group, Inc., Westport, Conn., from Milton Cantor and Bruce Laurie, eds., *Class, Sex, and the Woman Worker,* copyright © 1977 by Milton Cantor and Bruce Laurie and published in 1977 by Greenwood Press; and "Changing Education Strategies among New York Immigrant Generations: New York Italians in Comparative Perspective," *Journal of Social History* 15 (Spring 1982): 443–66.

Doing paid labor and maintaining a family life is hard, but I have had help in so many ways. My parents, Rebecca and Martin Cohen, have shown love and also respect for my work as a historian. I have had help with housework and childcare from Sara Amerson and Eleanor and Steve Kara. My wonderful daughters, Julia and Nora Hanagan, remind me all the time why love of family is so powerful. My husband, Michael Hanagan, has shaped his own career as a historian so that could I do the paid work I so enjoy and we could raise a family together. He has discussed this project at every stage, has read and reread many versions of the manuscript. Throughout its ups and downs, he has maintained faith and provided love. To him, I am most grateful.

MIRIAM COHEN

Poughkeepsie, New York

WORKSHOP TO OFFICE

ITALIAN-AMERICAN WOMEN:
A SOCIAL HISTORICAL ANALYSIS

In 1913 the social investigator Mary Van Kleeck described her interviews with several young Italian women in New York City. Her conversations reveal what life was like for many of these young women in early twentieth-century New York—the roles they played in the family and their understanding of their duties and obligations. One nineteen-year-old told Van Kleeck that in her family "there were two brothers, neither of whom had ever worked regularly. One of them, a boy of sixteen, was in the second year of high school, hoping to go through medical school. The older brother had just obtained his medical degree. His education had been a particular tax on the family. His sister said that during those years, while he was in medical school, she had brought home flowers from the shop and had worked sometimes until four or five o'clock in the morning, 'When he graduated,' she said, 'I cried all day I was so happy as though I had graduated myself.' "[1]

In 1950 the lives of adolescent females in New York were quite different. Marie Conti of Julia Richman High School, class of 1949, was listed in her graduating class as section captain, vice president of the school's model bank, and vice president of the sound (the cheering) squad. Under her picture the yearbook staff tried to give the reader a capsule view of the

---

[1] Mary Van Kleeck, *Artificial Flower Makers* (New York: Russell Sage Foundation, Survey Associates, 1913), p. 86. As will be seen in subsequent chapters, in 1913 having one son who already was a doctor and another hoping to follow in his footsteps was not typical of Italian families. The fact that the daughter in this family would work, sacrificing her personal ambitions so that the sons could be educated, is.

graduate: "Marie, striving for a career as secretary, enjoys dancing, reading and sports."[2]

The contrast between these two adolescents is striking. The day-to-day activities of the artificial flower maker involved long hours of wage labor; not only that, but her own schooling, however much she had received, was almost certain to have been secondary to the education of her brothers. Clearly, her energies had been devoted to the needs of others throughout her adolescence. She worked hard so that her brothers could be educated, and she expressed pleasure that her labors contributed to the immediate and long-term needs of other family members. In stark contrast, the daily life of Marie Conti was more focused on her own needs and her own future. Marie's time outside of school was spent on hobbies, recreation, and extracurricular activities. In school, she learned the skills she would need as a secretary—a very different kind of work than that of her predecessor.

This book analyzes how and why the behavior of Italian women like the flower maker and Marie Conti changed so greatly over the course of fifty years. At the same time it examines the continuities in the lives of these women as daughters, wives, and mothers. In short, it is a social historical study of significant changes in the family roles, work lives, and schooling patterns of two generations of Italian-American women in New York.

The process of adjustment to American life among the newly arrived and their offspring has interested scholars for generations. Immigrant studies done in the mid-twentieth century, including those on Italians, were heavily influenced by social scientists' acceptance of modernization theory. Premodern people who confront a modern world, according to this theory, undergo mental transformations, adopting modern values as they come into contact with an industrial world that is characterized by rational, impersonal market relations. To adjust to the new environment, people from traditional societies must leave behind their group loyalties and family ties. The change may begin slowly, but eventually urbanization, industrialization, and mass communication overwhelm and transform the premodern world; ultimately people abandon the old and embrace the new mentality.[3]

---

[2] Julia Richman High School Yearbook, *Spotlight* (1949), p. 17 (Julia Richman High School, Library Archives, New York City). All names from Julia Richman are fictional.

[3] For an important example of modernization theory see C. E. Black, *The Dynamics of Modernization* (New York: Harper and Row, 1966). The analyses put forth in the post–World War II era had their origins in the writings of sociologists as far back as the late

Scholars of American immigration, assuming that modernization theory was correct, emphasized the extent to which adjustment to American urban life meant abandoning Old World traditions of family loyalty for the new creed of individualism and personal autonomy. This was the underlying theme of works by Oscar Handlin and S. N. Eisenstadt on immigrants in general, and of those by Paul Campisi and William Whyte, among others, on Italians.[4] Almost all the studies that focused on families depicted the breakdown of solidarity that accompanied the transformation in values. "For the Italians of Greenwich Village," Caroline Ware concluded in 1935, "the disintegration of the old pattern was rapid and violent, while the confusion in the American situation gave little opportunity for the successful acquisition of new standards."[5]

Our understanding of the immigrant experience is no longer based on the assumption that it inevitably involved a breakdown and disorganization of basic institutions in the community. Two decades or more of social historical analysis has shown that European immigrants in the nineteenth and twentieth centuries came from villages that were not isolated, not untouched by modern social, economic, and political change.[6] Moreover,

---

nineteenth century. See Max Weber, *The City*, trans. Don Martindale and Gertrude Neuwirth (New York: Free Press, 1958); George Simmel, "The Metropolis and Mental Life," and Louis Wirth, "Urbanism as a Way of Life," both in Richard Sennett, ed., *Classic Essays on the Culture of Cities* (New York: Appleton Century Crofts, 1969); Emile Durkheim, *The Division of Labor in Society* (1933; reprint, New York: Free Press, 1964).

[4] See Oscar Handlin, *The Uprooted* (Boston: Little, Brown, 1951); S. N. Eisenstadt, *The Adaptation of Immigrants* (London: Routledge and Kegan Paul, 1954). On Italians, see Paul Campisi, "Ethnic Family Patterns: The Italian Family in the United States," *American Journal of Sociology* 53 (May 1948: 443–47; Laurence Pisani, *The Italians in America* (New York: Exposition Press, 1957). Also see William Whyte, *Street Corner Society* (Chicago: University of Chicago Press, 1943); Lydio Tomasi, *The Italian-American Family: The Southern Italian Family's Process of Adjustment to Urban America* (Staten Island, N.Y.: Center for Migration Studies, 1973); Leonard Covello, *The Social Background of the Italo-American School Child* (Totowa, N.J.: Rowman and Littlefield, 1972); Caroline Ware, *Greenwich Village, 1920–1930* (Boston: Houghton Mifflin, 1935).

[5] See Ware, *Greenwich Village, 1920–1930*, pp. 171, 172. See also W. Lloyd Warner and Leo Srole, *Social Systems of American Ethnic Groups, Yankee City*, vol. 3 (New Haven: Yale University Press, 1943); Marcus Lee Hansen, *The Immigrant in American History* (Cambridge: Harvard University Press, 1948); Irwin Child, *Italian or American? The Second Generation in Conflict* (New Haven: Yale University Press, 1943).

[6] See Josef Barton, *Peasants and Strangers: Italians, Rumanians and Slovaks in an American City, 1890–1950* (Cambridge: Harvard University Press, 1975). The best synthesis of the new literature on the European communities that sent emigrants is John Bodnar, *The*

reflecting a new appreciation for the durability of working-class and ethnic culture, studies in the 1960s and 1970s such as those of Herbert Gutman and Rudolph Vecoli argued that immigrants did not abandon modes of thought and behavior that they brought to America; instead, they used their traditions in adapting to modern industrial life.[7]

Yet in focusing on the continuity of immigrants' values and experiences, many of the new ethnic histories left unanswered the question, To what extent and how did change occur? Second-generation immigrants did not behave the same way their elders did. Italian women in New York City are a case in point; by 1950 second-generation Italian females were better educated than their mothers and entered different occupations. To understand such changes, scholars of immigration such as John Bodnar, Judith Smith, and Dino Cinel have adopted in the last decade a more dynamic approach, emphasizing transformations along with continuity.[8]

My analysis demonstrates that family strategies can account for both continuity and change in the behavior of New York Italian women. Throughout the period under study, 1900–1950, Italian parents were motivated by one basic goal—to raise their families to the best of their ability

---

Transplanted: A History of Immigration in Urban America (Bloomington: Indiana University Press, 1985).

[7] See Herbert Gutman, "Work, Culture and Society in Industrializing America," *American Historical Review* 78 (June 1973): 531–88; Rudolph Vecoli, "Contadini in Chicago: A Critique of The Uprooted," *Journal of American History* 51 (December 1964): 404–17. On Italians, see also Virginia Yans-McLaughlin, *Family and Community: Italian Immigrants in Buffalo, 1880–1930* (Ithaca, N.Y.: Cornell University Press, 1977); Rudolph Vecoli, "Le fonti americane per lo studio dell'immigrazione italiana," in Symposium di Studi Americani 3rd 1969, Florence [Rudolph Vecoli, ed.], *Gli Italiani Negli State Uniti* (Florence: Istituto di studi americani, Università degli studi, 1972), pp. 1–24; Richard Gambino, *Blood of My Blood* (Garden City, N.Y.: Doubleday, 1974).

[8] See, for example, Bodnar, *The Transplanted;* Judith Smith, *Family Connections: A History of Italian and Jewish Immigrant Lives in Providence, Rhode Island, 1900–1940* (Albany: State University of New York Press, 1985); Dino Cinel, *From Italy to San Francisco: The Immigrant Experience* (Stanford, Calif.: Stanford University Press, 1982). See also Elizabeth Ewen, *Immigrant Women in the Land of Dollars: Life and Culture on the Lower East Side, 1890–1925* (New York: Monthly Review Press, 1985); Kathy Peiss, *Cheap Amusements: Working Women and Leisure in Turn-of-the-Century New York* (Philadelphia: Temple University Press, 1986); Sydney Stahl Weinberg, *World of Our Mothers: The Lives of Jewish Immigrant Women* (Chapel Hill: University of North Carolina Press, 1988); Janice Reiff Webster, "Domestication and Americanization: Scandinavian Women in Seattle, 1888–1900," *Journal of Urban History* 4 (May 1978): 275–90.

and provide for their own old age and their offspring's future. In seeking to achieve that goal, the Italian families shifted their behavior in response to changing economic, social, and demographic conditions. In this book I examine the lives of mothers and daughters around 1905 and 1925 and then in the late 1930s to 1950s; I then touch more briefly on the lives of young women as they become wives in 1950. My analysis shows how greater economic resources in the household, changing family structures, and new opportunities for work and school affected family decisions about women's everyday life. The shifts in work and school patterns among Italian women, as well as the changes in the availability of leisure time, were outcomes of shifting family strategies.[9] By the same token, to the extent that Italian families experienced continuity in social conditions over the two generations, there were continuities, too, in their strategies and in women's roles.[10]

Italian families developed their strategies on the basis of experiences in southern Italy and Sicily, as well as the realities of life in Italian communities of New York. Most immigrants to New York arriving around 1900 came from Old World communities in which households depended on hard work and the financial contributions of as many members as possible. Working-class strategies were thus important to some degree for all immigrant groups, but ethnic circumstances were relevant as well. Each ethnic group brought different economic resources and skills; they often arrived in different periods and encountered different labor markets. Some groups gained a foothold in particular occupations because of the timing of their arrival; some, through unions, ethnic, or political networks.[11] Such factors, of course, affected the work and school patterns of

[9] See Louise Tilly, "Individual Lives and Family Strategies in the French Proletariat," *Journal of Family History* 4 (Summer 1979): 138.

[10] For a similar analysis of first- and second-generation immigrants, which focuses on how family strategies respond to change and continuity in economic and social conditions, see John Bodnar, "Materialism and Morality: Slavic-American Immigrants and Education, 1890–1940," *Journal of Ethnic Studies* 3 (Winter 1976): 1–19; Bodnar, *The Transplanted.*

[11] On the importance of occupational, political, other networks for the ethnic group, see Micaela di Leonardo, *The Varieties of Ethnic Experience: Kinship, Class, and Gender among California Italian-Americans* (Ithaca, N.Y.: Cornell University Press, 1984); Suzanne W. Model, "The Effects of Ethnicity in the Work Place on Blacks, Italians, and Jews in New York," Center for Studies of Social Change, New School for Social Research, Working Paper Series no. 7 (March 1985). How the structure of economic and political opportu-

Italian women. For many, moreover, identification with their ethnic group was important.

Although Italian family strategies were influenced by their particular ethnic experience, I do not view them, in contrast to one trend in contemporary ethnic scholarship, as the outcome of a well-defined and established system of ethnic values. Nathan Glazer and Daniel Moynihan on New York immigrants, Richard Gambino on Italians, Michael Olneck and Marvin Lazerson on Italians and Jews, just to name a few, have emphasized the extent to which cultural values unique to each group, carried over from the Old World, determined familial, occupational, and schooling patterns.[12] In this book I view culture more dynamically, in the words of John Bodnar, as "a constellation of behavioral and thought patterns which offer people explanations, order and a prescription for how to proceed with their lives."[13] Culture changes as individuals, networks, and circumstances interact.[14] To understand the work, school, and family lives of first- and second-generation immigrants in the early twentieth century, one must appreciate that ethnic culture was deeply pragmatic. It was born of the understanding that in America, as in Europe, families would have to shift behavior in order to survive.[15]

Women's behavior both in southern Italy and in New York reveals their profound pragmatism. A look at the ways in which Italians dealt with the daily realities of their lives provides new insight into women's roles and gender relations in ethnic working-class families. Because Italian women

---

nities in American cities has promoted ethnic identity is discussed in Ulf Hannerz, "Ethnicity and Opportunity in Urban America," in Abner Cohen, ed., *Urban Ethnicity* (London: Tavistock, 1974), pp. 37–76.

[12] Nathan Glazer and Daniel P. Moynihan, *Beyond the Melting Pot: The Negroes, Puerto Ricans, Jews, Italians, and Irish of New York City*, 2nd ed. (Cambridge, Mass.: M.I.T. Press, 1970); Gambino, *Blood of My Blood*; Michael Olneck and Marvin Lazerson, "The School Achievement of Immigrant Children, 1900–1930," *History of Education Quarterly* 14 (Winter 1974): 454–82. See also Corinne A. Krause, "Urbanization without Breakdown: Italian, Jewish and Slavic Immigrant Women in Pittsburgh, 1900–1945," *Journal of Urban History* 4 (May 1978): 291; and, to some extent, Thomas Kessner, *The Golden Door: Italian and Jewish Immigrant Mobility in New York City, 1880–1915* (New York: Oxford University Press, 1977).

[13] Bodnar, *The Transplanted*, pp. 208–9.

[14] See ibid., pp. 212–13. Di Leonardo, in *The Varieties*, makes a similar argument.

[15] Bodnar, *The Transplanted*, chap. 8 ("Conclusion: The Culture of Everyday Life"); see also di Leonardo, *The Varieties*, pp. 212, 213.

in the United States were tied to home and family activities, contemporary observers and modern scholars, both, have often attributed their behavior to the influence of Mediterranean patriarchal culture. Thus, in her study of Italian immigrant families in Buffalo, Virginia Yans-McLaughlin contends that in Italy patriarchal norms kept women from engaging in paid labor outside the home. The fact that Italian women were unlikely to be employed outside the home in Buffalo, New York, is seen as a carryover of this traditional culture.[16]

Like Buffalo's Italians, the women in New York City believed that familial values were fundamental; nevertheless, in Italy and the United States women acted in seemingly contradictory ways that cannot be summarized simply as outgrowths of patriarchal norms. Patriarchal ideals were strained, indeed, violated, as people struggled to meet the realities of everyday life. Within the family arena, the women never had been deferential and passive; they made important decisions about family members.[17] As the anthropologist Micaela di Leonardo notes in her study of second- and third-generation Italian Americans in San Francisco, "patriarchy is an evolving and variable set of social relations."[18] It is particularly difficult to shed the stereotype of Italian women because descendants identify ethnicity with an idealized past in which women stayed home and served the men. But the rhetorical nostalgia is just that — a romanticized image of the past, invoked most often (but not exclusively) by men, that denies the real context of ancestors' lives.[19] In neither southern Italy nor New York did Italian women live sheltered lives or remain in the shadow of their male kin. In both countries Italian women were called upon to work outside the home, and they were ready when needed to defend the family's interest in the marketplace and with law enforcement officers, school personnel, and representatives of welfare agencies.

---

[16] Virginia Yans-McLaughlin, "Patterns of Work and Family Organization: Buffalo's Italians," *Journal of Interdisciplinary History* 2 (1971), 303–12; Yans-McLaughlin, *Family and Community*.

[17] In her book *Family and Community* Yans-McLaughlin acknowledges that women had status and played an important role within the family; nevertheless, she contends that "the conservatism of female employment patterns [the fact that few worked full time, or outside the home], and the immigrants' understanding of them is clear evidence for continuing male domination" (p. 215).

[18] Di Leonardo, *The Varieties*, p. 227.

[19] Ibid., pp. 233–34.

The shift in occupations, and the increased schooling for women that occurred in the second generation by midcentury, can best be understood as pragmatic responses by the women to changing family needs and new job opportunities. Louise Lamphere found among contemporary Portuguese and Colombian immigrant families in Providence attitudes that have frequently been termed traditional and patriarchal: "men commanded special respect as household heads, and both men and women believed in inherent gender differences," yet such an ideology did not preclude flexible behavior. When needs dictated, the women of these poor communities shifted their productive and even their reproductive roles.[20] Similarly, among New York Italians the changes in women's behavior did not demand rejection of old patriarchal values or the acceptance of new, modern values such as individualism.

Recent studies of mass culture and immigrant communities, in providing an important critique of modernization theory, have pointed out that the adoption of individualist values was not the inevitable and necessary consequence of adjustment to modern life. The transformations of minority cultures were evidence of the power of capitalist institutions, including mass culture, to promote bourgeois, individualist values, which ultimately cut across class lines.[21] Although many have emphasized the negative consequences of this "cultural hegemony," some historians of working-class culture, including some feminist historians, have viewed it in a more positive light.[22] Two histories of Jewish and Italian women

---

[20] Louise Lamphere, *From Working Daughters to Working Mothers: Immigrant Women in a New England Industrial Community* (Ithaca, N.Y.: Cornell University Press, 1987), p. 267.

[21] On cultural hegemony, see Raymond Williams, "Base and Superstructure in Marxist Cultural Theory," *New Left Review* 82 (November–December 1973): 3–16; see also Kerby A. Miller, "Class, Culture, and Immigrant Group Identity in the United States: The Case of Irish-American Ethnicity," in *Immigration Reconsidered: History, Sociology, and Politics*, ed. Virginia Yans-McLaughlin (New York: Oxford University Press, 1990), pp. 96–129.

[22] As Charles Tilly points out, the process of modernization can be seen in both progressive and conservative terms. Conservative modernization models "nest neatly with models of protest, conflict and collective action as irrational responses to the stress and strains of rapid change. Progressive modernization models, on the other hand, articulate plausibly with a vision of awakening consciousness, of increasing integration into cosmopolitan world views." "Did the Cake of Custom Break?" in John Merriman, ed., *Consciousness and Class Experience in Nineteenth-Century Europe* (London: Holmes and Meier, 1979), p. 20. A number of leftist scholars, though they may see the move toward bourgeois liberal society, overall, as progressive, have emphasized the negative consequences of bourgeois cultural

have focused on the ways that the proliferation of mass culture and the exposure to the values of modern capitalism via mass media altered the women's sense of themselves. Participation in mass leisure pursuits, argue Kathy Peiss and Elizabeth Ewen, heightened desires for more autonomy from the family, and involvement in youth culture was a reflection of these new aspirations. In New York, according to Ewen, immigrants received a "daily dose of new American values at school and in the factory." The process of becoming American, for second-generation women, meant adapting the bourgeois, individualist values of capitalism, which ultimately pitted children against parents.[23] In her fascinating study of leisure pursuits among immigrant women in New York City, Peiss concludes that working girls used popular leisure to define a new style, which was neither a wholesale adoption of middle-class, American values, nor the maintenance of traditional ethnic values.[24] Though this new style did not "transform the web of gender and class relations," according to Peiss, it did in "some ways subvert the traditional bases of their dependencies as dutiful daughters in the patriarchal family, and as submissive workers in a capitalist economy."[25]

---

hegemony. See, for example, Stewart Ewen, *Captains of Consciousness: Advertising and the Social Roots of Consumer Culture* (New York: McGraw-Hill, 1977). Miller discusses the way bourgeois hegemony ultimately undermined the class counsciousness of Irish workers in "Class, Culture, and Immigrant Group," pp. 111-24. For a more positive view of the impact of consumerism on Jewish immigrants, see Andrew Heinze, *Adapting to Abundance: Jewish Immigrants, Mass Consumption, and the Search for American Identity* (New York: Columbia University Press, 1990).

[23] See Ewen, *Immigrant Women in the Land of Dollars*, p. 94 and chap. 11, especially pp. 186, 190, 205. Ewen's analysis is hardly a full-scale celebration of the loss of group values and the adoption of bourgeois individualism, but it does suggest that in fostering individualism, mass culture was a powerful factor in promoting women's autonomy in immigrant communities.

[24] Peiss's model of the process of cultural hegemony is thus similar to Raymond Williams's. Minority cultures do not merely take on an imposed middle-class ideology, but create something of an alternate culture, rather than an oppositional one, which "can be accommodated and tolerated within a particular effective and dominant culture." (Williams, "Base and Superstructure," pp. 9, 10.) For another fine analysis of the emergence of working-class leisure among men at the same period that emphasizes the differences between working-class and middle-class values, see also Roy Rozensweig, *Eight Hours for What We Will: Workers and Leisure in an Industrial City, 1870–1920* (New York: Cambridge University Press, 1983).

[25] Peiss, *Cheap Amusements*, p. 187.

I find Nancy Hewitt persuasive when she cautions against assuming that the vast scholarship on middle-class women that has emphasized their rejection of premodern notions of patriarchy for "modern" values such as the "growth of individualism and the search for autonomy" is relevant for poorer women.[26] In my analysis of social historical change, I have departed from all modernization models, whether the Americanization of immigrants is seen as a consequence of bourgeois hegemony, or the inevitable result of the adjustment to industrialization. I do not assume that people must undergo mental transformations to adopt behavior we would term modern, or bourgeois, nor do I assume that the absence of modern behavior signifies a different mind-set. Rather, I am convinced that, as Charles Tilly writes, "most of the time ordinary people have an idea, more or less clear, of their short-run interests, but they vary enormously in their capacity to act on their interests."[27] My analysis of two generations of Italian women attempts to answer Tilly's call for an alternative model to modernization theory, one that focuses on how "large social changes have altered the interests, capacities and opportunities of ordinary people."[28] By the same token, I also show how the lack of opportunity reinforced traditional strategies.

Throughout the first half of the twentieth century Italian Americans in New York remained working class. Given the opportunities available for Italian women, values that stressed individual autonomy had little meaning in their culture because they could not be translated, in Bodnar's terms, into prescriptions about how to proceed with one's life. By mid-century, however, the relationship between aspirations and the structure of opportunity had changed,[29] and second-generation Italian women more

---

[26] Nancy Hewitt, "Beyond the Search for Sisterhood: American Women's History in the 1980's," in *Unequal Sisters: A Multicultural Reader in U.S. Women's History*, ed. Ellen Carol Dubois and Vicky Ruiz (London: Routledge, Chapman and Hall, 1990), pp. 5, 7. Donna Gabaccia has also noted that individualism had little meaning for immigrant women. "Modern Americans," she warns, "feminists among them, have difficulties accepting a concept of self or identity that is created primarily through relation to others within families." "Immigrant Women: Nowhere at Home?" *Journal of American Ethnic History* 10 (Summer 1991): 70. See also Elizabeth Fox-Genovese, *Feminism without Illusions: A Critique of Individualism* (Chapel Hill: University of North Carolina Press, 1991).

[27] Tilly, "Did the Cake of Custom Break?" p. 20.

[28] Ibid.

[29] In *World of Our Mothers*, Weinberg makes excellent use of oral interviews to show the relationship between changing opportunities and aspirations among Jewish women.

commonly pursued goals that were personal. In doing so, they may well have defied their relatives, as has been suggested by Peiss and Ewen, and many more may have wished it were possible.[30] But the larger patterns of behavior in the community, which are the basis of this study, such as who worked and where, who would go to school and when, are evidence of important shifts in working-class familial strategies.

Though individual autonomy from male-dominated families had little meaning for Italian women, a female world apart from men was important; this was particularly so during the early years of settlement. Ardis Cameron, Judith Smith, and others have shown that female networks were critically important to working-class women, just as historians of middle-class women have demonstrated they were in that group.[31] In this study we will see that in Italy women spent months and years at a time without fathers, brothers, or husbands. In Italian communities in New York female networks were an important part of everyday life; women shared common perceptions about the world, especially the rights and responsibilities of women and men. But women's values separate from overall family values did not, at this time, have an important influence on patterns of life in terms of work, school, and family among Italian-American women. As Donna Gabaccia has noted, scholars of immigrant women tend to study them within a family context because the evidence, both oral and written, suggests that women generally identified with their families.[32] The ties among Italian women in New York were important precisely because they were rooted in cooperation among kin and neighbors that was critically important to the well-being of the entire community. They exemplify, as Hewitt has pointed out, the "sisterly bonds (in work-

---

[30] Although Peiss concedes that Italian women were less involved in popular culture than other groups, my study differs by suggesting that Italian women in the early decades of the century had such little leisure time that popular culture was not a significant part of their lives. Beyond that, I, unlike Peiss, have focused on the broad patterns of behavior over two generations and comment on women's attitudes only as they affect basic choices about work, school, and family roles.

[31] See Hewitt, "Beyond the Search for Sisterhood." On working-class women, see Ardis Cameron, "Women's Culture and Working-Class Activism," in *Women, Work and Protest: A Century of U.S. Women's Labor History*, ed. Ruth Milkman (Boston: Routledge and Kegan Paul, 1985), pp. 42–61; Judith Smith, "Our Own Kind: Family and Community Networks in Providence," in Nancy F. Cott and Elizabeth H. Pleck, eds., *A Heritage of Her Own: Toward a New Social History of American Women* (New York: Simon and Schuster, 1979), pp. 393–412.

[32] Gabaccia, "Immigrant Women: Nowhere at Home?"

ing class communities)" which "were often employed in the interests of men as well as women."[33]

My study of the relationship between family strategies and women's behavior begins by focusing on women's work and family roles in southern Italy (Chapter 1). In an economy organized around household production, women had important work roles and participated in decisions concerning domestic and economic activities while men were away at work. When Italian families settled in New York, women were still expected to contribute labor, but as the social and economic situations confronting the families was now changed, so, too, was the women's contribution to the family's welfare. Throughout the first half of the century a number of interacting factors affected female work and schooling: the family's economic need for female labor, its need for their services at home, employment opportunities for women in New York, the demographic characteristics of Italian households. In subsequent chapters each of these interacting factors is examined in turn, and their changing impact on the lives of the mothers and daughters is discussed.

Chapters 2 and 3 deal with women's work patterns for single adults and married women, respectively, between 1900 and the early Depression years. Both chapters also focus on the ways family strategies affected women's attitudes toward work, and the ways the women combined work, family, and leisure responsibilities.

An understanding of work and family responsibilities sets the stage for the discussion in Chapter 4 of Italians' poor school attendance during the early twentieth century. Daughters were kept at home because families believed that the kinds of skills females as workers or wives needed could be taught at home. To appreciate the social context in which Italian families made that assessment, we move beyond the social conditions of the family to an examination of the political economy of New York. Although New York State had some of the most progressive laws anywhere on child labor, the government's unwillingness to eradicate many forms of child employment meant that girls found strong demand for their labor. Moreover, despite mandatory school attendance laws, not until the New

[33] Hewitt, "Beyond the Search for Sisterhood," p. 7.

Deal years did Italian families in New York have reason to fear the authorities if they wished to keep children away from school.

Toward the end of the Great Depression social, demographic, and political changes created a new context for this Italian-American community. Italians responded with new expectations about how girls should spend their adolescent years. Chapter 5 explores the ways that the growing availability of white-collar work for women, changes in the household structure, and greater enforcement of labor and school laws on the national and local level encouraged families to send daughters to high school. By 1950 Italian schooling patterns reflected those of the population at large, with a greater proportion of females, as compared with males, obtaining high school diplomas. This chapter also assesses the high school experience of Italian-American girls and their aspirations for the future.

Chapter 6 outlines the work and family lives of the new generation of young adult Italian women in 1950 and touches on both the differences and similarities between the generations. To sort out the effects of class and ethnicity on family strategies and women's behavior, throughout the study I have made systematic comparisons of Italian women with Jewish women. The data on Jewish families I use is limited but is nonetheless suggestive of the ways that social and demographic circumstances affected the work and school lives of another group of immigrant women who arrived in New York around the same time. By the middle of the twentieth century the behavior of Italian and Jewish women had converged in significant ways, but differences between the two groups remained.

The analysis of Italian women in one city cannot, of course, tell us everything there is to know about this group in the United States. The experience of New York City Italians is significant because of the size of the community. Italian family strategies, however, are particular responses to the urban economy of New York City, the center of American corporate capitalism. The specific economic and social resources of the immigrant community that remained in the eastern port of entry were often different from the settlers inland, or on the West Coast.[34] By study-

---

[34] A recent study has argued convincingly that in generalizing from analyses of the

ing the interaction of specific social and political developments responsible for both change and continuity, this case study can, however, point the
way to a more general understanding of immigrant women in the first half
of the twentieth century. How this study can illuminate the more general
experience is discussed in the conclusion, after the story of Italian women
in New York is told.

Northeast, scholars have mistakenly attributed the fact that Italians were largely working
class at midcentury to Italian values, yet large Italian communities, such as that in San
Francisco, prospered and became middle class very quickly. See di Leonardo, *The Varieties.*

CHAPTER ONE

WOMEN AND THE FAMILY IN SOUTHERN ITALY

Peasant women know they must do whatever needs to be done.

—Ann Cornelisen, *Women of the Shadows: The Wives and Mothers of Southern Italy*

The majority of Italians who emigrated to the United States were from southern Italy, and most who settled in New York City during the peak years from 1900 to World War I were emigrants from the southern provinces of Campania, Basilicata, and Calabria and from Sicily.[1] My study concentrates on the Italians from southern Italy who congregated in the Little Italies of Lower Manhattan and East Harlem, and in the Greenpoint-Williamsburg, Red Hook, and Fort Greene sections of Brooklyn. Although southern Italians came from several regions, they shared a number of common characteristics with respect to economic and social background. Of particular interest here are the work roles of girls and women in the southern Italian economy and women's role in the Italian family. These roles were part of the traditional strategies for survival that the women brought to America.

[1] Most northern Italians settled in South America, although a number did come to the United States in the latter half of the nineteenth century. Northern Italians tended to be more prosperous; many were from urban areas. In New York City they colonized the edges of West Greenwich Village, around Washington Square, Bleecker, Sullivan, MacDougal and Thompson streets.

The Economy and the Peasant Family

The vast majority of Italian emigrants to the United States had lived in rural villages where life was a constant struggle and where organization of landholdings had far-reaching effects on family life. In the interior regions of Sicily, for example, large *latifondi* were worked by tenants and gang laborers, some of whom also owned small plots of land. The rest of the south was generally characterized by a large number of very small holdings.[2] The areas of out-migration were typically ones in which peasants worked their own small plots of land, sharecropped or rented small tracts from midsize property owners, hired themselves out as wage laborers, or combined some of these alternatives in order to make a subsistence or near-subsistence living.[3]

The southern peasant almost always worked on several plots, each of one crop, scattered throughout the village area. On one, the peasant might sharecrop a wheat field and on another he might work as a wage laborer picking grapes while on a third, which he owned, he might raise food for family consumption. Sharecropping and renting contracts tended to be very short term—most commonly one to three years. This pattern of scattered small holdings that were only temporarily transformed by an individual discouraged long-term investment in any one holding. There

[2] See Donna Gabaccia, *From Sicily to Elizabeth Street: Housing and Social Change among Italian Immigrants, 1880–1930* (Albany: State University of New York Press, 1984); Anton Blok, *The Mafia of a Sicilian Village, 1860–1960* (New York: Harper and Row, 1975), chap. 3; Sydel F. Silverman, "Agricultural Organization, Social Structure and Values in Italy: Amoral Familism Reconsidered," *American Anthropologist* 70 (1968): 1–20; Josef Barton, *Peasants and Strangers: Italians, Rumanians, and Slovaks in an American City, 1890–1950* (Cambridge: Harvard University Press, 1975), chap. 2; John S. MacDonald and Leatrice MacDonald, "Institutional Economics and Rural Development: Two Italian Types," *Human Organization* (Summer 1974): 113–18; J. S. MacDonald, "Some Socio-Economic Emigration Differentials in Rural Italy, 1902–1913," *Economic Development and Cultural Changes* 7 (1958): 61–75; Domenico Demarco, *La Calabria: Economica e Societa* (Naples: Edizione Scientifiche Italiane, 1966), chap. 2; Donald Pitkin, "Land Tenure and Family Organization in an Italian Village," *Human Organization* 18 (Winter 1958–59): 169–73.

[3] Silverman, "Agricultural Organization"; MacDonald and MacDonald, "Institutional Economics."

was no incentive for one peasant cultivator to cooperate with another who might be renting land on the same farm. Each family head was oriented not toward increasing value of the farm land as a whole, but toward accumulating earnings from his family's various enterprises in the region.[4]

Because they could not rely on others, family heads in the south turned to the members of their own households for the labor power needed to work the various enterprises. In most cases the household meant a nuclear family. In southern Italy property was traditionally divided among all offspring in the form of linens and furnishings as dowries for the daughters and land and tools for the sons. When each child married, he or she usually moved out of the parental family dwelling and established a separate nuclear household.[5] If the family owned too much land to be worked by the household alone, it might rent out part of the land or hire wage laborers during harvest time. If, on the other hand, the family did not have enough land to support it, its members might take land on a sharecropping basis, hire themselves out as wage laborers, or seek employment in other jobs. Artisanal work was one important source of non-agricultural work. Every village had its masons, barbers, and bakers, but often these jobs were passed from father to son. Some men found work as fishermen or shepherds; others traveled to work in the sulphur mines of

[4]Silverman, "Agricultural Organization"; MacDonald and MacDonald, "Institutional Economics."

[5]Silverman, "Agricultural Organization"; MacDonald and MacDonald, "Institutional Economics." Also see Charlotte Gowar Chapman, *Milocca: A Sicilian Village* (London: Schenkman, 1971), chap. 2; Phyliss Williams, *South Italian Folkways in Europe and America: A Handbook for Social Workers, Visiting Nurses, School Teachers, and Physicians* (New Haven: Yale University Press, 1938), chap. 6; Constance Cronin, *The Sting of Change: Sicilians in Sicily and Australia* (Chicago: University of Chicago Press, 1970), chap. 4. It should be noted that Cronin studied contemporary Italy, whereas Chapman considers the 1920s. Silverman's work also refers to contemporary Italy. I have tried to use information from these studies which the authors have indicated are applicable to Italians of earlier generations. My historical analysis also benefited from Donna R. Gabaccia, "Houses and People: Sicilians in Sicily and New York, 1890–1930" (Ph.D. diss., University of Michigan, 1979), p. 118, chap. 2. Anthropologist William Douglass has suggested that scholars have underestimated the extent of cooperation in joint family domestic groups. Joint family domestic groups were advantageous for Italian peasants. Nevertheless, as he points out, the ability to form such households was limited by the demographic realities of age or marriage, the birth rate, and life expectancy, as well as out-migration of young adult males. Thus, these joint households were not common. See "The South Italian Family: A Critique," *Journal of Family History* 5 (Winter 1980): 338–59.

Sicily or to other parts of Italy and Europe seeking jobs in factories, construction, urban services, or farming.[6]

During the latter half of the nineteenth century the resources of southern Italian families were strained by rapid population growth, an expansion of capitalist agriculture that increased competition and lowered prices, and a pylloxera epidemic that destroyed Sicilian grape vines. Children were increasingly unable to share in their parents' holdings, and many families found their properties inadequate. Since nonagricultural work was scarce, peasants were forced to migrate even farther from home, to North and South America. Until the early decades of the twentieth century, male migrants often traveled back and forth between their southern Italian villages and America, sending their wages to their families and saving to purchase land in southern Italy.[7]

Southern Italian peasants of the late nineteenth century were thus both tied to their small villages and yet very much involved in a large cash and wage economy. Either small property holders or propertyless laborers, they dreamed of becoming small landowners and were reluctant to sever ties with their native villages.[8] Trying to maintain traditional connections

---

[6]See Silverman, "Agricultural Organization." Also see MacDonald and MacDonald, "Institutional Economics"; Barton, *Peasants*, chap. 2; Leopoldo Franchetti and Sidney Sonnino, *La Sicilia nel 1876*, vol. 2: *I Contadini* (Florence: Vallecchi Editore, 1921), chap. 3. On peasant goals that involve balancing production resources and family consumption needs to maintain subsistence, or near-subsistence, levels, see Eric Wolf, "Types of Latin American Peasantry: A Preliminary Discussion," *American Anthropologist* 57 (1955): 452–71. Wolf's discussion of peasant behavior in the "open" community is most relevant to the Italian peasantry. Also see Eric Wolf, *Peasants* (New York: Prentice-Hall, 1966), chap. 2; Basile Kerblay, "Chayanov and the Theory of the Peasant Economy as a Specific Type of Economy," in Theodore Shanin, ed., *Peasants and Peasant Society* (London: Penguin, 1971), pp. 150–60.

[7]See Massimo Livi-Bacci, *A History of Italian Fertility during the Last Two Centuries* (Princeton, N.J.: Princeton University Press, 1977), pp. 192–200. See also Gabaccia, "Houses and People," p. 124; Blok, *The Mafia*, chaps. 2, 3; Barton, *Peasants*, chaps. 2, 3; Robert Foerster, *The Italian Emigration of Our Times* (Cambridge: Harvard University Press, 1919), chaps. 2, 3; Thomas Kessner, *The Golden Door: Italian and Jewish Immigrant Mobility in New York City, 1880–1915* (New York: Oxford University Press, 1977), chap. 2. Rudolf Bell also points to the improvement of transportation facilities in accounting for some of the increase in migration and emigration during the late nineteenth century. See "Emigration from Four Italian Villages: Strategy and Decision," in Pat Gallo, ed., *The Urban Experience of Italian-Americans* (Staten Island, N.Y.: American Italian Historical Association, 1977), pp. 9–35.

[8]Gabaccia, "Houses and People"; Barton, *Peasants*, chaps. 2, 3; Foerster, *The Italian Emigration of Our Times*, chaps. 2, 3.

to their settlements, peasants employed various strategies to earn a living. Everyone in the household, males and females, joined in the effort, adapting to the fluctuating, unstable circumstances. This was the context in which the work, school, and family experiences of southern Italian women unfolded.

Daughters, Sons, and Marriage in Southern Italy

Southern Italian and Sicilian women generally did not join the paid labor force, but they were partners in the family enterprise. For as long as anyone could remember the daily activities of southern Italian girls involved tasks that contributed to the family economy. Young girls helped their mothers sew clothes for the family, and in some areas they assisted in weaving and spinning. Girls helped in routine household chores such as washing and cleaning and herding small animals. In fishing families young girls along with their mothers did much of the work making lines and nets.[9] Girls rather than boys were expected to help do the chores around the house, and they began at an earlier age. Although boys often helped by tending animals, weeding, or clearing away stones, they enjoyed some leisure time until they were strong enough to assist their fathers in the fields.[10]

When youngsters reached adolescence, their contribution to the family economy increased. Farmers' sons assisted their fathers in the fields; sons of craftsmen helped in their father's shops. Boys from the poorest families often sought employment outside the family as herders or day laborers. As they grew up, many males found jobs elsewhere in Europe or abroad.[11] Adolescent girls generally remained under the supervision of their mothers, assisting them in household tasks, clothing production, food preparation, and the farm chores that could be done close to the house. If labor was badly needed, particularly among the poorer families,

[9] See Williams, *South Italian Folkways*, pp. 20–25; Cronin, *The Sting of Change*, chap. 6. Also see Leonard W. Moss and Walter H. Thompson, "The South Italian Family: Literature and Observation," *Human Organization* 18 (Spring 1957): 35–41.

[10] See Chapman, *Milocca*, p. 31; Williams, *South Italian Folkways*, p. 20.

[11] See Williams, *South Italian Folkways*, pp. 20–25; Gabaccia, "Houses and People," chap. 2.

southern Italian—including Sicilian—girls joined their mothers and other kin in the fields.[12]

As the responsibilities of adolescent girls grew, so did restrictions on their behavior. The proper adolescent female was expected to stay close to home under the strict supervision of her kin. A young woman in southern Italy who remained at home near her kin was considered virtuous, whereas a woman who wandered off and spent time socializing with peers, male or female, was considered immoral and an unattractive potential marriage partner. Such protectiveness had a very practical purpose. Women who remained close to their kin were valued because they displayed a sense of responsibility to family needs and a willingness to work hard; they could be expected to learn the proper skills to make a good marriage. Ignorance of the hardships of work may have been a feminine virtue for wealthier families, but not for peasants. "Well kept hands," wrote Phyliss Williams, of the features that made Italian women attractive to prospective grooms, ". . . were unknown among the peasants, for a girl could not be an industrious worker if she was able to keep her hands in a dainty condition."[13]

When necessary, Italian families sent young women to work away from the supervision of their mothers, though unlike their brothers, the daughters generally did not travel to other countries. The 1901 Italian census listed southern Italian women at work in textiles in Campania and in garment manufacturing in regions around Naples. Domestic service is often assumed to have been rare in southern Italian culture because of customary limits on women's activities outside the home, but the percentage of women employed outside who were domestic servants was 9.2 in Calabria, 18.9 in Campania, 23.5 in Basilicata, 34 in Sicily. In Sicily domestic service was the largest single female occupation outside of agriculture.[14]

---

[12] Williams, *South Italian Folkways*; Gabaccia, "Houses and People," chap. 2. See also Chapman, *Milocca*, p. 39.

[13] Williams, *South Italian Folkways*, p. 83.

[14] Direzione Generale della Statistica, *Annuario statisco italiano, 1905–1907* (Rome, 1907), pp. 12–115 passim, as quoted by Louise A. Tilly, "Comments on the Yans-McLaughlin and Davidoff Papers," *Journals of Social History* 7 (Summer 1974): 453–54. Edward Banfield also notes that young Italian women were employed as domestic servants in the 1950s. See *The Moral Basis of a Backward Society* (Glencoe, Ill.: Free Press, 1958), pp. 52, 149. For an example of the common assumption that southern Italian culture prevented women from taking on domestic service, see Virginia Yans-McLaughlin, "Patterns of Work and Family Organization: Buffalo's Italians," *Journal of Interdisciplinary History* 2

How many women among those who came to the United States actually had some experience with wage work outside the home in southern Italy is unknown, but there are some clues. The social investigator Louise Odencrantz reported in 1919 that about one-half of a group of 176 Italian women living in New York City who were at least fourteen years of age when they left Italy had contributed to their own support before arriving in America. Such a proportion was "not small," she noted, because many of the women had been under eighteen when they left their native homes. About one-half of the group had worked for wages at home, by taking part, for example, in the family enterprise, crocheting, weaving, or making shoes. The women who had worked outside their homes in rural regions had worked as farmhands or as apprentices to local dressmakers. But "whether they worked as farm hands for their own families or elsewhere," Odencrantz concluded, "they all agreed in their stories of heavy work, long hours, and child labor."[15]

"Girls never went to school," one New York woman recalled about her childhood in Italy, "but were made to work."[16] Certainly, although work was important in the lives of southern Italian youth, schooling was not. Educational opportunities for all Italians expanded after unification, but as late as 1907–1908 the Italian government reported that, for the country as a whole, only 20 percent of the appropriate population was enrolled in what would be the equivalent of the first three grades in the United

(Autumn 1971): 299–314; idem, *Family and Community: Italian Immigrants in Buffalo, 1880–1930* (Ithaca, N.Y.: Cornell University Press, 1977), chap. 7. Yans-McLaughlin has correctly pointed out that these figures offer no urban-rural breakdown and thus we cannot be sure that women workers were from peasant families. But we do know that the percentage of women workers who were servants in more urbanized areas of northern Italy was lower than in most parts of the south. In Piedmont, for example, the percentage was 16; in Lombardy, 12.5. See Tilly, "Comments," p. 453. If southern Italian patterns conform to those elsewhere in Europe, we can assume that most servants were rural migrants. On women's work in northern Italy, see Marie Hall Ets, *Rosa, the Life of an Italian Immigrant* (Minneapolis: University of Minnesota Press, 1970); Gary Ross Mormino, *Immigrants on the Hill: Italian-Americans in St. Louis, 1882–1982* (Urbana: University of Illinois Press, 1986), chap. 2. For other parts of Europe, see Louise Tilly, Joan Scott, and Miriam Cohen, "Women's Work and European Fertility Patterns," *Journal of Interdisciplinary History* 6 (Winter 1976): 447–76.

[15] Louise C. Odencrantz, *Italian Women in Industry* (New York: Russell Sage Foundation, 1919), pp. 27, 28.

[16] Ibid., p. 28.

States.[17] Conditions in the south made it particularly difficult to educate children. Schooling was possible only during the winter months, when children were not needed to assist in planting, cultivating, and harvesting.[18] And increased numbers of surviving offspring in the late nineteenth century accentuated the economic pressures on the family that made child labor so important.

School attendance was theoretically mandatory for Italian youngsters ages six to nine; however, both boys and girls attended poorly financed and badly organized schools where attendance laws were not enforced.[19] In some communities a large percentage of children received some schooling, but not beyond the lower grades.[20] This pattern was true of the private, Catholic schools as well. Most of the students in church schools were girls from wealthier families, who were sent to learn fancy embroidery and dressmaking. The very few high school classes in the south were by and large attended by boys who stayed on for technical training.[21] But for adolescents, especially the girls, the skills needed to help their families and set up their own households later could be taught at home; most parents saw little need to send their older children to school.[22]

Mothers taught daughters household skills as one part of the effort to ensure that they would attract proper mates. Like all parents, southern Italians were concerned that their children find suitable marriage partners. For the Italian woman, finding a good mate depended on her labor power, her ability to produce and raise children, and her inheritance. These resources were valued by the parents of a prospective bride, and

[17] Ministero della Pubblica Istruzione, Direzione Generale dell'Istruzione Primaria e Popolare, *L'istruzione primaria e popolare in Italia con speciale riguardo al'anno scholastico 1907–08* (Rome, 1960), 1:108, as quoted in John Briggs, *An Italian Passage: Immigrants to Three American Cities, 1890–1930* (New Haven: Yale University Press, 1978), p. 39.

[18] See Gabaccia, "Houses and People," p. 92; Williams, *South Italian Folkways*, p. 126.

[19] Boys and girls attended separate schools where the numbers were sufficient. See Leonard Covello, *The Social Background of the Italo-American School Child* (Totowa, N.J.: Rowman and Littlefield, 1972), chap. 8; Briggs, *An Italian Passage*, chap. 3; Williams, *South Italian Folkways*, chap. 2.

[20] Some communities sent large numbers of their young children to school, according to Briggs, *An Italian Passage*, chap. 3.

[21] Ibid., p. 63. There existed some seminaries for boys and convent schools for girls, run by orders, but they were not common. See Williams, *South Italian Folkways*, p. 128.

[22] Covello, *The Social Background*, chap. 3; Chapman, *Milocca*, chap. 2; Cronin, *The Sting of Change*, chap. 6; Williams, *South Italian Folkways*, pp. 20, 21.

they relinquished their daughter and dowered her only after they felt no urgent need for her service and when she had found a worthy husband.

Family needs sometimes meant that Italian parents delayed their children's marriages. A large proportion of Italian women did marry, but the mean age at first marriage for southern Italians at the turn of the century was about 23 years for women and about 27 for men, older than in the United States and about average in Europe.[23] The custom of late marriage was one important way that Italians controlled family size. Italians did not have an unusually high fertility rate. Italian demographer Massimo Livi-Bacci has found that even before the general decline in fertility that took place at the end of the nineteenth century, southern Italy as a whole had what he calls a "moderate" pattern, with about 5.8 children per married woman born before 1879. In one Sicilian community peasants averaged 4.6 children, while wealthy landowners averaged 6.1 and artisans averaged 4.7. This pattern was near or below that observed in many countries of central or northern Europe. We can speculate that, as in other peasant societies in Europe characterized by the wide distribution of property, rural southern Italians were concerned that too many offspring would dissipate their property holdings.[24]

When offspring finally left home, parents tried to prevent family wealth from being adversely affected by their children's marriages; the dowry system was one way for families to maintain or increase the economic position of their kin. A dowered daughter was eligible to marry a man who possessed equal or greater wealth; her family worked actively to ensure that such a spouse was found.[25] In fact, marriages of both sons and

[23] Livi-Bacci, *A History of Italian Fertility*, p. 107. See also Herbert Klein, "The Integration of Italian Immigrants into Argentina and the United States: A Comparative Analysis," *American Historical Review* 88 (April 1983): 306–29.

[24] Livi-Bacci, *A History of Italian Fertility*, 60–285. John Briggs, "Fertility and Cultural Change among Families in Italy and America," *American Historical Review* 91 (December 1986): 1129–45. On fertility patterns in European rural societies in general, see E. A. Wrigley, *Population and History* (New York: McGraw-Hill, 1969), chaps. 3, 4.

[25] Dowries in southern Italy varied; in some communities they included land, in others, furnishings and linens, or even houses. See Chapman, *Milocca*, p. 37; Williams, *South Italian Folkways*, pp. 73–90; Gabaccia, "Houses and People," p. 52; J. K. Davis, *Land and Family in Pisticci* (New York: Humanities Press, 1973), pp. 45, 46. For a general discussion of the role of the dowry system in agricultural society, see Jack Goody, *Production and Reproduction* (London: Cambridge University Press, 1976), chaps. 2, 3. Also see Jack Goody, "Inheritance, Property, and Women: Some Comparative Considerations," in *Family*

daughters were an important means of creating economic alliances between families. Eric Wolf has pointed out that among peasants, for whom
personal relationships serve as substitutes for the more formal economic
relationships of industrial societies, "relationships between two individuals do not merely symbolize the respective statuses and roles of the two
concerned, they involve a whole series of relationships which must be
evaluated and readjusted if there is any indication of change." This "over-
loading of personal relationships," as Wolf terms it, was characteristic of
southern Italian life; it pervaded the whole process of courtship and marriage.[26]

Parents of both daughters and sons carefully scrutinized prospective
mates and prospective in-laws; they closely supervised the courtship of
their sons and daughters to prevent their choosing spouses without parental approval. Single women were not allowed to meet alone with men
before a formal engagement had been announced; this way, families usually prevented a friendship that might lead to a marriage in disregard of
parental wishes on either side, or unpleasant confrontations between
child and parent. Even in Sicilian communities the loss of virginity before
marriage did not concern the parents of young women so much as the
public evidence of this loss — either in the absence of the requisite blood
on the sheets of the bridal bed or the presence of pregnancy.[27] If the latter
occurred, the family defended its honor by forcing marriage, even if it
was "too early" in terms of the bride's age and the family's economic
hopes.

Although parents played decisive roles in their children's marriages, it
was unusual for a family to select a spouse for a son or daughter against
the child's wishes or to veto a choice made by a son or daughter. Because
children associated only with community friends and kin, it was unlikely
that they would meet anyone without the appropriate social connections

---

and Inheritance, ed. Jack Goody, Joan Thirsk, and E. P. Thompson (Cambridge University
Press, 1976), pp. 10–36.

[26] Wolf, "Types of Latin American Peasantry," pp. 465–66. .

[27] Chapman, *Milocca*, chap. 5. See also Briggs, "Fertility and Cultural Change." According to Jane Schneider and Peter Schneider, "the use of the virginity test had as much a ritual
as a practical significance, and it is often the outward form of the ritual more than its sub-
stance that matters. People were well aware that the blood on the sheet could have come
from the bride's thumb." *Culture and Political Economy in Western Sicily* (New York: Academic Press, 1976), p. 94.

or wealth.[28] By the end of the nineteenth century, with the exception of Sicily where parents took the initiative, a young man or woman could begin the process of choosing a mate by reporting an interest in a particular person as a marriage partner to his or her parents. The parents would then make inquiries about the prospective mate's family—its wealth and reputation in the community, the character of the prospective spouse, and his or her economic expectations. If the answers to such questions proved satisfactory and if the other family was also interested, the two groups would meet to discuss details of the dowry and inheritance. After the agreement was reached, a formal engagement could be announced.[29]

The ritual surrounding marriage, however, could not be easily enforced in the case of poor peasants. Much of the contemporary literature on southern Italy stresses the family's tight control over the marriages of their children. These studies, however, are based on the experiences of property holders who remained in the village or who, formerly landless, succeeded in buying holdings after emigration had reduced population pressure on land. The ideal courtship pattern was established by landowners who had the resources to bargain for desirable mates and could afford to support their children until suitable spouses were found. Poorer peasants tried to emulate this pattern, hoping to improve their situation through the marriage of their offspring. In some cases a woman would be eligible for at least a somewhat wealthier husband if she had other qualities to substitute for an inadequate dowry such as beauty and charm, but more important, work discipline and household skills. To enhance their daughter's marriage prospects, parents encouraged hard work and proper behavior and prevented daughters from pursuing questionable activities that might cast doubt on their reliability.[30] But as the numbers of landless and land-poor peasants grew, it became more difficult for parents to influence the marriages of their daughters or sons. And land-poor peasants constituted a high proportion of those who emigrated from southern Italy.

[28] See Chapman, *Milocca*, chap. 5; Cronin, *The Sting of Change*, pp. 55–58; Williams, *South Italian Folkways*, pp. 73–90.

[29] See Chapman, *Milocca*, chap. 5; Cronin, *The Sting of Change*, pp. 55–58; Williams, *South Italian Folkways*, pp. 73–90.

[30] Sydel Silverman, "Life Crisis as a Clue to Social Functions," *Anthropological Quarterly* 40 (1967): 127–38. Also see Silverman, "Agricultural Organization," p. 16; Covello, *The Social Background*, pp. 202–4.

An exploration of the extent to which Italian families were losing control over the marriages of their offspring is beyond the scope of this study. An increase in the illegitimacy rate, a drop in the age of marriage, an overall increase in premarital and marital fertility in southern Italy might indicate that parents were increasingly unable to control the behavior of their children. But illegitimacy rates were always low in Italy, and those changes that did occur during the period were primarily a consequence of the redefinition of legal marriage.[31] Marital fertility as a whole declined in the second half of the nineteenth century, although very slowly. Some demographic evidence suggests that land-poor parents, less concerned about maintaining property than with a greater need for family workers, were more likely than others in southern Italy to have as many as six to eight children to a household.[32]

There is some other evidence indicating that families became less able to control their children's choice of partner. One of the chief mechanisms by which families in agricultural societies control marriage is by enforcing unions between men and women of the same communities; in this way, families could see to it that their properties would not be widely scattered. The greatest decline in endogamous marriages in Sicily did not take place until the twentieth century; nevertheless, in late-nineteenth-century southern Italian communities experiencing heavy rates of out-migration, the system of endogamous marriage was already breaking down.[33] The process of emigration itself, by disrupting the local sex ratio, forced women to move beyond their communities in search of a husband.

Emigration certainly disrupted norms concerning strict parental control over marriage and sexual behavior, but the process has yet to be systematically studied. We can speculate that under these circumstances, a woman's own freedom of choice regarding a prospective mate increased, and there is some evidence to indicate that sexual mores changed. Carlo Levi's account of life in a southern Italian village after the period of great migration is suggestive: "All that people say about the people of the South, things I once believed in myself: the savage rigidity of their morals, their Oriental jealousy, the fierce sense of honor . . . all these are but

[31] Livi-Bacci, *A History of Italian Fertility*, pp. 69–77.
[32] See ibid., pp. 77–98, 108.
[33] On the purpose of endogamous unions, see Goody, *Production and Reproduction*, p. 19; Barton, *Peasants*, 42.

myths. Perhaps they existed a long time ago, and something of them is left in the way of stiff conventionality. But emigration has changed the picture."[34] The closed, tightly controlled rural community that had so long been the popular image of the southern Italian village no longer existed.

Wives and Mothers in the Peasant Community

Once Italian women left their parents to become wives, their ability to control their own lives and those of others increased. That Italian women could exert such control runs counter to the conventional wisdom about patriarchal southern Italian culture. A careful look at the behavior of nineteenth-century southern Italian women reveals that although women were deferential in public, married women played very active roles within the family and took part in important decisions about the behavior of its members.[35]

Women with property had direct control over at least some economic decisions. Usually, the wife's dowry remained her property until she died; if she had no children at her death, it would return to her parental family. Her husband could not sell this property without her permission, and she typically decided how her property was to be divided among the offspring.[36] Women from landowning families could also bargain for husbands who would provide adequately for their material needs. Furthermore, these families had the prestige in the community to ensure that their daughters were treated with respect by their spouses.[37]

[34]Carlo Levi, *Christ Stopped at Eboli* (New York: Farrar, Straus, 1947), p. 102.

[35]Recent anthropological studies of contemporary peasant societies have described similar patterns. For the traditional view of the role of southern Italian women, see Covello, *The Social Background*, pp. 302–7; Blok, *The Mafia*, pp. 49, 50. My discussion has been influenced by Louise Lamphere, "Strategies, Cooperation and Conflict among Women in Domestic Groups," in Michelle Rosaldo and Louise Lamphere, eds., *Woman, Culture and Society* (Stanford, Calif.: Stanford University Press, 1974), pp. 99–100. See also Michelle Rosaldo, "Woman, Culture and Society: A Theoretical Overview," in ibid., pp. 17–42.

[36]See Chapman, *Milocca*, pp. 37, 97; Covello, *The Social Background*, pp. 202–8.

[37]See Ernestine Friedl, "The Position of Women: Appearance and Reality," *Anthropological Quarterly* 40 (1967): 93–108. See also Constantine Panunzio, *The Soul of an Immigrant* (1921; reprint, New York: Arno Press, 1969), p. 16.

All married women, whether propertied or not, were able to exert influence within the household. All women brought to their families a variety of important assets — labor power, domestic skills learned under rigorous training from their mothers, and the respect accorded women of good and industrious character. The Italian wife's ability to supervise domestic enterprises and to produce and raise children who could contribute to the family enterprise and take care of parents in their old age were her sources of domestic influence.[38] Although men held relatively more formal political power in the community than women, they lived in a hierarchical world in which peasants, regardless of sex, held no power. Political and social power rested in the hands of wealthy landowners and government officials who were remote and inaccessible.[39]

Within the peasant community the household was the most important social and economic unit; the division between the private and the public was therefore not distinct.[40] The Italian woman as wife and mother contributed to the work enterprise in various ways. She supervised household chores and organized the clothes making and food preparation. In addition, she often tended animals and tilled the garden, producing food for family consumption and for sale at the local market. Artisans' wives also assisted in the shop. In Sicily men traveled long distances to work in the fields, departing before sunrise and often not returning home except on weekends. The wives were thus left to supervise household tasks and care for children. Given their household tasks and responsibilities for child rearing, peasant wives found it difficult to work in the fields. It was a mark of poverty when women went to the fields, and a sign of status when wives remained in the home.[41] Nonetheless, poor families could not always achieve their ideals. Sicilian wives, particularly among the poorer families, helped during harvest periods picking fruits and nuts, threshing

---

[38] See Foerster, *Italian Emigration*, p. 95.

[39] See Schneider and Schneider, *Cultural and Political Economy*, chap. 8. Susan Rogers discusses the lack of political power in peasant society as it affects both men's and women's roles in "Female Forms of Power and the Myth of Male Dominance: A Model of Female/Male Interaction in Peasant Society," *American Ethnologist* 2 (1975): 727–56. See also Louise Tilly and Joan Scott, *Women, Work and Family* (New York: Holt, Rinehart and Winston, 1978).

[40] See Gabaccia, "Houses and People," chap. 7.

[41] See Williams, *South Italian Folkways*, chap. 26; Chapman, *Milocca*, chaps. 2, 5; Foerster, *Italian Emigration*, chap. 6; Moss and Thompson, "The South Italian Family," p. 38.

wheat, and husking almonds. In regions around Naples it was common for whole families to travel to the fields during the day. Rudolf Bell has suggested that in parts of Sicily and southern Italy infant mortality escalated during the harvest seasons partly because Italian mothers were unable to provide adequate nourishment and care while they were away in the fields.[42] In addition to working in the fields as the situation required, women earned needed cash by sewing clothes for wealthier families, and some became petty merchants, selling their wares from their homes or at market stalls.[43]

Given the connection between the ability to protect peasant women and notions of status, it is understandable that, in recalling their Old World roots, second- and third-generation Italian Americans in San Francisco stated categorically that the women in their families never worked. In the course of her interviews, anthropologist Micaela di Leonardo discovered quite complicated relationships between the ideal and the reality of the past concerning women's work. Understanding the everyday experience of Italian women in their homeland and during the early years in America is difficult, according to di Leonardo, because "the organic ethnic community—the patriarchal ethnic family and the total ethnic women are key elements in the language of rhetorical nostalgia." For Italians, therefore, the traditional notion that women never worked is part of an idealized past, not unlike the idealized past shared by many Americans about small-town life and the traditional nuclear family.[44]

Ann Cornelisen's incisive study of contemporary southern Italian women also reflects on women of earlier generations. "Peasant women were never afraid to work," she writes. One of her respondents, in describing her own work experience and that of her mother, demonstrated well her understanding of the disjunction between the ideal and the reality of married women's work:

---

[42] On married women's work in Sicily, see Franchetti and Sonnino, *La Sicilias*, pp. 76, 77; Chapman, *Milocca*, pp. 20–21; Williams, *South Italian Folkways*, p. 21. On southern Italy, see Silverman, "Agricultural Organization"; Foerster, *Italian Emigration*, chap. 5; Williams, *South Italian Folkways*, p. 23; Rudolf M. Bell, *Fate and Honor, Family and Village* (Chicago: University of Chicago Press, 1979), p. 40.

[43] See Gabaccia, "Houses and People," p. 86.

[44] Micaela di Leonardo, *The Varieties of Ethnic Experience: Kinship, Class, and Gender among California Italian-Americans* (Ithaca, N.Y.: Cornell University Press, 1984), p. 233.

> We had to do what came when it came. . . . Mamma worked at anything she could get and that's why she's so old now. . . . She worked — God alone knows how hard — and the only advice she ever gave me was "Face it. You're going to work all your life but don't ever work in the fields . . . they won't let you off till you're half dead and good for nothing else. . . ." When we got married, . . . [my husband] said no more work in the fields but I still did a lot of the time, especially when he didn't have work. Like I told him, we couldn't starve just because of his pride, so I'd go out by day — for good pay.[45]

Cornelisen's interview indicates more than just the Italian woman's understanding of the value of her work. It also suggests that women influenced important decisions in a day-to-day context.

One of the most significant areas where the wife could exert control was the family budget. As in many working-class families, the southern Italian wife was responsible for supervising the use of all her husband's earnings, except for a small amount he set aside for personal expenses. She also managed the income of other family members. In determining daily expenses, the wife made implicit decisions about how much would be contributed to each child's dowry or inheritance. Generally, the daily purchases for food and clothing were made by the woman on her own initiative; larger expenditures required the consent of both partners.[46] To the extent that surplus income was available, men may well have had greater authority in determining its expenditure. But because most of the household earnings went for food and clothing, the wife's role as budget director placed her in a strategic position. Constance Cronin has pointed out that in Sicily many husbands permitted their wives to make "secret" purchases with the family earnings precisely because they believed that all of the decisions were based on the women's best calculations about family need. Their attitude is demonstrated in the following excerpt from one man's account of his wife's use of family earnings:

> Tonight I see there is not a 1,000 lire bill in the money drawer and I ask my wife about it and she answers like this: "Well I bought thread for 100 lire and needles for 40 lire each and I bought three needles and pins for 55 lire . . ."

---

[45] Ann Cornelisen, *Women of the Shadows: The Wives and Mothers of Southern Italy* (New York: Vintage Books, 1976), pp. 36, 37.

[46] Williams, *South Italian Folkways*, p. 77. See also Chapman, *Milocca*, pp. 37, 38.

and when she finished it all adds up . . . to much more than 1,000 lire and yet the total value of the goods is much less than 1,000. So now what really happened? She bought some things and saved the rest and then makes my head swim with her accounting. So I let it go because I know my wife is a good woman and will not waste the money on foolish things, but will buy something for the children. . . . All the men do this and all the women.[47]

Although most rural Italians shared economic enterprises within the immediate family, they maintained ties to other members of the community as well. Ties to distant kin and neighbors were both competitive and cooperative.[48] Marriage was one way to solidify both kinds of connections, and women, because of their strategic positions, were at the center of this family effort. Because wives devoted many years to managing the welfare of their children, it seemed natural that when it came time for the children to marry, mothers would take a primary interest in the nuptial arrangements. But the most important reason for their central role in this activity was that mothers were in better positions than fathers to make the right connections, to find out the reputations of other families.

The wife's day-to-day activities brought her into contact with more people of varying status, whereas the majority of men worked away from the village for days, weeks, or even longer during most of the year. As day laborers, even more so as sharecroppers, these men came into contact with very few people, and those, usually other male farm workers. In her study of a Sicilian agricultural town, Donna Gabaccia has shown that although more prosperous women (wives of property owners and artisans) had relatively little contact with their neighbors, poor women in the course of their daily chores met many. They often worked alongside neighbors as they sat outside their small houses, supervising young children. Village women's gossip passed along information about community members and also set standards and reinforced norms about proper behavior.[49] Poor women even had the opportunity to interact with women

[47] Cronin, *The Sting of Change*, p. 75.

[48] The view that Italians depended solely on immediate kin was widely held until the 1970s. Most influential was Banfield, *The Moral Basis of a Backward Society*. By contrast, see Barton, *Peasants*; Gabaccia, *From Sicily to Elizabeth Street*, chap. 4.

[49] Gabaccia, *From Sicily to Elizabeth Street*, chap. 4; Cronin, *The Sting of Change*, p. 65. On the importance of female gossip for exchanging information about village families and for influencing public opinion, see Rogers, "Female Forms of Power"; Gabaccia, *From Sicily to Elizabeth Street*; Schneider and Schneider, *Culture and Political Economy*, p. 93.

and sometimes men who were their "social superiors." If they worked as laundresses, tailoresses, midwives, or petty merchants, they might visit the homes of wealthier families.[50]

Some Sicilian men acknowledged that their wives were better able to handle a variety of jobs precisely because they met more diverse people. "I'm alone in the fields all day. I have only the mule to talk to. What do I know about such things? My wife has more experience, go ask my wife," one man replied to Cronin's inquiries. A number of men, she reported, refused to participate in her study "on the grounds that they did not know how to talk correctly," but these men said "their wives should be excellent respondents."[51] Italian wives in Sicily were known as fast talkers and good arguers, and they used their skills in dealing with their husbands and others in the community. "Somehow they are the ones that understand the intricacies of local bureaucracy," writes Ann Cornelisen about the women of Lucania. "They sense who can be tricked, forced or cajoled. . . . They teach their children, and it is often the soundest teaching they will receive . . . [about] the 'proper ways' of the community."[52]

In the late nineteenth century, as in the twentieth, Italian women took complete charge of households when husbands migrated. In areas characterized by heavy migration, women were without husbands for months and years at a time. Women had to take charge of the economic projects at home, as well as the domestic chores. "The men have gone and the women have taken over," wrote Carlo Levi about a southern Italian community that had sent many men to the United States in search of work.[53] According to anthropologist Susan Rogers, this pattern can be generalized to other communities experiencing the male out-migration in the late nineteenth century. Under these circumstances, women "usurped formally male prerogatives such as overt household decision making."[54] One contemporary southern Italian woman described her responsibilities while her husband was away at work in Germany: "To me, my job is to see the land gets farmed, to raise up the children, . . . to teach them what is right and get work, as much work as I can get."[55] For wives of emigrant

---

[50] Gabaccia, "Houses and People," p. 86; Williams, *South Italian Folkways*, p. 77.

[51] Cronin, *The Sting of Change*, p. 73.

[52] Cornelisen, *Women of the Shadows*, p. 26.

[53] Levi, *Christ Stopped at Eboli*, p. 402.

[54] Rogers, "Female Forms of Power."

[55] Cornelisen, *Women of the Shadows*, p. 123. For a description of a similar situation in

men, doing domestic chores and overseeing the farm were inseparable parts of the job of maintaining the household.

Rogers's reference to formal male prerogatives does point to an important discrepancy between the actual behavior of Italian women and what the community acknowledged as proper relations between men and women.[56] The mores of the community paid lip service to the importance of showing respect to the male head even within the family arena. Folk sayings often declare that males were to be accorded ultimate authority in the household. And although actual incidents of wife beating were uncommon, Italian folk wisdom judged it a legitimate way of dealing with rebellious women.[57] In Sicily both public and private deference, or at least its appearance, was expected. The wife addressed her husband with the formal *voi* and waited on him at the table.[58] Sicilian women were not to speak with men in the public square or be seen in village cafes without their husbands. Women were more likely to attend church, and they clustered in groups segregated from the men.[59] Most poor women could not afford to stand on custom that dictated that females stay out of the public eye; unless a woman had servants, she had to go out to the village to market. Nonetheless, proper behavior of women in public was significant, and women who showed disrespect for their husbands were condemned by the community.

The discrepancy between the public rhetoric and private reality of Italian women's lives is an outgrowth of the fact that southern Italian society was very much a patriarchy in the legal sense—males acted as official representatives of the family to the public world. Males were recognized by the state as representatives of the family for census enumeration and as household heads for tax purposes. Men were conscripted as soldiers by

---

early Nantucket, when men were away whaling, see J. Hector St. John de Crevecour, "Peculiar Customs of Nantucket," in *Letters from an American Farmer* (1782; modern edition, Middlesex, England: Penguin, 1981), p. 157.

[56] Louise Lamphere found a similar discrepancy between the behavior and the rhetoric among Latin American immigrants in Providence, R.I., with respect to gender roles. See *From Working Daughters to Working Mothers: Immigrant Women in a New England Industrial Community* (Ithaca, N.Y.: Cornell University Press, 1987), chap. 6.

[57] Moss and Thompson, "The South Italian Family," pp. 36, 37; Cronin, *The Sting of Change*, chap. 5.

[58] Gabaccia, *From Sicily to Elizabeth Street*, chap. 4. See also Cronin, *The Sting of Change*, chap. 5.

[59] See Chapman, *Milocca*, p. 38.

the state. In most cases, beyond the dowry arrangements, land was registered in the name of husbands; the women could not sell it or make other contracts, such as land rental.[60] If the man could not command respect from his own family members, then his worthiness, and by implication the worthiness of the whole family, was suspect.

In a society where families had both to cooperate and to compete with one another, family prestige was particularly important. Reinforcing the prestige of the male head contributed to the family's public prestige; in part, this meant protecting the honor of women. In their discussion of the importance of honor in Sicilian peasant society, Jane and Peter Schneider have noted that although peasants were powerless to challenge the larger inequities of latifundism, they could challenge peers when they threatened the family's property by such acts as abusive grazing.[61] The concern for protecting women in public, or seeing to it that strangers did not violate the family by taking advantage of its women, the need for men to "right" the "wronged" family if women's honor was impugned, were similar: "It is in the competition between near status equals that honor plays an important role. It functions literally to even the score among people who are close enough to each other to feel envy."[62]

The idealization of female deference and reserve was greater among low-status peasants because these women had greater contact with people outside the family, beyond the indirect control of often absent males. Wealthier families, whose women were more secluded and whose men had larger roles in family networks among kin and neighbors, were less concerned about the public behavior of females. For example, wealthier women could dress in brightly colored clothes, and they could speak more freely with men when families visited one another.[63] One might argue that these women were permitted to be more gregarious precisely because it was clear that they, unlike their poorer sisters, exerted relatively less control over activities of economic consequence for the family.

---

[60] For an excellent discussion of legal patriarchy, see Joan Kelly-Gadol, "Family and Society," in Joan Kelly-Gadol, ed., *Women, History and Theory* (Chicago: University of Chicago Press, 1984), pp. 110–55.

[61] Schneider and Schneider, *Culture and Political Economy*, p. 100.

[62] Ibid.

[63] Gabaccia, *From Sicily to Elizabeth Street*, chap. 4; Schneider and Schneider, *Culture and Political Economy*, p. 152.

Peasant women understood the importance of maintaining the public posture. One New Yorker who had grown up in southern Calabria described what happened when his older brother took over as head of the family upon the death of the father:

> My brother who became head of the family had to take orders from her [mother]. But that was only in our home. On the street he tried to impress everybody that he was the boss of the family. . . . Also, as I remember, I could never make out why my mother would tell untrue things to other women in the street. She would always complain how strict our older brother was. She would say, "Oh my Rocco does not want me to do this," or "Rocco thinks so-and-so," or "Oh no, I must first ask Rocco." And so on. And she said these things while we knew perfectly well that the big bully Rocco would probably at the same time complain to my uncle saying how unreasonable, how impossibly crazy my mother was, and "Oh, if I only had the power, what I wouldn't do."[64]

In Sicily as well, although many families officially designated a male as family head to represent the family to the outside world and the person to whom relatives go for advice, the individual considered wise and perceptive is "invariably a female." One respondent whom Cronin termed typical reported: "My mother is the real chief. She is the intellect . . . she is recognized as having intelligence and clear sightedness. She is the one who has character and who is the ultimate arbiter of what is right and wrong."[65]

During the early part of the twentieth century many southern Italian wives traveled to the United States to join their husbands. The heritage southern Italian women brought with them included their vital role in the family economy, epitomized by their hard work. In Italy they were badly needed at home, and there was little opportunity for schooling, so young women stayed close to home. But Italian females, particularly married women, could not be excluded from the public world because the public and private realms were so closely intertwined. Navigating between the public and private spheres would be different in New York and would

---

[64] Covello, *The Social Background*, pp. 214, 215.

[65] Cronin, *The Sting of Change*, pp. 82, 83. Constantine Panunzio recalls that in his village near Molfetta his grandmother played a similar role. See *The Soul*, pp. 11, 12.

provide new challenges. The women brought to America years of experience helping to manage household economic enterprises, juggling domestic chores, and raising children under difficult circumstances. In the United States they mustered these resources to deal with more years of hardship and struggle in a new land.

WORK AND FAMILY IN
NEW YORK: DAUGHTERS

No one can be said to understand the economic conditions of this population who
fails to understand the important role played by the women.

—Robert Foerster, *Italian Emigration of Our Times*

In 1914 eleven-year-old Rose Peccara of Jones Street in Manhattan told a
social worker about her daily chores.

> I am a little girl, eleven years old. I live on Jones Street in a tenement. I
> have many sisters and brothers and we all help to do the work in our house.
> Every morning before school, I sweep out three rooms and help get
> breakfast. Then I wash the dishes.
> After school, I do my homework for an hour, then I make flowers. All of
> us, my sisters, my cousins, my aunts, my mother work on flowers. We put
> the yellow centers into forget-me-nots. It takes me over an hour to finish one
> gross and I make three cents for that. If we all work all our spare time after
> school, we can make as much as two dollars between us.
> In the mornings, on the way to school, I leave finished flowers at the
> shop, and stop for more work on the way home.
> In the summer, we do not make flowers. But I mind Danny, my baby
> brother, all the time. My mother says she would rather work in a shop than
> have to mind bad kids. But she does not go to work, she stays at home and I
> do lots of housework for her. Sometimes I do the washing.
> In the summer I don't have much time to play because always I must mind
> Danny. All during vacation, I carry lunch to my father. He works at a barber
> shop on 23 Street and every day in summer I walk there and back for him.

Sometimes I go to play a little while at night with the other children but I must mind Danny because he does not like to go to bed until we do. Then he gets so tired he goes right to sleep on my lap and I carry him up. I think my brother is very nice but I get tired minding him sometimes.[1]

Everyday life for New York Italian girls like Rose Peccara, her sisters, her cousins, and her aunts as well as her mother, meant juggling a variety of tasks, from sunrise to nightfall and beyond, in order to contribute to the maintenance of the family. These responsibilities affected women's attitudes toward wage labor, domestic roles, leisure life, and community life in New York.

Such arduous daily routines were nothing new to these immigrants— Italian women and children joining their relatives in the early years of the century brought with them the experience of hard work by all but the youngest family members. Some of the social investigators of the day understood this tradition. "As the wife and children of his forefathers have always worked in the fields," Elizabeth Shipley Sergeant wrote in 1910 about the Italian families huddled in New York City tenements, "and as the habit of familial labor is ingrained in his race and creed, the custom persists in spite of changed surroundings and conditions."[2] Sergeant's insight is not quite correct, however. Although the surroundings were indeed new and some conditions were different, the social and economic circumstances facing these households were similar in important ways. As in Italy, poor families in New York met the challenge of surviving by putting several members of the family to work in one capacity or another. Before examining the work experiences of, first, young Italian daughters

---

[1] Greenwich House, *Thirteenth Annual Report* (N.p.: n.p., 1913–1914), p. 8. Certainly, one must use evidence from settlement-house reports with great care. My study makes extensive use of survey material and government reports, as well as the records of private charities. The interests of those recording the information surely affects the way the material is presented. The voices of the respondents cannot be purely recorded; the tone is undoubtedly set by the desires of the recorders. Sometimes, as is probably the case here, investigators wished to emphasize the harsh aspects of family life involving sweated labor and the dangers of child labor. In other cases the descriptions of family life are deeply imbued with stereotypes about immigrant, working-class life. Aware of the biases and possible distortions, the historian must nonetheless make use of these materials because they are excellent systematic sources on immigrant working-class life.

[2] Elizabeth Shipley Sergeant, "Toilers of the Tenements: Where the Beautiful Things of the Great Shops Are Made," *McClure's Magazine* 35 (July 1910): 232.

and, then, adolescent daughters, we look at the social and economic circumstances of these families that set the stage for female work.

The Challenges Facing Italian Families

Southern Italian women usually came to the United States as part of a
delayed migration, joining men who had traveled to the New World first.
During the latter decades of the nineteenth century many men made the
voyage between America and Italy several times, either alone or in the
company of kin or fellow villagers (*paesani*).[3] When they accumulated
adequate funds, many settled permanently in the States and sent for other
family members. By the turn of the century large numbers of Italian immigrants lived as family groups in New York.[4] An analysis of a 5-percent
sample of the New York State Manuscript Census for three Italian neighborhoods—two in the heart of Manhattan's Little Italy on the lower West
Side and one in East Harlem—reveals that, like other migrant populations, this one was heavily dominated by adult men and women. In 1905
almost one-half of the foreign-born males and females were between the
ages of sixteen and thirty-six.[5] (For details about the sampling method,
see Appendix A.)

The wives' journeys to join their husbands in New York were invariably difficult; from the moment they left Italy, however, they faced new
responsibilities with characteristic determination. Leonard Covello recalls in his autobiography that his mother had never been more than a few
kilometers outside their native Avilgliano when in 1896 she made the

[3] See Robert Foerster, *The Italian Emigration of Our Times* (Cambridge: Harvard University Press, 1919); Betty Boyd Caroli, *Italian Repatriation from the United States,
1900–1914* (New York: Center for Migration Studies, 1973).

[4] Analyzing aggregate statistics on the emigration of males and females, Massimo Livi-
Bacci has estimated that Italian females arrived, on the average, one year and two months
after the males. See *L'Immigrazione et l'Assimilazione degli Italiani negli Stati Uniti* (Milan:
Dot. A. Giuffrè, 1961), esp. pp. 17–19.

[5] Another 19.37 percent of the foreign-born males were between thirty-five and forty-
four; only 15.5 percent were below age sixteen. For females, 20.6 percent were between
thirty-five and forty-four; 16.6 percent, below sixteen. New York State Manuscript Census,
1905.

Italian mother and child, Ellis Island, 1905. (Photograph by Lewis W. Hine, courtesy of the New York Public Library.)

long trip with her young children, first to Naples and then on the choppy seas for twenty days to New York. Nevertheless, "she accepted this with resignation as God's will." The family spent two days at Ellis Island waiting for Leonard's father to meet them, and during this time Mrs. Covello "hardly closed her eyes for fear of losing us in the confusion."[6]

But not all women who traveled to the United States were wives or mothers with small children. Single women sometimes came alone to join parents, siblings, uncles, aunts, even fiancés. Unlike Irish women of the nineteenth century, or even a significant proportion of Slavic women in the early twentieth, very few southern Italian females set out to establish themselves independently, even on a temporary basis.[7] Most Italian women in America lived in households with kin, the vast majority with immediate kin in nuclear families.[8]

Italian women in New York lived in households that were large and poor. Although my sampling of the 1905 and 1925 censuses produced a slight bias in favor of large families (see Appendix A), the figures nevertheless clearly indicate that Italian households were not small. In 1905 the

---

[6] Leonard Covello, *The Heart Is the Teacher* (New York: McGraw-Hill, 1958), p. 19.

[7] Hasia Diner, *Erin's Daughters in America* (Baltimore, Md.: Johns Hopkins University Press, 1983); Stephen Steinberg, *The Ethnic Myth: Race, Ethnicity and Class in America* (New York: Atheneum, 1981), chap. 6.

[8] "Household" is here a group of coresiding persons whether kin or not; "nuclear family" here is a coresiding married couple or married couple with their offspring or widowed person with offspring (see also Appendix A). In 1905 about 96 percent of foreign-born Italian women in the New York City sample neighborhoods lived in nuclear families headed by their husbands or fathers (families referred to here as the primary nuclear families; see Appendix A). The remaining 4 percent lived with a secondary nuclear family (see Appendix A), or, less frequently, with a family of boarders. Twenty years later a 1-percent sample of the same neighborhoods showed similar patterns. The neighborhoods in the sample were chosen because they were dominated by households rather than by boarding houses, as is characteristic of some immigrant settlements. (See Appendix A.) Therefore, they are no doubt biased in favor of women living in nuclear families. However, these findings are similar to results obtained by contemporary surveyors who sampled from among Italian women, rather than households. For example, of 1,095 Italian working women investigated by Louise Odencrantz in 1919, only 86 (7.8 percent) were found to be living outside of their families, three as domestic servants. These figures are particularly striking because the women were all wage earners and thus had greater potential to be living away from their families than the female population as a whole. See Louise C. Odencrantz, *Italian Women in Industry* (New York: Russell Sage Foundation, 1919), p. 17. In general, Italian neighborhoods dominated by boarding houses were overwhelmingly male. Thus my sample seems to accurately reflect the living situations of Italian women.

median household size was 6.3 people. This figure included a number of families with boarders, but in 1925, when very few households included boarders, the median size was still a high 5.4.[9] In 1930 in New York City as a whole, Italian households had a median size of 4.4, the largest for all the foreign groups in the city on which the census reported household size.[10]

These large families were headed by men with low earning capacity. A substantial number of Italian men in New York City, about one-quarter, were skilled workers—barbers, tailors, and skilled construction workers—but an even greater number were unskilled workers—street cleaners, dock workers, and construction laborers. In fact, among the Italian men the unskilled group was the largest of all the skill classifications. Of all married Italian men in the three sampled neighborhoods, 44 percent were unskilled laborers in 1905. The proportion was similar for all age groups—young single men, those who had families to support, and older males.[11] (For the skill classification, see Appendix B.) Unskilled labor usually meant low wages, and both unskilled and some skilled labor meant seasonal or irregular work. Many Italian men were likely to be out of work several months of the year. A 1909 U.S. Immigration Commission investigation of the social and economic conditions in the sampled Italian neighborhoods revealed the consequent economic problems for these families. Seventy-six percent of Italian households earned less than $600 per year; the average, $519, was one of the lowest among the immigrant groups surveyed and well below that estimated as necessary for a

[9] New York State Manuscript Census, 1905 and 1925.

[10] U.S. Department of Commerce, Bureau of the Census, *Fifteenth Census of the United States, 1930: Special Report on Foreign-Born White Families* (Washington, D.C.: Government Printing Office, 1933), pp. 171, 178.

[11] New York State Manuscript Census, 1905. Thomas Kessner drew a sample of Italian households from basically the same neighborhoods in 1905; he included a number of households from Kings County as well. His figures show a similar distribution of Italian male occupants, except that he found a greater percentage of men in what he termed "low white collar jobs" in 1905. In large part our differences are due to the fact that Kessner recorded peddlers as low white-collar workers whereas I have recorded peddlers as unskilled workers, placing only those who declared they were shopkeepers in the white-collar category. See Kessner, *The Golden Door: Italian and Jewish Immigrant Mobility in New York City, 1880–1915* (New York: Oxford University Press, 1977), p. 52.

Italian street laborers under the Sixth Avenue Elevated, New York City, 1910. (Photograph by Lewis W. Hine, courtesy of the New York Public Library.)

household of five to enjoy the "essentials of a normal standard of living in New York City."[12]

In 1925 foreign-born husbands still held humble jobs. Forty-eight percent were unskilled, and the percentages of skilled, semiskilled, and white-collar workers were essentially the same as in 1905.[13] My sample, drawn from neighborhoods in Manhattan only, is somewhat weighted in favor of poor households; nevertheless, my findings are corroborated by other studies, which suggest that the overall picture for Italian households in New York City was similar. An early 1930s study of some 27,000 Italian-born fathers in New York City, based on information from the birth certificates of their children, found that the most common occupation for the fathers was unskilled laborer (52 percent); skilled workers accounted for approximately 20 percent. Among a smaller group of younger Italian fathers, those with children born in 1931, most were also blue-collar workers, although by then only 32 percent were unskilled laborers.[14]

Because these families were in such vulnerable economic circumstances, it is not surprising to find that they depended on income from more than one wage earner. Italian-born (hereafter, first-generation) and native-born of foreign stock (hereafter, second-generation) adult sons were in the best position to contribute to the family income, and it was clearly expected that they would work. The overwhelming majority were employed, and, as a group, the sons were doing better than the household heads—more were employed in the higher echelons of blue-collar work.[15] In both census years, however, the majority of single men still held blue-collar jobs.[16] In any case, the problem of irregular earnings was characteristic of Italian skilled laborers as well as the unskilled, since so many

[12]The average annual family incomes for the other major immigrant groups: blacks, $439; Russian Jews, $520; Slovaks, $507; the older immigrant groups—Germans and Irish—averaged $676. See U.S. Congress, Senate, *Reports of the Immigration Commission*, vol. 26: *Immigrants in Cities*, S. Doc. 338, 61st Cong., 2d sess. (Washington, D.C.: Government Printing Office, 1911), 1: 228. On the standard of living of New York working-class families, see Louise Bolard More, *Wage Earners' Budgets: A Study of Standards and Cost of Living in New York City* (New York: Henry Holt, 1907).

[13]New York State Manuscript Census, 1925.

[14]See John J. Alesandre, *Occupational Trends of Italians in New York City*, Casa Italiana Educational Bureau Bulletin no. 6 (New York: Columbia University, 1935), tables 1 and 2.

[15]By definition, all single adult men in the primary nuclear family are sons of those families.

[16]New York State Manuscript Census, 1905 and 1925.

jobs such as bricklaying, stonemasonry, and carpentry were particularly vulnerable to dips in the market and changes in the weather.

By the end of the 1920s Italians were among the poorest ethnic groups in the city, as revealed in a 1930 U.S. census report that listed the median monthly rent paid by families for twenty-eight ethnic groups in New York City. Although rent is not a precise index of family prosperity, it is one of the chief items of family expense and hence is a rough index of family resources. The median rent paid by Italian families in 1930 was $32.59, the second lowest among immigrants in the city; Italians ranked at or near the bottom in each borough as well as for the city as a whole.[17]

Italian families in New York City could no more rely exclusively on the labor and earnings of males than they could in southern Italy. But they found that the urban economy of New York offered more opportunities for women to do wage labor than they had in their homeland. Many jobs were available in the small-scale industries that have been the traditional employers of women everywhere in the world. New York was the center of the American garment industry, and this industry remained the city's leading manufacturing sector throughout the first decades of the twentieth century.[18] New York was also an important center for the manufacture of consumer goods such as candy, tobacco, and artificial flowers. These industries, along with domestic service and textile manufacturing, were the arenas where women were most likely to find work.[19]

In a national economy rigidly segregated by sex, variations in the employment structure of American cities greatly affected the employment patterns of women.[20] That the economy of New York City was well suited

[17] U.S. Department of Commerce, Bureau of the Census, *Fifteenth Census of the United States, 1930: Special Report on Foreign-Born White Families*, pp. 171, 178.

[18] A systematic listing of New York City manufacturing from 1900 to 1930 was compiled by a Mr. Kingsbury, using the U.S. Census of Manufacturing and other sources, for the New York City Federal Workers Project (located in the Works Progress Administration, Historical Records Survey, Municipal Archives, New York City). See also Personnel Research Federation, *Occupational Trends in New York City: Changes in the Distribution of Gainful Workers, 1900–1930* (New York: National Occupational Conference, 1933).

[19] On women's occupations in the United States, see U.S. Department of Commerce, Bureau of the Census, *Women in Gainful Occupations, 1870–1920*, by Joseph A. Hill, Census Monographs no. 9 (Washington, D.C.: Government Printing Office, 1929), esp. chaps. 5, 6.

[20] Susan J. Kleinberg, "The Systematic Study of Urban Women," in Milton Cantor and Bruce Laurie, eds., *Class, Sex, and the Woman Worker* (Westport, Conn.: Greenwood Press, 1977), pp. 20–42.

Table 1. Percentage of urban immigrant women employed, 1900, 1910, and 1920

	First generation			Second generation		
Year	All cities 100,000+	New York	Buffalo	All cities 100,000+	New York	Buffalo
1900	23.2	27.2	18.0	32.4	33.4	27.8
1910	26.6	31.7	19.0	36.3	37.8	33.8
1920	22.4	25.7	16.0	37.0	41.0	32.4

Source: U.S. Department of Commerce, Bureau of the Census, *Women in Gainful Occupations, 1870–1920*, by Joseph A. Hill, Census Monographs no. 9 (Washington, D.C.: Government Printing Office, 1929), pp. 239, 240, 272, 273.

Note: All women sixteen years old or over. First generation = foreign born; second generation = native born of foreign parents.

for the employment of foreign-born women is suggested by the figures in Table 1. From 1900 to 1920 about 23–25 percent of foreign-born women living in the largest American cities were recorded by the U.S. census as gainfully employed; however, in New York, the proportion was about 25–30 percent. Virginia Yans-McLaughlin attributes the low level of Italian female employment in Buffalo, New York, to the Italian reluctance to allow women to work outside the home, but she concedes that the upstate city, dominated by heavy industry, had few jobs available for immigrant women.[21] Indeed, as Table 1 shows, labor force participation in Buffalo for all foreign-born women (first generation) and native-born women of foreign stock (second generation) was below the national average for large cities. Although all cities between 1910 and 1920 experienced a decline in the proportion employed among first-generation women, who were now clustered in older age groups and tended to be married, even the proportion of second-generation women, who tended to be in the prime age group for employment, decreased slightly in Buffalo between 1910 and 1920; in contrast, New York, a city of small-scale consumer industries, continued providing jobs for immigrant women and their daughters at a rate above the national metropolitan average.[22] Given the need and

[21] See Virginia Yans-McLaughlin, *Family and Community: Italian Immigrants in Buffalo, 1880–1930* (Ithaca, N.Y.: Cornell University Press, 1977), pp. 50–53.

[22] For another example of the decrease in women's employment that accompanies the expansion of modern industry in European cities, see Louise Tilly, "Urban Growth, Indus-

opportunity in New York City, wage labor dominated the lives of Italian women throughout the first three decades of the twentieth century.

Girlhood and Homework

Italian children began helping their mothers in wage labor as soon as they were able to take on the simplest tasks. The garment industry was highly decentralized, and its production processes, requiring little or no machinery, offered women and children the opportunity for wage work. Owners kept their shops and permanent work force small; contractors responsible for sewing garments that had been cut in the manufacturer's shop subcontracted finishing tasks to homemakers during the busy seasons.[23]

The extent of homework in Italian neighborhoods is hard to estimate because much of the work was illegal, and thus hidden. Nevertheless, the facts we have suggest that it was common and a significant part of the family economy. By 1904 laws required the families engaged in homework and the tenement buildings containing homework apartments to be licensed. By 1913 legislation prohibited the employment of children under fourteen at home, as well as homework on food, dolls, doll clothing, and infants' and children's wear. Violations of the law were the rule; perhaps 50 percent of homeworkers were operating illegally.[24] Enforce-

---

trialization and Women's Employment in Milan, Italy, 1881–1911," *Journal of Urban History* 3 (August 1977): 467–84.

[23] U.S. Congress, Senate, *Reports of the Immigration Commission*, vol. 11: *Immigrants in Industries, Part 6: Clothing Manufacturing*, S. Doc. 633, 61st Cong., 2d sess. (Washington, D.C.: Government Printing Office, 1911), p. 385.

[24] "To count the number of home workers has proved as baffling a task as to attempt to regulate their conditions of employment," wrote Mary Van Kleeck in 1908. In 1901 approximately 27,000 persons were legally authorized to practice homework, with as many as another 13,000 working illegally. This, of course, does not account for all the friends and relatives who might have been helping family members. In 1919 the New York State Department of Labor reported that close to 14,000 Italians were registered as homeworkers; most were women; 7,000 Jews were registered. See Mary Van Kleeck, "Child Labor in New York City Tenements," *Charities and the Commons* 19 (18 January 1908): 1–16; New York State, Department of Labor, *Annual Report of the Industrial Commission, 1918* (Albany, New York, 1919), p. 38 in "Report of the Division of Homework Inspection." See also

ment of regulations before the New Deal was lax, and manufacturers and workers were complicit in trying to hide much of the work (see chapter 4 for an examination of the impact of lax enforcement on Italian women). It is known that approximately one-fifth of the work force in the men's garment industry were female home finishers, almost all of them Italian women and their children. Overall, according to one study in New York City, homework was done in approximately one-fourth of Italian households. Three-quarters of the artificial flower making was carried on in the Italian district below Fourteenth Street. Italians also could be found shelling peanuts, embroidering, assembling baby clothes, and making pin cushions at home.[25]

In general, Italian mothers supervised homework. Sometimes they worked with other women who lived nearby, but invariably they were assisted by their children. "It is the opinion of this investigation," reported the New York State Factory Investigating Commission in 1912, that "all the children of a household where homework was done were drafted into this work."[26] Because homework was seasonal, families had to maximize their wages during the rush period. All available members of the family, including the young children, worked late into the night to increase output. "We all must work if we want to earn anything," reported a mother who worked with two daughters (ages three and four) and their grandmother assembling flowers. The women in this family had no work during the six months from April to October. In the busy season, however, they worked steadily until 8:00 P.M. in order together to earn up to $7.00 a week.[27]

Jeremy Felt, *Hostages of Fortune: Child Labor Reform in New York State* (Syracuse, N.Y.: Syracuse University Press, 1965), p. 147.

[25] U.S. Congress, Senate, *Report on Condition of Woman and Child Wage Earners*, vol. 2: *Men's Ready-Made Clothing*, S. Doc. 645, 61st Cong., 2d sess. (Washington, D.C.: Government Printing Office, 1911), pp. 35, 221; U.S. Congress, Senate, *Reports of the Immigration Commission*, vol. 26: *Immigrants in Cities*, 1: 20. See also Sergeant, "Toilers of the Tenements," pp. 239, 242; Mary Van Kleeck, *Artificial Flower Makers* (New York: Russell Sage Foundation, Survey Associates, 1913); Van Kleeck, "Child Labor in New York City Tenements," pp. 1–16.

[26] New York State Factory Investigating Commission, *Second Report of the Factory Investigating Commission*, vol. 3 (Albany, N.Y.: J. B. Lyon, 1913), p. 105. Also see Sergeant, "Toilers of the Tenements"; Van Kleeck, "Child Labor in New York City Tenements"; Donna R. Gabaccia, "Houses and People: Sicilians in Sicily and New York, 1890–1930" (Ph.D. diss., University of Michigan, 1979), chap. 5.

[27] Van Kleeck, *Artificial Flower Makers*, pp. 94–95. See also Van Kleeck, "Child Labor in New York City Tenements," pp. 1–16.

When boys reached ten, they were allowed, under New York State law, to go out to sell newspapers in the streets; many Italian boys took newsboy jobs, still others became bootblacks, or helped their fathers peddle goods.[28] For girls, homework remained an important responsibility. The U.S. Labor Bureau reported to the U.S. Senate that among Italian girl homeworkers under the age of fourteen 80 percent assisted their mothers on a regular basis, either full time or after school.[29] As soon as girls reached the age of twelve or thirteen, social investigators observed, Italian families would become intensely protective and insist that the females remain very close to home. Investigators of the period attributed this behavior to southern Italian values that dictated females be kept under close supervision.[30] Such commitments must be understood in the larger context of an ideology that, as Louise Lamphere found in her contemporary study of Portuguese and Colombian immigrants, stressed, above all, the importance of "hard work and family self-sufficiency."[31] In the same way, Italian attitudes about adolescent girls were intertwined with the needs of a community in which the daughters' share in wage work was absolutely necessary for family well-being.

Italian girls told the New York State Factory Investigating Commission about the long hours they spent helping their mothers do homework:

Angelina: "When I go home from school, I help my mother to work. I help her earn the money, I do not play at all. I get up at 6 o'clock and I go to bed at 10 o'clock."

Giovanna: "I get up at 5 o'clock in the morning. Then I work with my mother. At 9 o'clock I go to school. I have no time to play. I must work my feathers. At 10 o'clock I go to bed."

[28] Felt, *Hostages of Fortune*, pp. 158, 163; Van Kleeck, "Child Labor in New York City Tenements," p. 9.

[29] U.S. Congress, Senate, *Report on Condition of Woman and Child Wage Earners*, vol. 2: *Men's Ready-Made Clothing*, pp. 235–39. Only fourteen boys were reported employed as homeworkers, and only eight did homework on a regular basis.

[30] See, for example, Caroline Ware, *Greenwich Village, 1920–1930* (Boston: Houghton Mifflin, 1935); Greenwich House, *Annual Report*, various editions 1900–1935; Dorothy Reed, *The Leisure Time of Girls in a Little Italy* (Portland, Ore.: private published, 1932); Robert Park and Herbert A. Miller, *Old World Traits Transplanted* (New York: Harper and Brothers, 1921). Yans-McLaughlin, *Family and Community*, chap. 5, likewise believes such behavior was shaped by traditional values.

[31] Louise Lamphere, *From Working Daughters to Working Mothers: Immigrant Women in a New England Industrial Community* (Ithaca, N.Y.: Cornell University Press, 1987), p. 267.

Antonetta, age 9: "I earn money for my mother after school and on Saturdays and half Sundays. No I do not play. I must work. I get up at 4 o'clock in the morning and I go to bed at 9 o'clock."

Nicolina, age nine, cuts embroidery four hours every day and two hours at night. Her sister, age eight, helps too.[32]

Preteens and young adolescents also did such household chores as cooking and cleaning, and they cared for their younger siblings so that mothers could spend more time doing homework or, if necessary, working at the factory.[33] Often, like Rose Pecarra of Jones Street, they were responsible for several jobs at the same time. Just as in Italy, no distinction was made between family chores and those that produced income— young girls did these tasks as part of their expected duties. Italian families explained to family investigators in 1911 how they managed these various jobs.

Maria reported: "I have no time to play when I work by mother but when I don't work, I mind the baby and clean the house. . . ." Thirteen-year-old Michelina gets up at 5:30 every morning, prepares her father's breakfast and crochets Irish lace before going to school, works again two hours after school and takes care of the baby. . . . Little Camilla only three years old was found running ribbons in corset covers. Rose, her eleven-year-old sister, was taking care of the baby, while Elisa, age 6, and Camilla helped mother.[34]

Although these girls had no time to pursue recreation independently of their families, their lives were by no means joyless. Social investigators who were sensitive to the hardships that poverty imposed on immigrant daughters often did not appreciate the way that work and leisure were

[32] New York State, Factory Investigating Commission, *Second Report*, 1: 106. Also see New York State, Factory Investigating Commission, *Public Hearings in New York City: Second Series* (reprint from the *Preliminary Report of the New York Factory Investigating Commission*; Albany, N.Y.: J. B. Lyon, October 1911), pp. 1744–87.

[33] Reed, *The Leisure Time of Girls*, p. 52. Josephine Roche, "The Italian Girl," in *The Neglected Girl*, West Side Studies (New York: Russell Sage Foundation, Survey Associates, 1914); Albert Perceroni, "The Italians in the United States," *Forum* 45 (January 1911): 15–59.

[34] New York State, Factory Investigating Commission, *Second Report*, 1: 105–6.

intertwined in the lives of these girls. Family tasks could be a source of sociability as well as fatigue for young girls. A letter from one eleven-year-old East Harlem girl describing her activities at a settlement-house camp shows that she enjoyed her new experience but missed the satisfaction she felt at home taking care of her siblings and helping her mother: "Tell mama I am happy. I miss her and de kids. I ain't got no baby to hold. The nurse says she ain't got no babies to give out to us girls and says we must play. Flowers grow here like we makes, only better."[35]

Adolescence and Young Womanhood: Work Patterns

An Italian woman "works because the family relies on her to do her part," Louise Odencrantz wrote in her 1919 study of Italian women workers; her conclusion was echoed by other social investigators.[36] Many young, single women remained at home, assisting in household chores and homework until marriage. Others followed the pattern of most foreign-born and second-generation women, finding work in the New York workshops. In New York, as in Italy, family need was a powerful factor in determining the behavior of Italian women. In pursuing family goals, Italian daughters and their families adapted old strategies to new work patterns.

In New York City in 1905, according to my findings in a sample from the state census, 46 percent of all single Italian-born women over the age of sixteen were wage earners, twice the percentage for all single American women over the age of sixteen. Moreover, nearly 62 percent of women between the ages of sixteen and twenty-one, the largest group of single women living at home, reported occupations to the New York State census takers (see Table 2, part a). In 1925 matters had changed little: 43 percent of all single first-generation women worked outside the home, and the younger women again reported higher rates of gainful employ-

---

[35] Home Garden of New York City Settlement [Harlem House], *Annual Report* (n.p.: n.p., 1913), p. 9.

[36] Odencrantz, *Italian Women in Industry*, p. 179; see also Van Kleeck, *Artificial Flower Makers*, p. 35; Roche, "The Italian Girl," p. 109.

Table 2. Single Italian women at work, 1905 and 1925, New York City (percentage distribution)

	All	Aged 16–21	Aged 22–44	45 and older
a. First generation, 1905	(N=188)	(N=112)	(N=55)	(N=21)
Works outside home	45.7	61.7	27.3	9.6
Works at home	6.4	4.5	10.9	4.8
Does not work	47.9	33.9	61.8	85.7
b. First generation, 1925	(N=123)	(N=38)	(N=56)	(N=29)
Works[a]	43.4	63.2	46.4	13.8
Does not work	56.6	36.8	53.6	86.2
c. Second generation, 1925	(N=293)	(N=225)	(N=68)	[b]
Works	60.8	63.6	51.5	[b]
Does not work	39.2	36.4	48.5	[b]

Source: New York State, Manuscript Census, See Appendix A for description of sampling method.

[a]No single women are listed in the census as homeworkers.

[b]No single women over age forty-four are recorded.

ment (see Table 2, part b). Among the second-generation women, a sample dominated by young women, nearly 61 percent listed occupations (Table 2, part c).[37]

Italian families in New York did not insist that wage-earning daughters stay home to work rather than go to a factory. Homework was reserved for young children and mothers. Apparently, only about 6 percent of young adult females in 1905 were employed at home, mostly as garment finishers. The census figures are reinforced by contemporary investigations of New York factories, which indicated just how large a role the young Ital-

---

[37]Beause speed and dexterity were so important for factory work, females clustered in the younger age categories tended to work in greater proportions than older women. Given the fact that the population of second-generation Italians was by 1925 heavily clustered in the late adolescent category, it is not surprising that they worked in greater proportions than first-generation women in the same year. We cannot know why second-generation women aged twenty-two to forty-four worked in slightly greater proportions than first-generation women in the same age category. However, in 1925 first-generation women between the ages of twenty-two and forty-four were likely to be older.

ian women were playing in the workshops. The U.S. Bureau of Labor reported that half of the female shop force in the men's garment industry was Italian, and for the clothing industry as a whole (both men's and women's clothing), one-quarter to one-third of the female employees were Italian, the largest single ethnic group.[38]

The overall work patterns for Italians show just how well the women responded to employment opportunities. The fashion industries—garments, millinery, and artificial flowers—accounted for 80 percent of Italian female workers in 1905, with the remaining in paper box, candy, jewelry, and tobacco shops. In 1925, 64 percent of all Italian women (averaged for first and second generation) worked in the fashion industry, while another 21 percent worked in other factories. Almost no first-generation workers in 1925 reported work in nonfactory jobs of any kind; among second-generation workers less than 1 percent reported sales work and 11 percent did office work.

One typical area of female employment, domestic service, did not attract many Italian women. Why was this so? Yans-McLaughlin and others have suggested that Italian families were especially reluctant to allow their daughters to work in strangers' homes for fear doing so would compromise their virtue.[39] However, we have seen that in Italy, when familial need required, norms allowed for domestic service. In the United States by the turn of the century, servantry was not considered an acceptable option by many white working-class females. Manufacturing jobs meant shorter hours and at least some freedom from supervision, and such work allowed women to live at home with their parents.[40] As more factory work became available, females of all ethnic groups chose the workshops. Unlike many Irish women in the nineteenth century and Polish women in the early decades of the twentieth, Jewish and especially Italian women emigrated almost exclusively in family groups or to join family groups already in America. These family connections meant that

---

[38] On men's clothing, see U.S. Congress, Senate, *Report on Condition of Woman and Child Wage Earners*, 2: *Men's Ready-Made Clothing*, p. 45. For the clothing industry as a whole, see U.S. Congress, Senate, *Reports of the Immigration Commission*, vol. 11: *Immigrants in Industries, Part 6*, 372.

[39] See Yans-McLaughlin, *Family and Community*, chap. 7; Caroline Golab, *Immigrant Destinations* (Philadelphia: Temple University Press, 1977), p. 152.

[40] See Lucy Maynard Salmon, *Domestic Service* (New York: Macmillan, 1897).

Fourteen-year-old Italian girl working in a paper box factory, New York City, 1913. (Photograph by Lewis W. Hine, courtesy of the New York Public Library.)

Table 3. The employment status of single Italian women in New York by length of time since father's immigration, 1905 (percentage distribution)

Woman's employment status	Years since father's immigration		
	5 or less (N=31)	6–10 (N=28)	11 up (N=56)
Works out	67.0	57.0	44.6
Works at home	6.4	14.0	1.7
Does not work	25.0	28.0	50.0
In school	0	0	3.5

Source: New York State, Manuscript Census. See Appendix A for description of sampling method.

Note: This sample of daughters whose fathers are present in the household tends to correspond to but not match the 1905 sample of single women aged 16 to 21 in Table 2.

Jewish and Italian women did not need domestic service to supply room and board as well as wages.[41]

The overall pattern of Italian women's employment shows that, as in other immigrant communities, the family economy was operating in full force in the Italian community during the early decades of the century. The Italian family relied on the contributions of several members to feed, clothe, and shelter its members. Yet each family brought to its situation a different set of demographic and economic circumstances. More detailed analysis of census data highlights the variety of strategies Italian families employed in their struggle for security. That Italian family behavior regarding women's work was flexible and quite responsive to family need, rather than to a patriarchal proscription concerning women's work is perhaps best illustrated by the summary of Italian female work patterns in Table 3. If loyalty to traditional values discouraged women's work and value changes promoted it, then we might expect that the longer a family

[41] Such demographic characteristics as the sex ratio of migrant populations, as well as the age of marriage and proportion of women married, would give us some idea about the numbers of single women who had to earn a living independently of family groups. For example, Yans-McLaughlin notes that Poles in Buffalo, like Italians, were a population in which males outnumbered females, and thus Polish women could also depend on males if they wished, yet many worked in domestic service. But it is unlikely that the ratio of males to females was nearly as disproportionate as for Italians, because, as she indicates, at least 59 percent of Buffalo's Polish women under age thirty in 1905 were unmarried, as compared with 35 percent of Italian women. *Family and Community*, p. 209.

lived in the United States, the more likely it would be to permit an adult daughter to work. The longer in the United States, the more opportunity to absorb American ideals and attitudes about female behavior.[42] My analysis of the 1905 census strongly suggests that patriarchal traditions carried over from Italy did not inhibit daughters' employment. Indeed, a greater proportion of the daughters of *newly* arrived immigrants reported occupations; the longer the household head had been in America, the *less* likely it was that a daughter would do wage work outside the home. Newly arrived males, as a group, encountered the greatest difficulties in obtaining secure employment; it was the greater need among recent settlers that led families to turn to daughters as well as sons as wage earners.

Variations in the earning capacity of the male household head were not the sole factors affecting the employment patterns of Italian-American daughters, however. If we use the skill level of the father as a rough proxy for their wages, we find that there was not a higher proportion of women working in households headed by lesser skilled workers, as might be expected.[43] However, since the Italian family relied on the economic contributions of several members, we must look to the entire family unit to understand conditions that accounted for women's work. As will be shown in greater detail in the next chapter, most of the Italian families had many mouths to feed and bodies to clothe; in other words, they had many "consumers" at home. Some families, however, had more wage earners per "consumer" than did others. The data summarized in Table 4 are not conclusive, but they suggest that families with more wage earners per consumer, i.e., higher ratios, were more likely to keep single daughters at home. Comparing Italian nuclear families by the ratio of wage earners to consumers does not yield large differences; nevertheless, in both 1905 and 1925 the proportion of single women working decreased in a step-

[42] On women's work patterns as an expression of ethnic values, see Yans-McLaughlin, *Family and Community*; Golab, *Immigrant Destinations*; Barbara Klaczynska, "Why Women Work—A Comparison of Various Groups—Philadelphia, 1910–1930," *Labor History* 17 (Winter 1976): 73–87.

[43] Not only are there small numbers in the various categories, there are also other methodological problems in using occupational categories as a proxy for earnings. For a discussion of the problems in assigning status categories and skill levels for historical data, see Clyde Griffen, "Occupational Mobility in Nineteenth Century America: Problems and Possibilities," *Journal of Social History* 5 (Spring 1972): 310–30; Michael Katz, "Occupational Classification in History," *Journal of Interdisciplinary History* 3 (Summer 1972): 63–68.

Table 4. The employment status of single Italian women in New York by economic
strength of household, 1905 and 1925 (percentage distribution)

Woman's employment status	Ratio of male wage earners to consumers[a]		
	to .20	.21–.40	.41–.60
a. In 1905	(N = 103)	(N = 144)	(N = 66)
Works	72.8	67.2	66.0
Does not work	27.0	32.6	33.3
b. In 1925	(N = 170)	(N = 239)	(N = 105)
Works	71.1	69.0	67.6
Does not work	28.8	30.9	32.3

Source: New York State, Manuscript Census. See Appendix A for description of sampling method.

Note: First and second generations are combined.

[a]Derived according to the method employed in Karen Oppenheim Mason, Maris A. Vinovskis, and Tamara K. Hareven, by "dividing the number of adult men in the family by a weighted sum of all related individuals in the family, with children weighted less heavily than adults on the ground that their consumption needs were more modest. The weights used were .55 for children aged 0–4, .65 for children aged 5–9, .75 for children aged 10–14 and adults, those 15 and over, 1.0" See "Women's Work and the Life Course in Essex County, Massachusetts, 1880," in Tamara K. Hareven and Maris A. Vinovskis, eds, *Transitions: The Family and the Life Course in Historical Perspective* (New York: Academic Press, 1978), p. 194.

wise fashion as ratios of wage earners to consumers in their families increased (see Table 4).[44]

Finally, although *need* appears to have played a strong part in shaping Italian women's work patterns, a comparison with Jewish families suggests that job *opportunity* within the city also played an important role in accounting for women's employment. To test the impact of ethnic attitudes on female employment, I chose for analysis one area in New York's Lower East Side inhabited both by Jews and Italians. Both Jewish and Italian males who lived on this block were of relatively high occupational

[44]The method used here was employed originally by Karen Oppenheim Mason, Maris A. Vinovskis, and Tamara K. Hareven for their analysis of women's work in Essex County, Mass. See "Women's Work and the Life Course in Essex County, Massachusetts, 1880," in Tamara K. Hareven and Maris A. Vinovskis, eds., *Transitions: The Family and the Life Course in Historical Perspective* (New York: Academic Press, 1978), pp. 187–216.

status. In general, Jewish immigrants had a higher proportion of males occupied as skilled workers than Italian immigrants did, but on the Lower East Side, in the heart of New York's Jewish ghetto, the small group of Italians and Jews, randomly sampled, showed nearly the same high percentage of skilled workers.[45] Significantly, similar proportions of women were at work in both Jewish and Italian households. Contrary to what might be expected in a community so dominated by skilled workers, however, a large majority of women were working.[46]

One likely explanation, worth further investigation, is that work opportunities for women varied according to residential location within the city and in ways that were different than for men. There were many small-scale garment firms in the Lower East Side, so job opportunities for women were numerous. Jobs located very close to home were particularly attractive, for they made it easier for women to combine work and domestic chores. In their study of Essex County women Karen Mason, Maris Vinovskis, and Tamara Hareven found that among lower status families, where the pressures to combine earnings were greatest, single women who lived in towns where more *jobs* were available were more likely to work; among higher status families single women who lived where relatively high *wages* were available were more likely to be employed.[47] A similar pattern may exist for immigrant women in New York City. In other areas of the city a large proportion of Italian women worked at unskilled jobs as finishers and operators. In the Lower East Side, however, with its more prosperous men, all single women who worked listed skilled occupations: most were tailors; several, milliners.[48] Perhaps because these families lived near shops that needed skilled labor, they could make use of local contacts to secure employ-

---

[45] For comparisons of the occupational status of Jews and Italians in New York City, see Kessner, *The Golden Door*, chaps. 3, 4.

[46] In 1905 more than 60 percent of both the Italian and Jewish males in the families were skilled workers, but more than 90 percent of single women were engaged in paid labor. New York State Manuscript Census, 1905. The sample of Italian and Jewish households was drawn for 1905 and 1925, but there were not enough Italian single women in the 1925 sample to make any comparisons. See Appendix A for a description of the sampling procedure.

[47] See Mason et al., "Women's Work and the Life Course."

[48] Once again, census classifications are problematic because one cannot be sure if the census enumerators merely classified all garment workers as tailoresses or were careful to denote only those women who were actually doing skilled tailoring work as tailoresses. But

ment. Perhaps the families of skilled workers were attracted to these neighborhoods precisely because of the job opportunities available. These findings suggest how urban geography – in this case the location of work close to residence and the clustering of households of people with similar occupations – interacts with gender roles in accounting for variations in immigrant employment patterns within a city, as well as between cities.[49]

Adolescence and Young Womanhood: The World of Work

The pursuit of familial goals put thousands of adolescent and young adult Italian females in new surroundings, away from parental supervision for many hours a day. For an immigrant woman, this often was her first experience with wage labor. Contemporary writers were concerned that "industrial work . . . tends to destroy the unity of family life and leads to the destruction of the Italian ideal of the home."[50] Recent studies of immigrant females at the turn of the century have shown that work did not destroy familial attachments.[51] Moreover, in the clothing shops of New York there were few opportunities for Italian women to develop the "initiative, creativity and autonomy" so well described by Susan Benson in her study of female department store employees.[52] Because going to work

in this neighborhood, so heavily populated by Jewish tailors, it is likely that a large majority of these women were also employed in highly skilled work in the small shops of the area. At any rate, in no other block were female garment workers so consistently listed in one category.

[49] For a discussion of recent efforts to analyze how gender affects the use of urban space, see Linda Kerber, "Separate Spheres, Female Worlds, Woman's Place: The Rhetoric of Women's History," *Journal of American History* 75 (June 1988): 36–37.

[50] Gino Speranza, "Italians in Congested Districts," *Charities and the Commons* 20 (April 1908): 55. See also Ware, *Greenwich Village*; Roche, "The Italian Girl," esp. p. 116; Greenwich House, *Ninth Annual Report, 1909–1910*, p. 17; Reed, *The Leisure Time of Girls*; Yans-McLaughlin, *Family and Community*, pp. 184–201.

[51] See, for example, Leslie Woodcock Tentler, *Wage-Earning Women: Industrial Work and Family Life in the United States 1900–1930* (New York: Oxford University Press, 1979).

[52] Susan Benson, *Counter Cultures: Saleswomen, Managers and Customers in American Department Stores, 1890–1940* (Urbana: University of Illinois Press, 1986). On nurses, see

did not take them very far outside the world they already knew, Italian women may have found their work setting especially confining.

Many Italian women found work in industries familiar to them. For example, girls who had helped their mothers make flowers or sew garments at home often went to work in artificial flower factories or clothing stores.[53] Most took jobs located very close to home; flower shops, paper box plants, and garment factories were but a few short blocks from the Italian neighborhood. These firms were well located to attract the single adult population and close enough to the residential areas so that mothers and young children could carry homework back and forth from tenement to shop.[54] As late as 1924 some 88 percent of the shops in the men's garment industries were located in the lower Broadway area, just north of the heart of major Italian neighborhoods. The highest concentration of women's garment shops was farther uptown, but not more than a short subway ride from Italian areas.[55] Women made these trips back and forth to work with kin and friends from their own block who were employed in the same or nearby shops.[56]

The work environment was not a stark contrast to the home environment for many women who had grown up sewing garments at home. Most Italian women workers sewed garments or assembled patterns in small shops or, more likely, in even smaller contract shops located in Lower Manhattan. Consumer goods industries everywhere, but particularly in New York City, were small scale, with little heavy or complex machinery. The

---

Barbara Melosh, *The Physician's Hand: Work Culture and Conflict in American Nursing* (Philadelphia: Temple University Press, 1982).

[53] Odencrantz, *Italian Women in Industry*.

[54] See Greenwich House, *Third Annual Report, 1903–1904*; idem, *Seventh Annual Report, 1907–1908*; idem, *Twelfth Annual Report, 1912–1913*; Van Kleeck, *Artificial Flower Makers*, p. 13; Odencrantz, *Italian Women in Industry*, chap. 3.

[55] New York State, Department of Labor, *Homework in the Men's Clothing Industry in New York and Rochester*, New York State Department of Labor Special Bulletin no. 147 (Albany, N.Y., 1926), pp. 43–44; Harry Best, *The Men's Garment Industry in New York and the Strike of 1913*, University Settlement Studies (New York: University Settlement Society, 1914), p. 12; Joint Board of Sanitary Control in the Cloak, Suit and Skirt Industries, *Tenth Annual Report* (New York: n.p., 1911), no pagination.

[56] See Roche, "The Italian Girl," pp. 95–98. Robert Park and Herbert Miller observed that in Chicago, Italian women traveled in groups on the streetcars to and from garment shops. *Old World Traits Transplanted*, p. 152.

Forming flower wreaths in an artificial flower factory, New York City, circa 1913.
(Photograph by Lewis W. Hine, courtesy of the New York Public Library.)

Corner of a Broadway flower factory workroom, circa 1913. (Photograph by Lewis W. Hine, courtesy of the New York Public Library.)

high rents and seasonality of the industry made investment in large plants or a permanent work force very risky. Garment manufacturers kept investment and other costs low by decentralizing — sending the coats, vests, and pants that had been cut by skilled men to subcontractors for assembling and cutting. The "contract shop" system was more common in New York City than in any other city in the country. As late as 1915, 70 percent of the garment sewers in men's clothing worked in contract shops rather than in manufacturing plants.[57] The women's garment industry was similarly organized, but because of changing fashions, more supervision by the manufacturer was required. In the women's cloak and suit industry, therefore, the subcontractor often supervised his own work teams in space provided inside the manufacturer's shop.[58]

In the contract branch of the men's garment industry, where most Italian women worked, 40 percent of the workers were employed in shops of fewer than 20 employees in 1925; another 44 percent, in shops of 21 to 50 employees. Women who sewed garments in manufacturers' shops tended to work in slightly larger groups — about 45 percent worked in shops of 21 to 50 people, and 50 percent worked in shops of 51 to 100 people.[59] Slightly different figures available for the other fashion industries show similar patterns. In 1910 the average number of workers in women's clothing factories was 27; this level persisted after World War I.[60] In 1930 the average number of workers per shop for all New York City industries was 23, the lowest figure for any city in the state.[61]

[57] New York State, Department of Labor, *Homework in the Men's Clothing Industry*, p. 39, quoting the Survey of Amalgamated Clothing Workers of America.

[58] For men's clothing, see U.S. Congress, Senate, *Report on Condition of Woman and Child Wage Earners*, vol. 2: *Men's Ready-Made Clothing*, p. 416. For all clothing (men's and women's), see U.S. Congress, Senate, *Reports of the Immigration Commission*, vol. 11: *Immigrants in Industries, Part 6*, pp. 385, 386.

[59] New York State, Department of Labor, *Homework in the Men's Clothing Industry*, p. 42. This study is based on eighty-nine firms representing all aspects of the industry.

[60] For 1910, see Joint Board of Sanitary Control in the Cloak, Suit, Skirt, Dress and Waist Industries, *Monthly Bulletin* 1 (October 1919): 7–8. See also U.S. Congress, Senate, *Reports of the Immigration Commission*, vol. 11: *Immigrants in Industries, Part 6*, pp. 384, 389, quoting the New York State Factory Inspector Report of 1907. In 1929, 77 percent of the workers in the artificial flower and feather industry were employed in shops of fewer than 20. See New York State, Department of Labor, *Homework in the Artificial Flower and Feather Industry*, in *New York State*, Part II, New York Department of Labor Special Bulletin no. 199 (Albany, N.Y., 1938), pp. 21–22.

[61] New York State, Department of Labor, *The Trend of Employment in New York State*

Within the small shops Italian women sometimes worked in mixed groups of Italian and Jewish women but usually worked alongside other Italians. Since Italian women, like other immigrants, commonly used family and neighborhood networks to find jobs, it is not surprising that large proportions worked together in these shops.[62] One investigation of Italian women workers found that factories employing any Italian women were likely to employ many. In the men's garment industry, for example, Italians dominated the female work forces in 22 out of the 27 that employed Italian women. In the women's cloak and suit shops containing Italians, they consituted 68 percent of the work force, and in the flower and feather shops, 35 percent of the female employees.[63]

Thus the patterns of family, residence, and work frequently coincided. In fact, going to work in the early years did little to expose Italian women to Americanizing influences. A new worker could learn the trade from kin and establish friendships without moving beyond her own ethnic group. She did not even need to speak English in order to get along in New York factories; indeed, many workers, particularly during the early part of the century, spoke only Italian.[64] The world of Italian women workers had expanded beyond the block where they lived, but it was still quite limited.

The nature of the jobs—poorly paid, exhausting, and requiring long hours—meant that unmarried Italian women did not have the resources to enable them to pursue the leisure lives often associated with single life in the city.[65] The majority of Italians, like most women who did factory work, performed semiskilled or unskilled tasks. In the garment shops skilled men were employed as cutters, and in New York men usually tended the sewing machines that were used to assemble the large pieces of

---

from 1914–1929, New York State Department of Labor Special Bulletin no. 206 (Albany, N.Y., 1930), p. 67.

[62] On the importance of ethnic networks in hiring patterns, see Suzanne W. Model, "Work and Family: Blacks and Immigrants from South and Eastern Europe," in *Immigration Reconsidered: History, Sociology, and Politics*, ed. Virginia Yans-McLaughlin (New York: Oxford University Press, 1990), pp. 130–59.

[63] Odencrantz, *Italian Women in Industry*, pp. 60–61.

[64] Ibid., p. 59.

[65] On the leisure lives of working girls of this time, see Kathy Peiss, *Cheap Amusements: Working Women and Leisure in Turn-of-the-Century New York* (Philadelphia: Temple University Press, 1986).

a garment and to do the complicated stitching. Some Italian women used the dressmaking skills they had learned at home; they worked in custom dressmaking shops and as fine hand sewers in the ready-made garment factories. But most did the unskilled jobs of lining garments, sewing on buttons, trimming threads, and pulling bastings by hand. In the candy industry men and sometimes native-born American women did the skilled labor hand dipping and operating the heavy machinery; Italian women were relegated to candy wrapping, sorting, shelling nuts, and carrying trays. In the paper box industry men and some native-born American women did the skilled work while Italian women pasted labels, stuffed finished boxes with tissues, and tied them with ribbon. Finally, in artificial flower shops men were the highly skilled dyers, and although some Italian women did skilled flower arranging, most did the less skilled tasks of assembling flowers and petals.[66]

New York's Italian women, newly arrived, without the networks to provide them with better jobs, and under intense pressure to take any available employment, were clustered in the lowest wage categories. In 1915 the New York State Factory Investigating Commission estimated that a single woman residing alone needed to earn $10 weekly to maintain a minimal standard of living. Italian women over eighteen earned an average weekly wage of $6.76 in 1910; only 35 percent earned more than $7.50.[67] The problem of low wages was compounded because Italian women could not work full time every week. Clothing factories and candy

[66] On the garment industry, see U.S. Congress, Senate, *Report on Condition of Woman and Child Wage Earners*, vol. 2: *Men's Ready-Made Clothing*, pp. 202–12. On men's clothing, see U.S. Congress, Senate, *Reports of the Immigration Commission*, vol. 11: *Immigrants in Industries, Part 6*, pp. 384–87; for other industries employing large numbers of Italians, such as the paper box, candy, and artificial flower industries, see Odencrantz, *Italian Women in Industry*, pp. 38–44; New York State, Factory Investigating Commission, *Third Report of the Factory Investigating Commission* (Albany, N.Y.: J. B. Lyon, 1914), 3: 73–78, 110–14; also on artificial flowers, see Van Kleeck, *Artificial Flower Makers*, pp. 15–17; New York State, Department of Labor, *Homework in the Artificial Flower and Feather Industry*, p. 31; New York State, Factory Investigating Commission, *Preliminary Report of the New York State Factory Investigating Commission* (Albany, N.Y., J. B. Lyon, 1912), 1: 275.

[67] New York State, Factory Investigating Commission, *Fourth Report of the Factory Investigating Commission* (Albany, N.Y.: J. B. Lyon, 1915), 4: 1472; U.S. Congress, Senate, *Report of the Immigration Commission*, vol. 11: *Immigrants in Industries, Part 6*, pp. 375–77.

and paper box plants, as well as flower shops, had slack periods for several months during the year in which there were reductions of 15 to 50 percent of the work force. Most of the clothing industries had regular seasons, but some trades could not predict their labor needs in advance. Their employees never knew when they might be out of a job. Since one-half of the industrial wage earners that Louise Odencrantz later interviewed were out of work for at least one-sixth of the year, she estimated that their stated weekly salaries should be reduced by 17 percent to approximate full-time work.[68] Wages improved slightly for Italian women during the second two decades of the century, partly because of union organization but also because Italians eventually moved up the skill hierarchy. In men's garments actual and real wages for finishers, basters, and operators improved steadily during the early 1920s, reaching a peak around 1925 and 1926. Real and nominal wages decreased after 1926, however, because of market fluctuations; seasonality continued to be a problem.[69]

The difficulties encountered by immigrant women in factories have been well documented and need only brief reiteration here. Whether one had to work at a machine or by hand, the task had to be done quickly; employers were constantly trying to fill orders on short notice. There was constant pressure to increase the pace, and most workers were paid by the piece. An Italian shirtwaist worker told one investigator: "You may have to do only part of the waist, sleeves, or hem . . . [but] . . . you will have to do it fast at that one thing."[70] The atmosphere in candy and paper box factories was similar. In one candy factory that employed Italian females, Odencrantz reported that candy wrappers each packed about 180 pieces of candy per box into sixty or seventy boxes, that is, 10,000 to 12,000 pieces of candy, every day.[71]

Many factories required the women to work while standing. Women stood as they packed candy, clothing, or feathers, pasted labels, folded

[68]Odencrantz, *Italian Women in Industry*, p. 116.

[69]U.S. Bureau of Labor Statistics, *Wages and Hours of Labor in the Men's Clothing Industry, 1911-1930*, Bureau of Labor Statistics Special Bulletin no. 557 (Washington, D.C.: Government Printing Office, 1932). See also Louis Levine, *The Woman's Garment Workers* (New York: International Ladies Garment Workers Union, B. W. Heubsch, 1924); Irving Bernstein, *The Lean Years* (Boston: Houghton Mifflin, 1960), chap. 1.

[70]Odencrantz, *Italian Women in Industry*, p. 39.

[71]Ibid., p. 77.

garments, and pressed clothes. Those who needed to bend over to do their tasks, such as garment finishers or flower makers, were provided with chairs. But these women had other problems; for example, they often suffered from severe eye strain brought on by hours of close work in poor lighting conditions.[72] Not only the work processes but also the materials that Italian women used in the shops were dangerous to their health. In paper box factories glue fumes caused nausea; in the flower factories the aniline dyes irritated throats and skin; in the feather factories swirling fluff caused bronchitis, asthma, and eye disease. Many of the work materials were highly flammable, yet fire escapes were rickety and inaccessible. Discarded materials in paper box factories, food processing shops, feather and flower workrooms littered the floors for days. Since most of the shops were too small to provide lunchrooms, workers simply ate their meals on the work tables, mixing crumbs with work materials.[73]

Italian women were exposed to the dirt, the physical exhaustion, and the dangers of work for long hours each day, six days a week. These workers had precious little time for recreation. In her study of immigrant women and leisure in New York City, Kathy Peiss attributed increased leisure activities for factory women to enactment of the fifty-four-hour work week law in 1900. The law was not well enforced, however, and many Italian women working in nonunion small contract shops did not experience significant reductions in their working hours until the New Deal.[74] Pushed by employers desperate to increase output in the busy season and impelled by family need, many Italian women worked overtime on a regular basis. During the busy season employers frequently violated the law limiting the work week in order to keep up with demand. While only 7 percent of the firms in the artificial flower and feather trade

[72] Ibid., p. 73.

[73] New York State Factory Investigating Commission, *Preliminary Report of the Factory Investigating Commission*, 1: 275; Odencrantz, *Italian Women in Industry*, p. 68; U.S. Congress, Senate, *Report on Condition of Woman and Child Wage Earners*, vol. 2: *Men's Ready-Made Clothing*, p. 325.

[74] Peiss, *Cheap Amusements*, chap. 2. Some improvements occurred, particularly around the time of World War I, when an expansion of the garment industry forced improvements in the safety standards of the shops, as well as a reduction in the work week. New regulations, however, were effective mostly in shops where unions were strong; many of the tiny contract shops, where Italians worked, were exempted from the regulations. Moreover, the unions suffered major setbacks during the employers' counteroffensives of the 1920s.

routinely worked more than 54-hour weeks, 63 percent required overtime that increased the work week to a total of anywhere from 55 to 72 hours. Workers added hours by taking work home at night. Such practices occurred in the garment trades but were particularly common in artificial flower manufacturing. Odencrantz found that 57 percent of the artificial flower workers took work home with them at night after they had completed a full day in the shop. A plume maker reported that she worked until one or two o'clock in the morning five nights a week during the busy season; another Italian feather maker, eighteen years old, reported having worked every night until eleven o'clock for six weeks.[75]

Yans-McLaughlin has suggested that, because it was seasonal, Italian women's work in Buffalo was considered supplemental to male labor.[76] Yet males, too, faced the problem of irregular earnings. Precisely because there were slack periods for all, several members of the family had to work. Women like Rose Cellini, therefore, could not use the slack period for rest or leisure, but instead: "She was much run down from the strain and worry of her irregular work. Three times within the year immediately past she had undergone the harrowing experience of losing a job and hunting a new one, only to return each night to her tenement home . . . where a large family was clamoring for her earnings."[77] Mary Lombardini, age eighteen, and her seventeen-year-old sister Millie were the principal wage earners for a twelve-member family. Mary had worked at seven places during the year, Millie at eight. Some Italian women worked two jobs during the busy season, as a hedge against future unemployment. The New York State Factory Investigating Commission found one group of Italian women in a bathing suit factory whose work day lasted from 8:00 A.M. to 6:00 P.M.; they then returned home to crochet slippers each night until 10:00 P.M.[78]

Families clearly depended on the earnings of Italian daughters just as the daughters depended for their well-being on the resources of the family group. We turn next to the ways in which the interdependence of elders and daughters affected the leisure and community lives of Italian women.

---

[75] Odencrantz, *Italian Women in Industry*, p. 119.

[76] Yans-McLaughlin, "Patterns of Work and Family Organization: Buffalo's Italians," *Journal of Interdisciplinary History* 2 (Autumn 1971): 299–314.

[77] Odencrantz, *Italian Women in Industry*, p. 119.

[78] New York State Factory Investigating Commission, *Second Report*, 3: 108.

Social Life and Leisure for Italian Women

Popular amusements for New York's working class flourished during the early years of the twentieth century; dance halls, pool halls, and movies were all vehicles for recreation. Historians of working-class women have drawn attention to the importance of peer culture. By organizing social clubs, socializing in the streets, and patronizing new forms of popular amusements, the young working class created a youth culture that "structured their social relations and expressed a distinct crystallization of values and concerns." Italian girls according to Peiss, were "curtailed by conservative cultural traditions"; nevertheless, even in Italian families, "young women carved out spaces in their lives for . . . independent and unsupervised social interaction." On the basis of public surveys and private charity reports, she concludes that even the limited forms of recreation available to Italians undermined "the traditional bases of daughters' dependency."[79]

My own reading of the same materials leads me to a different conclusion. First, it is impossible to tell to what extent the new forms of leisure changed individual attitudes about self-fulfillment. Furthermore, the extent to which popular culture is adopted depends a great deal on the social context. Given the constraints on their time and the lack of opportunities available to Italian girls, theirs was not a world in which new values about autonomy from the family could flourish.

Working outside the home certainly gave Italian women opportunities to make new friends. Workplace sociability mitigated the negative aspects of their jobs. The fast pace, the almost constant supervision, and sometimes the noise of machinery made the interaction difficult. Nevertheless, for Italians, as for other employed women, working in a group of women allowed many the first opportunity to speak freely with peers outside the presence of their elders.[80] Within this female world they discussed current boyfriends or the latest romantic novels and magazines.

Conversations about boyfriends and news of impending marriages also preoccupied women as they walked home together from the shops, but these interludes with coworkers after work were usually brief.[81] Re-

---

[79] Peiss, *Cheap Amusements*, pp. 57, 69, 70, 187.
[80] See Tentler, *Wage-Earning Women*, chap. 3.
[81] Roche, "The Italian Girl," pp. 95–100.

formers worried that working women would pursue recreational activities that were dangerous to moral, mental, and physical health. That was not very likely for Italian young women, who went directly home after work rather than going out with friends. The hour was usually late, the women were exhausted, and family obligations claimed their time even in the evenings and on Sundays. Older daughters who held outside jobs were expected to assist in household chores; if their mothers did homework, daughters often spent evening hours as extra hands.

Though opportunities for an independent social life were very limited for these young women, they did find time for some recreation. They could socialize informally while doing family tasks; they could visit with girlfriends on the tenement stoop, for example, while watching younger brothers or sisters who were playing in the streets. Young women took walks and attended movies whenever possible. Because movies were so popular among working-class immigrants, historians have been particularly interested in their impact on audiences. Elizabeth Ewen has suggested that in providing images of different ways of life and raising expectations, movies in particular undermined familial values and fostered conflict between first- and second-generation immigrants.[82] Yet the degree to which film can enhance one's expectations depends not only on the power of the medium but also on the ability of consumers to see the "alternatives" as plausible. For Italian women, movies offered images of wealth, sometimes of daring heroines, and great romance; they were often sexually titillating. Evidence of the extent to which movies affected Italian young women's attitudes and aspirations is hard to come by; definitive conclusions are simply not possible, but, in any case, there were few prospects that these women could act on desires for personal freedom. As one girl explained when she was asked in 1914 why she enjoyed the movies so much: "We don't get no chance to live that way and you can pretend when you see the picture that it's you."[83]

What Italian women could do was try to imitate the way movie stars looked and dressed. Films and magazines taught first- and second-generation immigrants how to fix their hair, put on makeup, decorate a home,

---

[82] Elizabeth Ewen, *Immigrant Women in the Land of Dollars: Life and Culture on the Lower East Side, 1890–1925* (New York: Monthly Review Press, 1985), esp. chap. 11; see also Peiss, *Cheap Amusements,* pp. 158, 185.

[83] Reed, *The Leisure Time of Girls,* p. 47.

and, perhaps most importantly, how to dress. Italian women, like other immigrants, wanted to look like American women and were often embarrassed by the foreign mannerisms of their elders. Because cheap consumer goods were available, many Italian women could dress in style. With its "beguiling modernity," consumer culture, according to Peiss, "challenged parental authority over manners and mores."[84] In the case of the Italians I am struck by the willingness of families to adjust to new challenges in order to maintain an important tradition of authority, that of parental supervision of earnings. Even girls whose lives were very much dictated by family needs could assert themselves when it came to clothing.[85] Like working-class women from other ethnic groups, Italian women spent more money on clothes than did other members of the family. Italian families spent only about 15 percent of the family income on clothing, but, according to one study, female wage earners spent from 20 to 25 percent of their earnings on clothing.[86] Daughters usually turned over their pay to their mothers, but this did not mean that they lost all control over their income. Where family income permitted, working daughters openly set aside a portion of their income for personal clothing expenses. Parents allowed daughters to retain a portion of their income for personal expenses because they knew that daughters could and would secretly withhold wages if conflicts arose.[87] In this way Italian parents made concessions to the realities of wage labor and to the fact that their daughters had the desire for and ready access to the artifacts of popular culture.

New York factory women spent money on clothes for a variety of reasons. Adequately warm clothing was an important protection against possible illness. Factory operatives generally required nimble hands, and wearing heavy clothes meant that women could arrive warm at the workshops on cold winter mornings. Also, working women frequently had to replace their outer garments, which were subjected to the damp and dirt

---

[84] Peiss, *Cheap Amusements*, p. 72; see also p. 69.

[85] See Judith Smith, *Family Connections: A History of Italian and Jewish Immigrant Lives in Providence, Rhode Island, 1900–1940* (Albany: State University of New York Press, 1985), chap. 2.

[86] See Louise Polard More, *Wage Earner's Budgets* (New York: Henry Holt, 1907), p. 77. Robert Coit Chapin, *The Standard of Living among Workingmen's Families in New York City* (New York: Russell Sage Foundation, 1909), pp. 172–79; Odencrantz, *Italian Women in Industry*, p. 202.

[87] Smith, *Family Connections*, chap. 2.

of the factories day after day. But less practical reasons than these were no less important. Working-class women in New York dressed well as a way of maintaining self-respect. It was obvious that the well-dressed woman was "received with more courtesy in the outside world than her poorly clad sisters," reported the New York State Factory Investigating Commission.[88] Many Italian women were aware of the latest styles, not only through the movies and other media, but because they worked in the fashion industry. Even though most did rather menial tasks in the shops, many were talented dressmakers. Like other working-class women, Italians dressed well in hopes of attracting a beau.

Finding a husband was a high priority for young Italians, as it was for most women; the issue of dating probably caused more tension between the generations than clothing. Here, too, Italians adopted new strategies for maintaining a traditional goal—securing suitable husbands for their daughters. In the small villages of Italy families were well acquainted with the pool of prospective mates for their offspring. The families of future marriage partners could establish formal links with one another and discuss mutual obligations. In New York, however, families often did not have much information about prospective suitors, and premarital pregnancy had greater consequences because families were less able to force marriage. Parents were thus apt to be very wary about allowing their daughters to form casual friendships with men. As in Italy, these poor families wanted to keep their daughters at home until they could afford to do without their wages. When parents desperately needed a daughter's wages, they were even stricter about her social life.

Despite the disapproval of parents, Italian daughters often made casual contact with single men. Italian women mentioned walks around the block and trips to the park or local museums when asked how they spent time with male companions. In the summer they traveled to local beaches to meet boys. Courting also took place in the streets and in tenement hallways.[89] Conflicts between parents and daughters over such practices sometimes were referred to openly. One young woman, Lucy, complained to her friends that her father "had no use" for her new boyfriend and would not let her out at night. "If I got a husband," she moaned, "he takes

---

[88] New York State Factory Investigating Commission, *Fourth Report*, 4: 1525, 1527.
[89] Ware, *Greenwich Village*, pp. 185–91; Roche, "The Italian Girl," p. 95.

you out." Another female reported, "I ain't allowed to do nothing but sit—They'd kill me if I even thought of a boyfriend and I could never go home if they found out I met him."[90] Italian daughters often handled the issue of dating, not by confronting their elders, but by evasion. Investigators reported that it was common for young women to go off to the park with girlfriends, where they would "coincidentally" meet their boyfriends. Some women slipped away to neighborhood dances. One woman obtained her father's permission to go to the Metropolitan Museum, where she would secretly meet her boyfriend. Another told her mother she was going to church when she had a date.[91]

Such subterfuge was relatively easy because Italian families understood that total supervision was both impossible and ultimately undesirable—very few families had the resources for constant surveillance of their daughters, and parents had to be flexible if they wished their daughters to find suitable mates. They were resigned to the fact that unsupervised sociability was impossible to avoid completely. As early as 1930 Caroline Ware reported that seventeen out of a group of twenty-two women she studied had gone out with their future husbands alone before they were engaged—to the movies, the park, on bus rides, or walks.[92]

Meeting and socializing with men on their own gave Italian women in New York greater freedom to decide on prospective husbands than they would have had in Italy, as well as a much larger pool of eligible bachelors to choose from. Even the limited possibilities for meeting men gave them new opportunities to use public space. Family considerations, however, were still relevant for immigrant daughters. The ability to choose one's mate in accordance with personal rather than familial needs has often been associated by historians of immigration with the adoption of new values about marriage. The emphasis on difference between premodern and modern marriage patterns often underestimates the extent to which seemingly new, personal, and independent decisions about prospective spouses continued to be intertwined with family strategies. In industrial society abstract notions of good character are more important than property in determining suitable mates. The greater leisure available to "modern," more prosperous families allows for the "cultiva-

---

[90] Roche, "The Italian Girl," p. 95; Reed, *The Leisure Time of Girls*, p. 38.
[91] Ware, *Greenwich Village*, pp. 186, 187.
[92] Ibid., pp. 405–6.

tion of some kinds of sentiment," as E. P. Thompson has noted, "but economic necessities have only been masked or distanced."[93] Parents (and daughters) still tried to ensure that young women would find suitable mates and expected that husbands would support their wives. Good character, the right training, commitment to one's own family and ethnic group, all were important signs of the potential husband's acceptability.[94] Middle-class Americans tried to affect their children's marriage choices by sending children to the right schools or belonging to the right religious and social organizations. Italians tried to do the same by bringing their daughters into contact with people they or their friends and relatives knew.

During the early years of settlement Italian families did not have to worry much that their daughters would bring home husbands from strange and unexpected backgrounds. As with other immigrant groups, young Italians met their future mates at ethnic affairs sponsored by organizations to which their parents belonged, or at gatherings with families and friends. Italian daughters, like other working-class women living with families, seldom went to commercial dance halls; instead, they attended social affairs of the local Italian benefit societies, lodges, and clubs.[95] Neighborhood events, such as street fairs, were typical opportunities for sociability.

The atmosphere at these gatherings of family and friends encouraged casual mixing between the sexes. Pietro DiDonato has vividly described the wedding of a widow and a middle-aged man in his social novel about Italian immigrant life, *Christ in Concrete*. The wine flowed and enormous amounts of food were served, accompanied by dancing and jokes.

---

[93] Edward P. Thompson, "Happy Families," *New Society* 8 (September 1977): 501. Robert Lynd and Helen Merrill Lynd make this same point about the seemingly new attitude toward marriage in the 1920s. See *Middletown: A Study in Modern American Culture* (New York: Harcourt, Brace and World, 1929), chap. 10.

[94] On the family strategies of American middle-class families, see Mary Ryan, *Cradle of the Middle Class: The Family in Oneida County, NY, 1790–1865* (New York: Cambridge University Press, 1981).

[95] On commercial dance halls in New York City, see Peiss, *Cheap Amusements*, chap. 4. For Italians, see Robert Orsi, *The Madonna of 115th Street: Faith and Community in Italian Harlem, 1880–1950* (New Haven: Yale University Press, 1985); Marie J. Concistre, "Adult Education in a Local Area: A Study of a Decade in the Life and Education of the Adult Italian Immigrant in East Harlem, New York City" (Ph.D. dissertation, New York University, 1943), pp. 25–28.

Married men and women were not at all loathe to engage in sexual banter. Young, single adults of both genders flirted. After eating and drinking, the guests turned to song:

> In fine voice the Lucy started the suggestive popular Sicilian song, and guitar, accordion and the rest quickly caught up with him.

> > "With high moon far out at sea
> > Each mother's daughter desires ma-tri-mony—
> > And if to her we give the fisherman . . .
> > Forever more with his fish in hand she'll stay' e"

> While in the dining room they indoe-ah-ed . . . those in the kitchen lilted . . .

> > "Peasant women mine, peasant women mine
> > Barefoot sweated and bovine
> > Spread on a summer stack of hay
> > I loved with you to play"

> Later it was time to dance:

> > ! Tarantell!! Tarantell! Twirl
> > about swinging hips—twisting swaying torso
> > pushing ahead and circle gay friendly lusty
> > bump of buttocks away and around to face
> > and skip forward and circle now bent forward
> > and now fall backward and stamp Tarantell![96]

The passage evokes the sexually expressive dancing popular among working-class youth at turn-of-the-century dance halls in New York.[97] In the case of Italians "dirty dancing" was part of older peasant culture, but in contrast to the women of the dance halls, Italian women socialized within family settings. Surrounded by observant elders, they were able to enjoy a mildly erotic good time. "The party went on all night," DiDonato continues, until at last: "In the chill isle of Dawn the paesanos were tangled one upon and cross the other with snoring lips wide in burned out exhaustion amongst the children on coats and hats and piles of clothing throughout the room."[98]

---

[96] Pietro DiDonato, *Christ in Concrete* (New York: Bobbs-Merrill, 1937), pp. 259, 266–69, 270.

[97] Peiss, *Cheap Amusements*, chap. 4.

[98] DiDonato, *Christ*, pp. 259, 266, 269–70.

Italian Women and Community Activities

If Italian women participated only marginally in a peer culture away from home and family, so, too, were they only marginally involved in educational and recreational activities sponsored and run by New York reformers. Contemporary explanations reflected popular views about peasant family life. "Tradition in some southern Italian families was so strong," wrote Louise Odencrantz, that "some girls were not allowed to go out unless accompanied by the father or mother."[99] Settlement-house workers liked to point out that Italian daughters were interested in participating in activities but were hindered by family strictness; their assumptions legitimated the reformers' convictions about the needs of working-class females. "They intend to be American girls," noted the annual report of the Greenwich House Settlement in 1910, but "sometimes girls are beaten if they go out at night."[100] What social workers viewed as overzealous protectiveness on the part of Italian families toward females, however, stemmed partly from the elders' convictions that settlement-house activities kept daughters from their chores at home. When evening schools and settlement houses offered courses in areas considered useful to the family, such as fancy dressmaking, families were more willing to permit their daughters to go out. Carmela, for example, could attend evening classes in dressmaking because they proved of practical value to the family: "She contributed to the family resources by making a blue serge dress for her younger sister, thus saving a dressmaker's bill."[101]

Reformers conceded that parents' attitudes were often beside the point in understanding the girls' behavior. Young Italian women told investigators that they were "much too tired at night" for outside activities. Teresa, an Italian student in a local evening school, explained that she dropped out because she no longer had the time to go out: "After coming home from the factory, she was obliged to wash the dishes and make up the folding beds for a family of eight." Greenwich House workers admitted

[99] Odencrantz, *Italian Women in Industry*, p. 203.

[100] Greenwich House, *Tenth Annual Report, 1910–1911*, p. 14. See also Ware, *Greenwich Village*, p. 181.

[101] Mary Van Kleeck, *Working Girls in Evening Schools* (New York: Russell Sage Foundation, Survey Associates, 1914), p. 26. See also Greenwich House, *Thirteenth Annual Report, 1913–1914*, p. 23.

that establishing classes for the Italians was difficult partly because "having worked all day along, the women had no interest in classes that involved particular mental effort."[102]

The absence of Italian women in community activities was in marked contrast to the behavior of Jewish women who lived nearby. Because they were also a newly arrived immigrant group and a prime target for social reformers, Jewish women were often compared with their Italian counterparts. Like modern scholars, reformers were struck by the fact that Jewish families showed a greater appreciation of cultural enrichment and education for both men and women than did the Italians, and that such values were reflected in the behavior of women.[103]

A number of Jewish women shared labor activism and feminist convictions with women reformers.[104] Convinced that the days of unbridled pursuit of self-interest were a thing of the past, reformers devoted their lives to encouraging a sense of responsibility on the part of Americans, not just for one's family, one's social group, one's enterprise, but for the community at large. The public commitment on the part of the politicized Jewish community, so unlike the family-oriented Italian community, was greatly admired by progressives. Women activists who themselves were carving out new societal roles found immigrant women's social awareness and political involvement especially thrilling. Mary Van Kleeck, like others, frequently compared Jewish with Italian girls, as she did in this description of artificial flower makers:

> The Jewish girl has a distinct sense of her social responsibility and often displays an eager zest for discussion of labor problems. The Italian girl will answer all questions graciously but briefly, considering work in the flower trade as only one of many interesting topics of conversation. It is vital to her not as a general industrial problem but as a means of supplying her family, to whose welfare she is traditionally inclined to subordinate her individual

---

[102] Greenwich House, *Tenth Annual Report, 1911*, p. 14.

[103] For the modern scholarship, see, for example, Kessner, *The Golden Door*, chap. 4; Nathan Glazer and Daniel P. Moynihan, *Beyond the Melting Pot: The Negroes, Puerto Ricans, Jews, Italians, and Irish of New York City*, 2d ed. (Cambridge, Mass.: M.I.T. Press, 1970).

[104] For a recent treatment of these activist women, see Nancy Schrom Dye, *As Equals and as Sisters: Feminism, the Labor Movement and the Women's Trade Union League of New York* (Columbia: University of Missouri Press, 1980).

desires. The Jewish girl, on the other hand, will probably plunge at once into a discussion of her trade, its advantages and disadvantages, wages, hours of work and instances of shabby treatment . . . or of unsanitary conditions in the workrooms. . . . She has the foundation of that admirable trait, "public spirit," and a sense of relationships to a community larger than the family and the personal group of which she happens to be a member.[105]

Why did Jewish women join the new politics of early-twentieth-century New York when their Italian counterparts in the garment industry did not? First, they brought with them to the United States different social and political traditions. In eastern Europe Jewish daughters had, until recently, been under the strict supervision of elders just as Italians had been, but radical political and social movements that swept the Jewish Pale of Settlement (the area where Russian Jews had been confined since the eighteenth century) at the end of the nineteenth century fostered changes in family control. Many of the Jewish adults who arrived in New York in the wake of the revolutionary upheavals of 1904 and 1905 and the subsequent purges had been caught up in an atmosphere that fostered open questioning of traditional orthodox Jewish customs and woman's place in Jewish society. As part of the revolt against Jewish traditions, young Jewish women learned to read and write in Russia and often attended political meetings.[106]

Second, in New York, the differences between Italian and Jewish parents were reinforced by the greater prosperity of the Jewish community. Not only did more Jewish men hold skilled jobs, but Jewish women benefited by the fact that their ethnic group dominated the garment industry at both the employer and employee levels. Through community and family contacts, Jewish women were likely to get better jobs. For example, in the men's clothing industry, more Jewish women than Italian women were employed in the higher paying category of operator, but even in the most unskilled categories Jewish women had higher wages. In 1910 adult Jewish women in the clothing industry (both men and women's apparel) earned, on average, a weekly wage 25 percent greater than did the Italians. Jewish adolescents aged fourteen to eighteen were 32 percent better

[105] Van Kleeck, *Artificial Flower Makers*, pp. 34, 35.

[106] See Ezra Mendelsohn, *Class Struggle in the Pale: The Formative Years of the Jewish Workers' Movement in Tsarist Russia* (New York: Cambridge University Press, 1970).

off.[107] The average yearly wages of Jewish female workers was $115 more than that of their Italian counterparts.[108] Because Jews were better paid than Italians, the women did not have to put in long hours of extra work. Many more Italian mothers, as will be shown more fully below, were engaged in homework trades, and they needed their daughters' assistance to a greater extent than did the Jews. As a result Italians could not afford to be as liberal about their daughters' free time as were Jews. The Italian daughter's presence at home was too crucial for the family's survival for her to be free to pursue activities away from home.

Nowhere was the difference between Italian and Jewish females more apparent than in their attitudes about and involvement in union organizing. When the shirtwaist workers were preparing their massive strike in 1910, leaders found that mass meetings were always more heavily attended by Jewish women than by other women. In fact, so many Italian women crossed the picket line that employers were able to break the strike. At the last minute labor leaders attempted to buy off Italian families in hopes of getting them to support the strike. Activists went from tenement to tenement offering partial compensation to Italian families to enable female garment workers to stay home during the strike. The plan failed miserably.[109]

Most observers made use of stereotypical notions about Italian women to explain their role as strikebreakers. The traditional Italian female "was willing to accept conditions no matter how bad"; docile and obedient at home, she was likewise passive in the face of exploitation at the shop.[110] A recent discussion of the relative lack of union activism among Italian women, echoes this earlier explanation: An ability to keep the power struggles of the public world from entering into the private, as well as "familial restrictions and an emphasis upon dependency," discouraged la-

[107] U.S. Congress, Senate, *Report on Condition of Woman and Child Wage Earners*, vol. 2: *Men's Ready-Made Clothing*, p. 195; U.S. Congress, Senate, *Reports of the Immigration Commission*, vol. 11: *Immigrants in Industries, Part 6*, pp. 375–77. See also Best, *The Men's Garment Industry in New York*, p. 10.

[108] Even if we control for the length of time that the employees have been in the United States, the Jewish women in the men's garment industry still earned more than the Italians. On the wages of Italians and Jewish families, see U.S. Congress, Senate, *Reports of the Immigration Commission*, vol. 26: *Immigrants in Cities*, 1: 225.

[109] See Edwin Fenton, *Immigrants and Unions: A Case Study, Italians and American Labor, 1870–1920* (1957; rpt. New York: Arno Press, 1975), p. 485; Adriani Spadoni, "The Italian Working Woman in New York," *Collier's* 49 (March 1912): 14–15.

[110] Van Kleeck, *Artificial Flower Makers*, p. 3.

bor activism among Italian women, according to Yans-McLaughlin.[111] A focus on the traits of Italians, however, fails to account for the fact that most American women were not organized. And recent scholarship has shown that explanations that focus on the docile attitudes of women in order to explain their lack of participation in the labor movement are inadequate.[112] Women workers, including Italians, faced the problems of combining work and family responsibilities that left little time for union activity. Most working women, like the Italians, worked full time for only part of their adult lives. Under such circumstances, stable organizations were hard to maintain.[113] Finally, in all immigrant families where women worked, wages were a vital part of the budget. Families were reluctant to forgo their earnings for the sake of a strike.[114]

Studying the exceptional cases in which women were active in strikes and labor organization, such as Jewish women in turn-of-the-century America, provides insight into the conditions that promote activism. Scholars of working-class women have recently emphasized the special experiences and perspectives that women brought to the labor movement. It has been noted that Jewish women had connections with the growing women's movement of the day.[115] But equally important for understanding why Jewish women, in particular, were so active, was the fact that in New York City they belonged to a highly organized community in which local ethnic institutions had well-established connections with the burgeoning labor movement. Skilled Jewish workers had been hard at work since the

[111] Virginia Yans-McLaughlin, "Metaphors of Self in History: Subjectivity, Oral Narrative, and Immigration Studies," in *Immigration Reconsidered: History, Sociology and Politics*, ed. Yans-McLaughlin, (New York: Oxford University Press, 1990), pp. 281–82.

[112] Leslie Woodcock Tentler focuses on docility and dependence as an explanation for the lack of organization among most working women in the early decades of the century. See *Wage-Earning Women*, pp. 13–80.

[113] One of the best discussions of these issues is Alice Kessler-Harris, "Where Are the Organized Women Workers?" *Feminist Studies* 3 (Fall 1975): 92–110.

[114] For a discussion on how the dependence on wages from various family members affected attitudes toward union militancy among Slavs in Pittsburgh, see John Bodnar, "Immigration, Kinship and the Rise of Working Class Realism in Industrial America," *Journal of Social History* 14 (Fall 1980): 45–65.

[115] See, for example, Dye, *As Equals and as Sisters*. Mary Blewitt explores the differences between male and female activists in the nineteenth-century New England shoe industry. See *Men, Women and Work: Class, Gender and Protest in the New England Shoe Industry, 1780–1910* (Urbana: University of Illinois Press, 1988).

1880s organizing the garment trades. In contrast to their Italian counterparts, Jewish newspapers and mutual aid societies had been active in the labor movement for twenty-five years before the massive organizing of the International Ladies Garment Workers Union (ILGWU), which took place during the first decade of the twentieth century.[116] Thus, for Jewish women, politics was part of their community. Most Jewish women, like their Italian counterparts, remained close to family and friends in their own neighborhoods, but these family links were not necessarily a conservative force. Family and community were important arenas for mobilizing Jewish women and men. Particularly in Jewish families, unlike Italian ones, both men and women worked in the garment trades; thus, for the Jewish women ethnic, familial, and class ties were intertwined.[117]

The very setting that fostered activism for Jewish women was initially a barrier for the Italians. The major ILGWU organizing coincided with the early movement of Italians into the garment trades. At that time the union structure was firmly in the hands of the Jewish community.[118] Meetings were run by Jewish men and some women entirely in Yiddish. Ethnic prejudices were common; Jewish women tended to be contemptuous of the Italians, viewing them as "slow and stupid."[119] One Jewish organizer in the artificial flower industry, for example, explained why Italian women had no interest in the union in these words: "If they were more civilized, they wouldn't take such low pay. But they go without hats and gloves and umbrellas."[120] In the early years Jewish garment workers refused to address the question of organizing the Italian community at all; the word *Italian* does not appear in the union proceedings at all

[116]On Jews and the organization of the garment trades, see, among others, Levine, *The Women's Garment Workers*; Joel Seidman, *The Needle Trades* (New York: Farrar and Rinehart, 1942); Melvyn Dubofsky, *When Workers Organize: New York City in the Progressive Era* (Amherst: University of Massachusetts Press, 1968); Irving Howe, *World of Our Fathers* (New York: Harcourt, Brace and Jovanovich, 1976).

[117]Susan Glenn makes a similar point about the role of family and ethnic community in promoting Jewish women's labor activism. See *Daughters of the Shtetl: Life and Labor in the Immigrant Generation* (Ithaca, N.Y.: Cornell University Press, 1990), pp. 200–206. See also Carole Turbin, "And We Are Nothing but Women: Irish Working Women in Troy," in *Women of America: A History*, eds. Carol Berkin and Mary Beth Norton (Boston: Houghton Mifflin, 1979), pp. 202–20.

[118]See Fenton, *Immigrants and Unions*, chap. 4.

[119]Ibid., p. 485.

[120]Quoted in Van Kleeck, *Artificial Flower Makers*, p. 37.

until 1910.[121] It is no wonder that union leaders had a difficult time getting Italians to support the 1910 strike.

The lessons of the 1910 failure, however, did not go unheeded. Organizing the Italian employees would be crucial to union success in New York's garment industries. In the next few years leaders in both the women's and the men's garment unions worked vigorously to organize Italians. Italian locals were established, and some Italians were brought into all levels of leadership, particularly during strikes. Union newspapers put out Italian-language editions, and during strikes and lockouts the union made an effort to publicize and praise the enormous sacrifices that Italian families made for the good of the union.[122] Activists outside the Italian community took note of the role Italian women were now playing in the union movement. Mary Heaton Vorse wrote about the determination, well embedded in the women's world of Italian women garment workers, during the lockout in the men's garment industry in 1920–1921. Though very different from the less numerous women who came from the more politicized world of northern Italy, southern Italian women were now caught up in the spirit of unionism.

"These were the women on whom the lockout presses heaviest." A civilization separated them from the fiery women from the north [Italy] who talked of [revolutionary] Russia and looked forward to an Italy that was industrially free. But they knew . . . what the Amalgamated had done for them. . . . there in this intimate gossip you hear the real spirit of the workers. Here at eight o'clock in the morning, here they voice daily their unalterable decision: "We will never go back to the old slavery."[123]

As Italians' participation grew, their community mutual-aid societies and newspapers lent their support, thus reinforcing Italian ties to the gar-

---

[121] Fenton, *Immigrants and Unions*, p. 483.

[122] Ibid., chap. 4.

[123] Mary Heaton Vorse, "At the Employment Bureau," *Advance* 4 (14 January 1921): 2 (reprint in Amalgamated Clothing Workers of America archives, Ithaca, N.Y.). See also Vorse, "How Do They Do It?" *Advance* 5 (1 April 1921): 7 (reprint in ACWA archives, Ithaca, N.Y.). For another discussion of how women's networks fostered labor militancy in southern Italian immigrant communities, see Ardis Cameron, "Beyond Bread and Roses," in Ruth Milkman, ed., *Women, Work and Protest: A Century of U.S. Women's Labor History* (Boston: Routledge and Kegan Paul, 1985), pp. 42–61.

ment unions. Once the community at large was integrated into the unions, the problem of Italian women strikebreakers disappeared. From the time of the great garment strikes of 1919 Italian working women, along with the Italian men, were well-organized and loyal participants in the labor movement. The ranks of Italian female garment workers never produced as many union activists as their Jewish counterparts. Even among Jews, however, women's careers as activists were short-lived. They, too, as others have shown, experienced difficulties in combining family and work roles, and they had to organize in the face of a male leadership that, at best, was ambivalent about high-level roles for women in the union.[124] Thanks largely to the intensive organizing drive during the second decade of this century, Italian women can boast of having one of the longer union traditions among American working women.

The Italian Woman and the Family

Throughout the early decades of the twentieth century the family group dominated the life of the Italian woman. Whether or not she did paid work outside the home, the way she related to her job, what she did in the hours she was not earning wages, all were shaped by familial demands. Most immigrant families in early-twentieth-century America devised collective strategies because survival depended on their pooling resources. Family obligations were important for all Italian children; nevertheless, Italian boys and girls did not experience childhood and youth in the same way. Both the boys and the girls took on wage work at an early age, but the girls were expected to make extra sacrifices. Although Italian sons nor-mally only paid board — generally about half of their wages — to the fam-ily, daughters automatically turned over all or most of their pay to their mothers. Even though many girls withheld some of their earnings for clothing, they more than their brothers were counted on for regular con-tributions. Sons also did fewer household chores after work and thus had more free time than their sisters. Like the young flower maker introduced

---

[124] See, for example, Alice Kessler-Harris, "Where Are the Organized Women Work-ers?"; idem, "Organizing the Unorganizable: Three Jewish Women and Their Union," *Labor History* 17 (Winter 1976): 14–23.

at the beginning of this study, Italian daughters often worked extra hours so that their brothers might stay in school and pursue advanced training.[125]

Clearly, daughters did not benefit from family strategies as much as sons did. Like parents in other ethnic groups, Italian parents invested in their sons' education because it meant greater financial rewards for the family. But even for families where parents invested little in schooling either sons or daughters, the fact that males had greater earning potential than their sisters gave them greater flexibility. Male youths in Italian families earned on the average approximately 40 percent more than females. They, more than their sisters, had "extra" spending cash to use during their free hours. Parents feared that if they demanded too much from their sons, they would leave home before marriage. Unlike their sisters, the sons could afford to live on their own.[126]

Beyond the differences in the financial circumstances of sons and daughters, Italian females contributed to the family out of a sense of social responsibility handed down from mother to daughter. Within the family Italian females were active participants in what many scholars have termed a women's culture. Alice Kessler-Harris has defined women's culture as the way women perceive and organize the meaning of social order, construct family relationships, act out their own roles, and socialize with one another.[127] Italian women's lives, so rooted in the family, reinforced ties between daughters and elders. Born of constrained circumstances that were different from men's, the commitments of these women gave them a positive and not unrealistic self-image as shapers of their own experience rather than as oppressed victims.

Italian women believed that they were more capable and more reliable about performing family responsibilities than men were. One expressed the sentiment clearly when she discussed the contributions that fathers

---

[125] On the relatively greater freedom accorded sons in Italian families in New York, see Odencrantz, *Italian Women in Industry*, pp. 204–5; Van Kleeck, *Artificial Flower Makers*, p. 86; New York State Factory Investigating Commission, *Third Report*, p. 101. See also Roche, "The Italian Girl," p. 109.

[126] For another analysis of how greater individual resources affect family obligations, see Michael Anderson, *Family Structure in Nineteenth Century Lancashire* (Cambridge: Cambridge University Press, 1971).

[127] Alice Kessler-Harris, "Problems of Coalition Building: Woman and Trade Unions in the 1920's" in Milkman, ed., *Women, Work and Protest*, p. 118.

made to the family income: "Of course they don't give all they make. They're men and you never know their ways."[128] Females, on the other hand, were supposed to be dependable, no matter what the situation. Women bore the children and raised the offspring. Daughters prepared for their roles by acting out familial rather than personal goals from a young age, and they accepted active and even assertive roles in caring for the family. Mario Puzo in his autobiographical novel, *The Fortunate Pilgrim* offers a striking account of such behavior. This story of an immigrant family in New York focuses on the efforts of two women, Lucia Santa and her eldest daughter Octavia, in their struggle with poverty, illness, and death. Puzo's picture of the Italian women offers a contrast to the image of the passive, subordinate female depicted by reformers. Octavia's stepfather is mentally ill, and her eldest brother is out much of the time chasing women: Octavia, alone, must assist her mother in raising the younger children. She assumes the role with gusto, seeing to it that the younger children clean the house and do their schoolwork, while the adolescent boys do their part to boost the family income. On the night before a new school term she lectures her siblings: "I want everyone upstairs from the street when I come home from work. . . . Anybody not in the house by 6 o'clock will get the hell kicked out of them. . . . No card playing or fooling around until homework is done and I check it. And you, Vino, Gino and Sal, take a night each helping your mother with the dishes. Give her a break." When her stepfather is permanently hospitalized, Octavia decides that she must "take care of the family," abandoning her plans to leave the garment factory and pursue a teaching certificate.[129]

Solidarity among female kin and even neighbors is common in working-class communities. Especially where male incomes are unsteady or where the presence of men in the household is sporadic, sharing domestic tasks and financial resources is crucial for survival.[130] Although most Italian households in New York were male headed, the income of the head of household could not be relied on because of unstable employment. Higher adult male mortality and the fact that men often traveled south in

[128] Odencrantz, *Italian Women in Industry*, pp. 204, 205.

[129] Mario Puzo, *The Fortunate Pilgrim* (New York: Atheneum, 1965), pp. 148–49.

[130] Elizabeth Bott, *Family and Social Networks: Roles, Norms, and External Relationships in Ordinary Urban Families* (London: Tavistock, 1957); Carol B. Stack, *All Our Kin: Strategies for Survival in a Black Community* (New York: Harper and Row, 1974).

the winter months to find outdoor laboring jobs meant that mothers often were left to raise children alone. In the early decades of the century most immigrant women did not have their mothers to rely on, so they turned to their sisters and cousins.[131] As their daughters matured, mothers turned to them. Puzo describes a scene in the family kitchen after Lucia Santa and Octavia have put the younger children to bed. Mother and daughter are together. This is a female world, dominated by family concerns but inhabited by strong women, confident of their ability jointly to manage affairs without the aid of men:

> The women were in perfect ease and contentment, chiefs of an obedient tribe. Everything was running smoothly; they were both in rapport—the daughter a faithful but powerful underling; the mother undisputed chief, but showing respect and admiration for a clever and faithful daughter's help. It was never said, but the father's banishment had relieved them of a great deal of tension and worry. They were almost happy he was gone, and their rule now absolute.[132]

We turn now from the daughters to a detailed look at the lives of Italian wives and mothers in New York.

---

[131] Smith discusses this phenomenon in *Family Connections*, chap. 3.
[132] Puzo, *The Fortunate Pilgrim*, p. 151.

WORK AND FAMILY DURING THE EARLY DECADES: WIVES AND MOTHERS

Lucia Santa makes the family organism stand strong against the sands of time: the growth of children, the death of parents and all changes of worldly circumstance.

— Mario Puzo, *The Fortunate Pilgrim*

"On fine summer days," reporter Ralph Foster Weld began his description of the typical Italian street in Brooklyn, "young mothers sat on doorsteps, babies at their breasts; children swarmed the streets; neighbors sought the sunshine and exchanged confidences."[1] Indeed, Italian-American women spent most of their adult lives as wives and mothers. Among the first generation of immigrants the average age at marriage was low, around twenty, and the proportion who married, high.[2] This young age was typical for migratory groups that were dominated by males; most

[1] Ralph Foster Weld, *Brooklyn Is America* (New York: Columbia University Press, 1950), p. 138. The period being described is c. 1935.

[2] Actual mean age at marriage is unknown because the census does not record date of or age at marriage. One can only know an estimated average, or singulate mean age at marriage. "The singulate mean age at marriage is an estimate of the mean number of years lived by a cohort of women before their first marriage. The statistic is calculated from the proportion of males or females single in successive age groups reported on a census schedule." See U.S. Department of Commerce, Bureau of the Census, *The Methods and Materials of Demography* vol. 1, 3d printing rev. (Washington, D.C.: Government Printing Office, 1975), p. 295. The complete method used for such calculations can be found in *The Methods and Materials*, 1: 295. Calculations from the New York State Manuscript Census sample reveal that in 1905 a singulate mean age at marriage for New York Italian women was 20.5 years.

adult females came to the new land specifically to join fiancés and husbands; the age of marriage rose by 1925, to around twenty-three years, suggesting the reemergence of parental control as the community in New York took root and parents sought to keep children at home as long as possible.[3]

Whether earlier or later, the vast majority of the Italian women throughout these years married, and once they did, the way they used their time changed.[4] The traditional tasks of raising children and caring for the household became their highest priorities. In order to fulfill these priorities, however, Italian wives often took on jobs that went beyond traditional roles. Many juggled paid labor with the far greater responsibilities they faced now that they were no longer single. Italian wives and mothers had even less time than their daughters to pursue activities independent of the family. Within the family, nevertheless, they were assertive participants, making critical decisions about family strategies that affected all members of the household. One source of strength came from their connections to female networks of relatives and neighbors.

Family Patterns and Work Patterns

Expectations about gender roles in the immigrant community interacted with the demographic and economic circumstances of this particu-

[3] Calculations using the New York State Manuscript Census for 1925 reveal a singulate mean age of marriage of 22.75. This result appears consistent with the findings of demographer Massimo Livi-Bacci. Using actual marriage records, he calculated the mean age at first marriage for Italian women at 24.8 between 1919 and 1934 in the state of New York, including New York City. See *Immigrazione et l'Assimilazione degli Italiani negli Stati Uniti* (Milan: Dot. A. Giuffrè, 1961), p. 56. On the efforts and capacity of working-class families to keep children at home to contribute to the family, see also John Modell, Frank Furstenberg, Theodore Hershberg, "Social Change and Transitions to Adulthood in Historical Perspective," in *Philadelphia: Work, Space, Family and Group Experience in a Nineteenth-Century City*, ed. Theodore Hershberg (New York: Oxford University Press, 1981), pp. 311–41; Frank Furstenberg, John Modell, and Douglas Strong, "The Timing of Marriage in the Transition to Adulthood: Continuity and Change, 1860–1975," in John Demos and Sarane Spence Boocock, eds., *Turning Points: Historical and Sociological Essays on the Family* (Chicago: University of Chicago Press, 1978), pp. S120–50; Michael Katz and Ian Davey, "Youth and Early Industrialization in a Canadian City," in ibid., pp. S81–S119.

[4] In 1905, 90 percent of all adult Italian women in the sample were married; in 1925, 93 percent were married.

lar community to shape married women's work patterns. Even though the family's need for wage earners might be great, a woman's child-care responsibilities were so enormous that it was difficult for her to engage in paid labor. In 1905 the average twenty-year-old Italian woman could expect to have at least six children before her child-bearing years were over.[5] Even when compared with the statistics for other immigrant groups, this was a large number.[6]

Over the twenty years from 1905 to 1925 the fertility level for New York Italians dropped but remained comparatively high. In 1925 calculations from the census show that Italian women could expect to bear 5.2 children.[7] Such a figure, based on 1925 age-specific fertility estimates, is higher than what would be the actual child-bearing patterns of the younger women in the ensuing years, because the Depression years saw a marked decrease in child bearing for Italians as well as for other Ameri-

[5] This figure is based on a 5-percent sample of three Italian neighborhoods, primary nuclear families in households analyzed. New York State Manuscript Census. N = 698 wives. Since the census does not record the number of children ever born to a woman, we can only estimate the fertility of this population, on the basis of the number of children under the age of five as recorded in the 1905 census, per married women. A raw ratio based on the number of children under five per 1,000 women ages 20–49 is calculated. The population analyzed here is one containing a disproportionate number of married women in their younger, child-bearing years. Thus, in order to get a true picture of the overall fertility of these women, we standardized the ratio, on the basis of a standard age distribution for married women in the population. Standardized according to the procedure used by Tamara K. Hareven and Maris A. Vinovskis, "Marital Fertility, Ethnicity and Occupations in Urban Families: An Analysis of South Boston and South End in 1880," *Journal of Social History* 8 (Spring 1975): 69–93. The resulting ratio was 1064.5 children (per 1,000 Italian women). The childbearing *estimate* is not an actual *completed* fertility figure for any group of Italians, but an estimate of what the completed fertility picture for a mother would be, on the basis of the child-mother ratio derived for the population at one point in time: in this case I have used the 1905 census. The completed child-bearing estimate is a minimum figure because the census records only children alive at the time of the count. The method for calculating the completed fertility can be found in Hareven and Vinovkis, "Marital Fertility."

[6] Comparing Italians' fertility rates to the fertility rates of other ethnic groups in late-nineteenth-century Massachusetts that have been age-standardized by use of the same procedure, we find Italians to have a higher rate than do the Irish, French, Canadian, all other foreign-born Americans, as well as the native born. See Hareven and Vinovskis, "Marital Fertility." The fertility for all Italians in the United States was 5.4. See Livi-Bacci, *Immigrazione et l'Assimilazione*, p. 58.

[7] This figure is based on 5-percent sample of three Italian neighborhoods, Manhattan, 1925, primary nuclear families in household analyzed. New York State Manuscript Census. N = 591 wives.

cans. But Italian fertility was relatively high throughout the 1920s. One study of New York immigrants from the 1930 census reported a gross fertility rate of 23.5 per 1,000 for Italians; the rate for Jews in New York was a much lower 11.4.[8]

Most Italian wives, like their counterparts throughout white America, left the workplace after marriage to raise their children. In 1905 the census recorded only 7.3 percent of New York's Italian-born wives at work, two-thirds of them doing homework.[9] Large numbers of wives, however, did paid labor at one time or another that went unrecorded in the census.[10] The census missed these workers for several reasons: one, families often concealed this source of income; second, some census takers simply neglected to record homework; third, much of the census was enumerated during slack periods in the garment industry, when homeworkers were least likely to be employed. Contemporary surveys done by both public and private agencies provide a more complete picture of the extent to which Italian women availed themselves of employment opportunities in the garment industry. One study of the men's garment industry in New York found that 17 percent of all women employed were homeworkers, almost all of them Italian wives and mothers. A survey of Italian neighborhoods, which includes some of the very blocks used in my 1905 census sample, found homework in one-quarter of the apartments. Homework in artificial flowers, an important aspect of that industry, was also dominated by Italian women.[11]

The low earning capacity of husbands and the seasonality of their work

---

[8] See "Vital Indices and Their Relation to Psychological and Social Factors," *Human Biology* 5 (February 1933): 118. A gross fertility rate is not standardized by the age distribution of the population, but the age structures of the Italian and Jewish immigrant populations were similar.

[9] This percentage is based on 5-percent sample, three Italian neighborhoods in Manhattan, New York Manuscript Census, 1905.

[10] For example, almost all the homeworkers recorded in the census sample were clustered in one neighborhood, particularly on Elizabeth Street in the Mulberry district, just south of Houston, data that reflect the large percentage of homeworkers found in that same area by the Immigration Commission. In her study of the same section of Manhattan, Donna R. Gabaccia found that, depending on the block, anywhere from 14 to 60 percent of the women were home finishers. See "Houses and People: Sicilians in Sicily and New York, 1890–1930" (Ph.D. diss., University of Michigan, 1979), pp. 195, 196.

[11] On the men's garment industry, see U.S. Congress, Senate, *Report on Condition of Woman and Child Wage Earners*, vol. 2: *Men's Ready-Made Clothing*, S. Doc. 645, 61st Cong., 2d sess. (Washington, D.C.: Government Printing Office, 1911), pp. 35, 221. For the immigrant neighborhood survey, see U.S. Congress, Senate, *Reports of the Immigration*

were often cited by the women as reasons for doing finishing at home. A twenty-eight-year old garment finisher explained to a U.S. Bureau of Labor investigator that "she and her husband were penniless when they reached America and her husband owed money for the passport and ticket and it was necessary for her to go to work." Another men's clothing finisher, working at home, told the bureau that she went to work "because her husband was not employed during the winter months and it was necessary for her to increase the family income." Older wives stated similar reasons for working. One fifty-two-year-old finisher said her husband was sick, which obligated her to go to work to support her family.[12]

Precisely how economic need encouraged married women to take on paid labor can be seen through an analysis conducted for the Senate by the Bureau of Labor of families connected with the men's garment industry. The bureau studied close to three hundred families that were headed by Italian men and that contained at least one single daughter sixteen years or over who worked in the men's garment industry. The investigators published the data, by family, with information on the employment status, earnings, age, education, and marital status of family members. I was able to analyze the mothers in these families as a subset of the survey, comparing household characteristics of working and nonworking mothers. (For a detailed discussion of the data, see Appendix C.) The mothers were recorded only either as at work or at home; undoubtedly, many listed as being at work were doing paid work as finishers at homes. Table 5 indicates, nevertheless, significant differences in the earning power of the Italian husbands whose wives were at work and the husbands whose wives were not employed. Table 6 also shows statistically significant differences with respect to the earnings of the entire household. The wealthier families had a smaller proportion of wives engaged in paid labor.

Commission, vol. 26: *Immigration in Cities*, S. Doc. 338, 61st Cong., 2d sess. (Washington, D.C.: Government Printing Office, 1911), 1: 204. On artificial flowers, see Mary Van Kleeck, *Artificial Flower Makers* (New York: Russell Sage Foundation, Survey Associates, 1913).

[12] The U.S. Bureau of Labor surveys were done for U.S. Congress, Senate, *Report on Condition of Woman and Child Wage Earners*, vol. 2: *Men's Ready-Made Clothing*, pp. 241–42. See also Louise C. Odencrantz, *Italian Women in Industry* (New York: Russell Sage Foundation, 1919), pp. 134–35.

That family economic needs were more important than ethnic values in determining employment patterns of Italian wives is suggested by com-

Table 5. The employment status of Italian mothers of female garment workers, by earnings of the fathers, 1910 (percentage distribution)

Employment status of mother	Earnings of father[a]			All female garment workers' families (N=204)
	to $200 (N=83)	$201–$400 (N=80)	$400 up (N=41)	
At work	49.4	51.6	24.4	45.1
Not working	50.6	48.8	75.6	54.9

Source: U.S. Congress, Senate, *Report on Condition of Woman and Child Wage Earners*, vol. 2: *Men's Ready-Made Clothing*, S. Doc. 645, 61st cong., 2d sess. (Washington, D.C.: Government Printing Office, 1911), pp. 781–807.

Note: Recorded as significant at .01 level with a Goodman and Kruskal Tau measure of strength at .0438.

[a]All are Italian born.

Table 6. The employment status of Italian mothers of female garment workers, by earnings of the rest of the household, 1910 (percentage distribution)

Employment status of mother	Household earnings						All female garment workers' families (N=257)
	to $200 (N=7)	$201–$400 (N=49)	$401–$600 (N=62)	$601–$800 (N=46)	$801–$1,000 (N=32)	$1,000 up (N=61)	
At work	57.1	63.3	61.3	28.3	34.4	21.3	42.8
Not working	42.9	34.7	37.1	65.2	56.3	75.4	53.3
Absent or deceased	0	2.0	1.6	24.3	9.4	3.3	3.9

Source: U.S. Congress, Senate, *Report on Condition of Woman and Child Wage Earners*, vol. 2: *Men's Ready-Made Clothing*, S. Doc. 645, 61st cong., 2d sess. (Washington, D.C.: Government Printing Office, 1911), pp. 781–807.

Note: Recorded as significant at .0002 level with a Goodman and Kruskal Tau measure of strength at .1140.

paring this group of women to the mothers in eighty-eight households of Jewish females in the garment industry. Only 4 percent of the Jewish mothers were at work. Again, we do not know the proportion doing homework as opposed to factory labor; nevertheless, even if all the Italian working wives could be accounted for by homework, a pattern that presumably would be consistent with traditional attitudes about the impropriety of permitting women to leave the house, the tiny percentage of Jewish working wives, in comparison with the 45 percent of the Italians, would still be surprising. It has been suggested that unlike southern Italian families with their abhorrence of married women's work, Jewish families were much more willing to allow wives to work because in eastern Europe Jewish women were often active in small family businesses.[13] Yet if one understands married women's work as an expression of economic need, the difference between the two groups is not surprising; the earnings of Italian husbands were substantially lower than those of the Jews. More than one-third of the Jewish men earned above $400 annually; 16 percent earned more than $600. Among Italians, only one-fifth of the men earned more than $400 annually; only 6 percent, more than $600.[14]

A comparison of Jewish and Italian families in the small sample of Lower East Side families, discussed in Chapter 2, suggests that where there are comparable economic conditions in the households, similar employment patterns will prevail among the wives. In 1905 both the Italian families and the Jewish families in this sample, it will be recalled, were more prosperous than the Italians elsewhere in Manhattan, as indicated by the large percentages of skilled workers among the Italian and Jewish males. In both ethnic groups none of the wives, in contrast to their daughters, worked for wages.[15]

[13] See, for example, Charlotte Baum, Paula Hyman, and Sona Michel in *The Jewish Woman in America* (New York: Dial Press, 1976).

[14] Calculated from U.S. Congress, Senate, *Report on Condition of Woman and Child Wage Earners*, vol. 2: *Men's Ready-Made Clothing*, pp. 781–807. The ethnic origin of wives is determined by the birthplace of the husband. Since the ethnic intermarriage rate among Italian foreign-born men between 1908 and 1912 was only 1 percent, it seems safe to identify these women as Italian. (It is also likely that in 1909 few, if any, of these women were second-generation immigrants.) On intermarriage rates, see Julius Draschler, *A Statistical Study of the Amalgamation of European Peoples* (New York: Columbia University, 1921).

[15] New York State Manuscript Census, 1905.

Italian wives also contributed to the family income at home by taking in boarders; in immigrant working-class communities, providing room and board for male migrants who arrived in the United States without families was common. In 1905, 15.2 percent of all households with wives present had boarders, and it was the wife who prepared the meals and often washed the clothes of lodgers.[16]

The availability of homework in the garment industry and the need for unattached males to find lodging meant that many Italian wives could combine paid and unpaid labor in a family setting, just as they had done in Italy. Yet Italian wives also responded to the demands of the huge garment industry and the needs of their families by taking paid labor outside the home. Contrary to all our expectations about Italian culture and women's work, Italian wives and mothers took jobs outside the home to a greater degree than most other females. One study of Italian working wives in 1914 reported that as many as one-third were employed outside the home.[17] In a special study of some 500 working wives with relatives in the men's garment industry, the Bureau of Labor recorded, among other things, the age of the women, their exact occupations (in this case, distinguishing homework from other occupations), the earnings of their husbands, the number of children in the family and their ages, and the earnings, if any, of children. (See Appendix C.) The vast majority, some 80 percent, were homeworkers, but of those working outside the home, almost all were Italians.[18]

An ever-changing balance between economic need and domestic responsibilities appears to have determined the women's choices about working at home or in the factory. What separated the smaller group of women who worked outside the home from homeworkers was not greater

---

[16] Almost all boarders listed in the census samples were males living without female relatives. New York State Manuscript Census, 1905. Interestingly, in the neighborhood of skilled Italian and Jewish workers on the Lower East Side one-quarter of the Jewish households and one-third of the Italian households had boarders or lodgers. On the importance of boarding in these immigrant communities, see also U.S. Congress, Senate, *Report on Condition of Woman and Child Wage Earners*, vol. 2: *Men's Ready-Made Clothing*, pp. 282, 281.

[17] Odencrantz, *Italian Women in Industry*, p. 152.

[18] These calculations are based on survey data for 549 families with working wives. U.S. Congress, Senate, *Report on Condition of Woman and Child Wage Earners*, vol. 2: *Men's Ready-Made Clothing*, pp. 842–59.

Mrs. Battaglia, Tessie (12), and Tony (7) working at home on Mulberry Street, 1908. "They are finishing men's trousers. Mr. Battaglia was crippled by a fall and cannot work. The mother works in a shop except on Saturdays when the children sew with her at home. They are paid two or three cents for a pair of trousers. Together they earn $1–$1.50 each Saturday." (Photograph by Lewis W. Hine, courtesy of the New York Public Library; legend found in the Lewis W. Hine Collection.)

economic need; families of female factory workers were actually earning more in weekly wages, exclusive of the wife's income. Rather, fewer female factory workers (17 percent) had children of preschool age than did homeworkers (62 percent).[19]

The proportion of Italian wives doing wage work decreased over time. The 1925 Manhattan census sample shows even fewer wives listed with occupations than in 1905; 2 percent of the foreign-born wives were recorded at work, while none of the small group of second-generation women was working. Undoubtedly, the fact that no homework was recorded at all in 1925 accounts for most of the change. The decrease also suggests that the earnings of the husband combined with the earnings of older children were high enough to make it more likely that wives would remain at home. Even in the 1920s, however, in the poorest Italian households married women were still taking on employment. All the Italian wives living in the Lower East Side block sampled from the 1925 state census were married to unskilled workers, not surprising since this neighborhood was in decline; five of those thirteen married women were also found at work, naturally enough, in the garment industry.[20] A private charity in New York reported that 21 percent of the wives in the Mulberry Street district, in the heart of one Italian neighborhood, were at work, 16 percent working in factories, stores, or at domestic service, 5 percent doing homework.[21]

Throughout these decades, moreover, Italian women continued to do homework that went unreported in the census. In 1926 the industrial commissioner of New York reported that 13 percent of all workers in the men's garment industry were still employed at home. The number of homeworkers actually increased in the mid-1920s—at a faster rate than

[19] The per capita weekly earnings of family members, *less* the earnings of the wife, averaged $2.52 for families of women working outside the home, $1.71 for women working inside the home. Calculations from ibid., pp. 842–59.

[20] Figures are based on a sample one-square block in Manhattan's Lower East Side. New York State Manuscript Census, 1925. Two families had boarders; in one of these families the wife was also working. No Jewish wives were at work, but five families had boarders. On the basis of the occupational status of males, this Jewish population, as might be expected, was economically weaker than the Jewish sample in 1905 but was still more prosperous than the Italian.

[21] John J. Gebhardt, *The Health of a Neighborhood: A Social Study of the Mulberry District* (New York: New York Association for Improving the Condition of the Poor, 1924), p. 9.

shopworkers, as the garment industry recovered from the post–World War I recession. Much homework was still being done illegally, and the commissioner's report added that even the official figure of 15,000 registered homeworkers was an underestimation of the actual conditions, as "not only the immediate family, but relatives and friends often work upon the garments given out to one person who calls at the factory."[22]

The need for Italian women to seek work was heightened during the harsh years of the Great Depression. In 1930 in the heart of Little Italy on Mulberry Street, 16.5 percent of the families had no adult wage earners working full time. In 1932 the figure was up to 47.6 percent.[23] To meet the crisis, every adult member of the family tried to find any kind of employment possible. Most single women sought factory work in the fashion industries; some found employment in service jobs such as office cleaning and waitressing. However, regular work of any kind was not easy to find.[24] On Mulberry Street 85 percent of the single women aged sixteen to twenty in 1930 reported that they considered themselves gainfully employed. Two years later the percentage had dropped to 75. In both years, only about 12 percent actually held full-time employment throughout the year.[25]

By contrast, the percentage of married women working actually increased during the early years of the Depression. When the younger women of the Mulberry district were having a hard time finding employment, their mothers returned to wage earning as homeworkers.[26] Indeed, during the height of the Depression, while the number of factory jobs

[22] New York State, Department of Labor, *Homework in the Men's Clothing Industry in New York and Rochester*, New York State Department of Labor Special Bulletin no. 147 (Albany, N.Y., 1926).

[23] See the social survey of Italian households conducted by the Fred J. Lavenburg Foundation, Hamilton House, "What happened to 236 families who were compelled to vacate their dwellings for a large housing project" (New York, 1933; reprint in the New York City Public Library Collection); Gwendolyn H. Berry, *Idleness and the Health of a Neighborhood* (New York: New York Association for Improving the Condition of the Poor, 1933), p. 25. See also John J. Alesandre, *Occupational Trends of Italians in New York City*, Casa Italiana Educational Bureau Bulletin no. 6, (New York: Columbia University, 1935), table 1.

[24] See "What happened to 236 families," pp. 4–5; Berry, *Idleness and the Health of a Neighborhood*, p. 17.

[25] Berry, *Idleness and the Health of a Neighborhood*, pp. 10–16.

[26] Ibid., p. 17.

shrank, the more poorly paid, irregular forms of employment—in particular, homework in the garment and artificial flower industries—rose dramatically. The expansion of homework was so noticeable that it
engendered labor agitation by garment unions in New York and eventually led to stiffer federal and state labor legislation, which is discussed in
later chapters. What was so noticeable and disturbing to labor leaders
seemed logical and normal to the Italians in these beleaguered households. Italian wives and mothers were just doing what they had always
done; in response to great family need, they found work in the interstices
of the economy.

In sum, throughout the early twentieth century married women's wage
work was a hardship for Italians, as for most American women, because it
took mothers away from the children in their care and violated norms
about gender roles. Most wives chose not to earn wages at all, if possible—but that choice was not always possible. Unlike immigrant mothers
in cities characterized by heavy industry, many New York Italian women
were able to do paid garment work at home while caring for their families. But homework was not the only way they could contribute badly
needed income; if necessary, these women could take on factory jobs.
How did wives juggle the many responsibilities in their daily lives?

Paid Work and Family Chores: Striking a Balance

Like all married women who did paid labor, Italian women were victims of the double day; they were still responsible for taking care of the
home and raising the children. Mothers theoretically could call on relatives to care for young children if they needed to go outside to work. But,
as already noted, very few first-generation wives had mothers or
mothers-in-law in New York. Sometimes sisters and cousins cared for
children; more often, older daughters helped tend to the younger ones.
Even with some help, mothers of young children were so heavily taxed by
duties at home that full-time, regular employment was impossible. One
study of Italian working wives reported that 44 percent had lost twelve
weeks or more during the year, compared with 25 percent of the single
women. And one-third of the married and widowed women workers had

been unemployed during the week previous to the interview, compared with 13 percent of the single females. "The reasons for their unemployment show their divided duty between home keeping and wage earning," the investigator concluded. "Over one-third were idle for personal reasons," she reported, such as illness and home responsibilities; only about one-fourth of the single women were idle for such reasons.[27]

For the majority of women who chose homework, the geography of immigrant neighborhoods made it relatively easy to combine their paid and unpaid jobs. They could walk a few short blocks to pick up and return the material daily. Many females continued the same trade, such as flower making, that they had worked in as single women in the shops.[28] Yet the opportunity to take materials home did not mean a marked improvement in the work environment. Most mothers labored with their children in tiny kitchens or bedroom areas; the U.S. Bureau of Labor found that about one-fourth of the rooms they visited were in dirty condition; about one-fifth had insufficient lighting for the work. They also found that during the winter many women worked in unheated rooms, and illnesses were common among Italian home finishers during the cold months.[29]

Like their children, Italian mothers spent long hours at paid labor in an effort to maximize earnings during the rush seasons. Sixty percent of the men's garment finishers in 1910 were found to be working more than eleven hours daily. As late as the 1930s the New York State Department of Labor found that more than one-half of the Italian flower makers were working forty or more hours a week; close to one-fifth were working between thirty and forty hours. Two-thirds stated that they had worked five days or more in the week prior to the investigation; 54 percent had worked six days or more.[30]

[27]Odencrantz, *Italian Women in Industry*, pp. 20–21.

[28]U.S. Congress, Senate, *Report on Condition of Woman and Child Wage Earners*, vol. 2: *Men's Ready-Made Clothing*, pp. 282–85; Van Kleeck, *Artificial Flower Makers*, pp. 91–92. See also Gabaccia, "Houses and People," chap. 4; Van Kleeck, *Artificial Flower Makers*, p. 97. For a discussion of new scholarship on gender and geography, see Linda Kerber, "Separate Spheres, Female Worlds, Woman's Place: The Rhetoric of Women's History," *Journal of American History* 75 (June 1988): 9–39.

[29]U.S. Congress, Senate, *Report on Condition of Woman and Child Wage Earners*, vol. 2: *Men's Ready-Made Clothing*, pp. 252, 296.

[30]Ibid., p. 241; New York State, Department of Labor, *Homework in the Artificial Flower and Feather Industry*, in *New York State*, Part II, New York Department of Labor Special Bulletin no. 199 (Albany, N.Y., 1938), pp. 104–5.

Carrying home materials for making flowers, circa 1913. (Photograph by Lewis W. Hine, courtesy of the New York Public Library.)

The work day, moreover, for most Italian homeworkers was longer than the cited eight to ten hours. Many women without older children to run errands were forced to spend time going to and from the shop for work. They often had to wait around the shop for the materials. Housework, caring for children, washing clothes, cooking, and tending to boarders, if there were any, also interrupted the day's paid work. The "complicated routine of duties thus prolongs the day of the homeworker into the night," reported the Bureau of Labor investigators, "even if she does only put in six to eight hours a day." More than one-third of a group of Italian artificial flower makers reported that during the week prior to being surveyed they had worked after 10:00 P.M. Among the late-night group, two-thirds had worked past 3:00 A.M. at least once during the week.[31]

The pressure to put in such long hours was due not only to the irregularity of employment, but to the fact that homeworkers' earnings were very low. In 1910 the men's garment finishers, for example, earned on the average $3.43 a week; with some help from her children, the homeworker could hope to earn about $4.10. Forty percent earned between $25 and $100 annually; a similar proportion earned between $100 and $175. Wages were only a little better for homeworkers in the artificial flower industry.[32] They improved somewhat over the years, but they remained far below shop salaries. In 1925 the men's garment finishers earned between $7.00 and $12.00 per week at home, about one-half the wages of female factory workers.[33]

Over and above the rigors of paid labor, the women had to struggle to care for the family and keep the household clean because of crowded conditions. In order to increase income, families were willing to put up with extremely cramped living quarters by taking in boarders, or as Gabaccia shows in her study of Elizabeth Street, living in partner households, where two or three families shared a single apartment.[34] One family of five, for example, sublet a part of their three-room apartment to

[31] U.S. Congress, Senate, *Report on Condition of Woman and Child Wage Earners*, vol. 2: *Men's Ready-Made Clothing*, pp. 241–42; New York State, Department of Labor, *Homework in the Artificial Flower and Feather Industry*, p. 55.

[32] U.S. Congress, Senate, *Report on Condition of Woman and Child Wage Earners*, vol. 2: *Men's Ready-Made Clothing*, pp. 225–26; Van Kleeck, *Artificial Flower Makers*, p. 106.

[33] New York State, Department of Labor, *Homework in the Men's Clothing Industry*, appendix.

[34] Gabaccia, "Houses and People," chap. 4.

a couple and their children; another three-member family living in three rooms took in nine boarders. "Eight members of the Caruso family lived in a three room apartment," Odencrantz reported, "which they occupied in return for Mrs. Caruso's services as a janitress." In order to increase their income by $3.50 a month, they took in one lodger. "The crowding of eight people into three rooms would have seemed bad enough," she said, "but less than one-fifth of the families with boarders who were asked, considered it an 'inconvenience' to live under those conditions."[35]

Under such circumstances, it is not surprising to find that Italian wives did not measure up to the housekeeping standards of middle-class observers. "I have known only two Italian women, out of fifty," wrote Lillian Betts, "who were good housekeepers." The Italian wife, she continued, "does not fret; dirt and disorder, noise and company never disturb her."[36] The U.S. Bureau of Labor investigators suggested a greater understanding of the problems facing Italians, although the disapproving tone of their observations also is evident. They described the problems of home finishers in the men's garment trades:

> Overburdened mothers became negligent in their homes, filth results, and their already subnormal standard of living drops still lower. . . . They can make no distinction between workrooms and living rooms—kitchens and bedrooms. You may find work in a kitchen where lodgers sleep; on the bed mixed with family's soiled bedding and clothing—and even loaves of bread and other food on the bed, too—or on the dirty floor. . . . One is not surprised that homes are dirty most of the time—the surprising thing is that they are ever clean and that these tired women take Saturdays or Sundays to wash the house.[37]

Modern plumbing freed Italian women from some of the most rigorous cleaning chores they had known in southern Italy, but, as Gabaccia has pointed out, the fact that in New York all work tasks, from food preparation to laundry to sewing, were performed indoors, in tenement flats, instead of out on the village street made homes even more cramped, crowded, and dirty.[38] The Bureau of Labor did concede that on a cleanli-

[35] Odencrantz, *Italian Women in Industry*, pp. 184–85.

[36] Lillian Betts, "The Italians in New York," *University Settlement Studies* 1 (October 1905–January 1906): 94.

[37] U.S. Congress, Senate, *Report on Condition of Woman and Child Wage Earners*, vol. 2: *Men's Ready-Made Clothing*, p. 296.

[38] See Gabaccia, "Houses and People," chap. 4.

ness scale from poor to good, almost one-half of the kitchens and bed-
rooms visited in homeworking households received a good rating; almost
two-thirds were rated either good or fair.[39] And in better-off families Italian wives, with more time and resources for housekeeping, became eager
participants in working-class domesticity. Caroline Ware describes the
homes of Italian women who had prospered during the 1920s and had
moved out of Manhattan.

> The homes of girls who had married and left the locality reflected care,
> effort, expenditure. . . . "She's forever fussing about the house and hasn't
> any time for me," complained a young husband as his wife proudly displayed
> to the interviewer, the lavender bathroom, the green kitchen, the pink bed-
> room, and the red and gold spun runner on the living room table. In describ-
> ing her friends who had moved to various outlying boroughs, a young
> married woman had nothing to say about their husbands, their children, or
> any of their activities—nothing except that each and all had "lovely homes."[40]

Italian mothers also struggled, within their limited means, to raise
healthy children. A look at food-consumption patterns shows that, despite
the disapproval of middle-class observers, they did not do badly with respect to diet. Criticism reflected prevailing standards of what was considered healthy food, which—ironically—have been greatly modified in the
past few decades. Contemporary writers criticized the Italian food because it was high in starch and made abundant use of olive oil, which we
now know is a healthy substitute for saturated fat. Italian menus tended to
depend on vegetables, starches, and dairy products, while other low-
income families relied more on meat. Italians used macaroni and dried
beans to furnish protein, which would be heartily approved today, along
with milk and cheese.[41]

[39] U.S. Congress, Senate, *Report on Condition of Woman and Child Wage Earners*, vol.
2: *Men's Ready-Made Clothing*, p. 252.

[40] Caroline Ware, *Greenwich Village, 1920–1930* (Boston: Houghton Mifflin, 1935), p.
195.

[41] Odencrantz, *Italian Women in Industry*, p. 198; Louise Bolard More, *Wage Earners'
Budgets: A Study of Standards and Cost of Living in New York City* (New York: Henry Holt,
1907), p. 97; Ware, *Greenwich Village*, p. 191; U.S. Congress, Senate, *Report on Condition of Woman and Child Wage Earners*, vol. 2: *Men's Ready-Made Clothing*, p. 283.
Dorothy Wiehl, "The Diets of Low Income Families in New York City," *Milbank Memorial
Fund Quarterly* 11 (October 1933): 320–24; Robert Coit Chapin, *The Standard of Living
among Workingmen's Families in New York City* (New York: Russell Sage Foundation,
1909), pp. 172–79.

Italian family at supper, New York City, 1915. (Photograph by Lewis W. Hine, courtesy of the New York Public Library.)

Living in households where families engaged in homework probably had negative effects on the children's health. For mothers forced to resume work soon after childbirth, home finishing was certainly more attractive than factory work because women at home could nurse their babies.[42] Inadequate heat, poor ventilation, and crowding, however, all contributed to the high rate of infant and child mortality in the Italian homework districts.[43] The larger proportion of Italian mothers (compared with other groups) engaged in homework may have been a factor in accounting for the high mortality among Italian children.[44] From the moment they were born, many homeworkers' children inhaled swirling pieces of feather fluff or chemical fumes from their mothers' work. Frequent lung infections, one of the major causes of child mortality at the turn of the century, were a consequence of this unhealthy environment.[45]

The Social Supports of the Married Woman

"The mother had no recreation," wrote Louise Odencrantz about the Italian wives she studied in the early part of the century, "and the father took his alone."[46] The actual experience was surely more complicated than this description allows; nevertheless, the combination of paid work, household chores, and child care left Italian mothers, like their daughters, with little time for formal recreation. If, as Ware noted in her community study of Greenwich Village in the 1920s, "the great mass of Italian [married] women belonged to no organizations at all," they certainly met

[42] Henry White, "Perils of the Home Factory," *Harper's Weekly* 55 (February 11, 1911): 10. Betts, "The Italians in New York," p. 94.

[43] U.S. Congress, Senate, *Report on Condition of Woman and Child Wage Earners*, vol. 2: *Men's Ready-Made Clothing*, pp. 296–97; New York City, Department of Health, *Influence of Nationality upon the Mortality of a Community with Special References to the City of New York*, by William Guilfuy, M.D., New York City Department of Health Monograph Series no. 18 (New York, November 1919), pp. 10–11.

[44] New York City, Department of Health, *Influence of Nationality.*

[45] Van Kleeck, *Artificial Flower Makers*; New York State, Factory Investigating Commission, *Public Hearings in New York City, Second Series* (reprint from the *Preliminary Report of the New York Factory Investigating Commission*; Albany, N.Y.: J. B. Lyon, October 1911), p. 1441, testimony of Dr. Antonia Stella.

[46] Odencrantz, *Italian Women in Industry*, p. 203.

frequently with other women, combining paid work, unpaid domestic labor, and sociability.[47] Many women did housework with other adult females, often relatives who shared an apartment or lived in the same tenement.[48] And while they did laundry or cared for the babies, Italian wives talked to female kin and neighbors sharing problems, news of their families, and advice. Weld's description of Italian streets in Brooklyn could be applied throughout the city. Writing about the time she spent living among Italians in New York, Lillian Betts noted that even though the location for a woman's activities had changed with the move from southern Italy, many of her behavior patterns, adapted to the new surroundings, remained essentially the same. "A tenement hall in New York is a substitute for the village road, where she and her neighbors can communicate."[49]

Adult women continued to use social interactions as a means of reinforcing community values. "Each tenement was a village square," wrote Mario Puzo, describing the Italian Tenth Avenue neighborhood that is the setting for *The Fortunate Pilgrim*. "Each had its own group of women, sitting on stools and boxes and doing more than gossip. They recalled ancient history, argued morals and social law."[50] Lucia Santa, the heroic Italian mother of the novel, frequents one of these circles to listen to her neighbors' stories, to pass along her own news, to offer advice on other women's problems, and to receive some useful advice about her own troubles.[51]

Just as mothers depended on their daughters for help during crises, so, too, they relied on women neighbors for help during emergencies. A

[47] Ware, *Greenwich Village*, p. 176.

[48] See Gabaccia, "Houses and People," chap. 4, 5; Marie J. Concistre, "Adult Education in a Local Area: A Study of a Decade in the Life and Education of the Adult Italian Immigrant in East Harlem, New York City" (Ph.D. diss., New York University, 1943), p. 326.

[49] Betts, "The Italians in New York," p. 94.

[50] Mario Puzo, *The Fortunate Pilgrim* (New York: Atheneum, 1965), p. 6.

[51] Ibid. On female friendship networks among working-class families, see Elizabeth Bott, *Family and Social Networks: Roles, Norms, and External Relationships in Ordinary Urban Families* (London: Tavistock, 1957); Michael Young and Peter Wilmott, *Family and Kinship in East London* (London: Routledge and Kegan Paul, 1957); Herbert Gans, *The Urban Villagers* (New York: Free Press, 1965); Mirra Komarovsky, *Blue Collar Marriage* (New York: Random House, 1964). On Italians, see also Judith Smith, "Our Own Kind: Family and Community Networks in Providence," in Nancy F. Cott and Elizabeth H. Pleck, eds. *A Heritage of Her Own* (New York: Simon and Schuster, 1979), pp. 393–411; Concistre, "Adult Education," p. 326.

death in the family, a sudden illness would send neighbors, especially nearby kin, running to offer assistance. They might help cook for the household, care for a sick family member, or even help deliver a baby.[52] Women's networks gave wives much-needed material aid and emotional support, not only in caring for the elderly and the young, but in dealing with husbands as well. In one case a wife's sister moved into a couple's two-room apartment with her three babies when she was deserted by her husband. In another, her family discovered a young bride slaving away at homework while her new husband made no effort at all to find himself a job; a quick visit to the groom by her angry aunt sent him off to find employment.[53] In these ways family members attempted to maintain the ability to enforce norms of proper behavior, just as they had in the towns of southern Italy.

Female relatives and neighbors shared in the good as well as bad times. Popular religious celebrations were one of the most important arenas for socializing. The relative indifference to the institutional church and organized church activities so characteristic of other American immigrant communities was a carryover from southern Italy, where anticlericalism was intense and religious education was minimal.[54] As Robert Orsi notes in his seminal study of religion among New York Italians, "historians and scholars have been waiting for Italians to get into church and start behaving like other American Catholics." Yet an understanding of religion in this community begins with the recognition that while they faithfully attended important ceremonies, "going to church was not so important to them." Italians, nonetheless, "considered themselves good and faithful people, and Catholics," and especially among the first generation, popular religion was very important.[55]

The planning, preparation, and celebrations surrounding weddings, christenings, and holidays were an important part of married women's

[52] Josephine Roche, "The Italian Girl," in *The Neglected Girl*, West Side Studies (New York: Russell Sage Foundation, Survey Associates, 1914), pp. 99–102; Gabaccia, "Houses and People," chap. 4.

[53] Betts, "The Italians in New York," pp. 97, 94.

[54] See Constantine Panunzio, *The Soul of an Immigrant* (1921; reprint, New York: Arno Press, 1969), pp. 18, 19; Rudolph Vecoli, "Prelates and Peasants: Italian Immigrants and the Catholic Church," *Journal of Social History* 2 (Spring 1969): 217–68.

[55] Robert Orsi, *The Madonna of 115th Street: Faith and Community in Italian Harlem, 1880–1950* (New Haven: Yale University Press, 1985), p. xvi.

lives.[56] The women of the community organized street *festas*, rooted in traditional celebrations of local patron saints. The annual feast of the Madonna in East Harlem, for example, became a neighborhood affair with bands, parades, special food. Each year young and old women took part in the street procession celebrating the power of the Madonna to overcome family catastrophes. The women used this ritual, according to Orsi, to honor their own contributions to family survival. Holding candles connected by ribbons, the women proclaimed their ties to kin and neighbors.[57]

The female world of relatives and neighbors was an important part of women's lives; men, too, had their own, separate social world. Men spent more time in recreational activities than did women. They went to neighborhood saloons to play cards or to parks for bocci ball.[58] They brought their male friends home, usually to the kitchen, for talk and games. But as Gabaccia has pointed out, New York wives probably interacted with their male relatives to a greater extent than women did in southern Italy. Although some Italian men in the United States traveled long distances on a seasonal basis for work, most, in contrast to their compatriots in Italy, were employed close to home in shops, on the streets, or on the docks.[59] When leisure time was available in New York, wives went with their families on weekend days to the park for picnics, to the movies, or to Coney Island.[60]

Wives could also turn to their husbands for help in domestic and work chores. Italian husbands are often pictured as hard taskmasters who expected their wives to take care of all family chores because these were uniquely female obligations. No doubt this was true for some Italian men, as it is true for some families in many cultures.[61] Nevertheless, as Louise Lamphere so well shows in her study of Latin American immigrants in

[56] On weddings and holidays, see Roche, "The Italian Girl," pp. 112; Concistre, "Adult Education"; Puzo, *The Fortunate Pilgrim*; Pietro DiDonato, *Christ in Concrete* (New York: Bobbs-Merrill, 1937).

[57] Orsi, *The Madonna*, chap. 7.

[58] Concistre, "Adult Education," chap. 1.

[59] Gabaccia, "Houses and People," p. 242. See also Chapter 3, above.

[60] See Chapin, *Standard of Living*, p. 211; Kathy Peiss, *Cheap Amusements: Working Women and Leisure in Turn-of-the-Century New York* (Philadelphia: Temple University Press, 1986), chap. 5.

[61] For a discussion of the unequal distribution of household responsibilities in contemporary couples, see Heidi Hartmann, "The Family as the Locus of Gender, Class and Political Struggle: The Example of Housework," *Signs* 6 (Spring 1981): 366–94.

modern-day Providence, whatever the popular views of ethnic families, poor people cannot afford to stand on ceremony about what is considered traditionally a male or female job.[62] Like families in southern Italy, the New York settlers often maintained an outward adherence to a code of gender differences, partly because a breakdown in roles was a sign of poverty. But those who went into Italian homes often found that a rigid separation of activities by sex was not being carried out. There simply was too much work that had to be done if these households were going to survive. Husbands were seen in the evenings helping their wives with household chores: "Together they will wash the dishes or he will take the baby out . . . the mother . . . washes clothes until midnight. The husband . . . carries the tub to hang the clothes on the pulley. [This scene is repeated] . . . in ten kitchens in this tenement."[63] The men were often good cooks, and they enjoyed preparing meals. And, according to one study, Italian husbands also "shared with the mother in the intimate care of the children, and in the close watchfulness over them."[64] Finally, though homework was traditionally a female occupation, males would often lend a hand during rush season if they were temporarily unemployed.[65]

Italian Wives and Their Families: The Rhetoric and the Reality of Power

Married women's responsibilities kept them among kin, close to home, far more than their daughters. But their strong attachment to the family

[62] Louise Lamphere, *From Working Daughters to Working Mothers: Immigrant Women in a New England Industrial Community* (Ithaca, N.Y.: Cornell University Press, 1987), chap. 6.

[63] Betts, *The Italians in New York*, p. 94. See also Micaela di Leonardo, *The Varieties of Ethnic Experience: Kinship, Class, and Gender among California Italian-Americans* (Ithaca, N.Y.: Cornell University Press, 1984), chap. 2.

[64] Roche, "The Italian Girl," p. 108. Also, conversation with Ronald Suny on oral interviews with Italian workers for the Immigration Labor History Project, City College of New York Oral History Project, the late Herbert Gutman and Virginia Yans-McLaughlin, directors. DiDonato, *Christ in Concrete*.

[65] See Odencrantz, *Italian Women in Industry*, p. 221; New York State, Factory Investigating Commission, *Public Hearings*; photographs submitted by National Child Labor Committee, U.S. Congress, Senate, *Report on Condition of Woman and Child Wage Earners*, vol. 2: *Men's Ready-Made Clothing*, pp. 235–38.

did not mean that they were docile females subject to the dictates of their husbands. Within the home mothers dominated family life, and they were able to make important decisions about the behavior of others.

By and large, wives controlled the family finances. Every wage earner in the family turned his or her earnings over to the mother, who then doled out the money to pay for family expenses.[66] Most of the family budget went for essentials like food and shelter, and wives had chief responsibility in this area. Their control in this arena was not complete, however. Husbands might keep money for recreational purposes. Single adult sons might take about one-half of their wages for personal expenses. As we have seen, daughters would withhold for clothing part of their earnings from the family fund. Finally, some wage earners might also practice subterfuge, but only on a small scale to avoid being caught. With control of the major part of the family income, the wife had a great deal to say about the behavior of her husband and daughters, and at least partial authority over her sons' activities, from recreational to personal or educational.

Because wives knew how the family's money was being allocated, they could influence decisions about how any surplus would be spent. Among Italian working-class families where resources were scarce, conflicts about the use of any disposable income inevitably rose and certainly the desires of men often triumphed. Italian women, like most wives, were subject to the real economic threat that the chief breadwinner might desert the family altogether, or use physical coercion. But within these limits, Italian women, when necessary, sought and found other means to extract financial support from reluctant husbands. They turned to kin for help in pressuring the men, or sometimes they struck out violently themselves. When these approaches failed, in defiance of what all Italians had learned and believed about government, embattled women went to the state for help. Linda Gordon has shown that in Boston, for example, Italian women enlisted sympathetic social workers and the social service bureaucracy as allies in their domestic battles.[67]

---

[66] U.S. Congress, Senate, *Report on Condition of Woman and Child Wage Earners*, vol. 2: *Men's Ready-Made Clothing*, p. 281; Odencrantz, *Italian Women in Industry*, p. 163; Roche, "The Italian Girl," pp. 98–109. In one case a mother and daughter kept a separate fund for their own business. See also Orsi, *The Madonna*.

[67] See Linda Gordon, *Heroes of Their Own Lives: The Politics and History of Family Violence in Boston, 1880–1960* (New York: Viking Press, 1988), chaps. 8, 9.

Italian wives had authority in other important domestic matters besides family finances. "The mother is almost always on duty," reported one investigator, "delegating the housekeeping and the tending of babies to the daughter."[68] And the mother often took the main role in deciding how all of her children spent their time, which children worked, and when. Indeed, it was the mother who gave her daughter the skill and the confidence to manage family affairs. Nowhere is the Italian wife as confident, aggressive family manager, an image so different from that of submissive female, better illustrated than in Puzo's *Fortunate Pilgrim*. "That men should control the money in the house, have the power to make decisions that decided the fate of infants—what folly!" thinks Lucia Santa, the mother in the family and central character in the novel. "Men were not competent. Moreover, they were not serious."[69] She, on the other hand, was quite serious, and she saw to it that the children were clothed, fed, and healthy. Lucia Santa had to assume these responsibilities completely because her husband was ill, but she was certain that all married women played similar roles. Once, angered by her daughter's excessive interfering, Lucia told her: "If you want a house to give orders to, get married, have children . . . then you can beat them, then you can decide when they will work, and how, and who works."[70]

Lucia Santa calculates constantly to make sure that everyone is provided for; at the end of one summer she sits down to plan for the fall: "Now school would begin. There must be white shirts for the children, trousers, mended and pressed. Shoes must be worn instead of sneakers patched with tape. Hair must be cut and combed. Winter gloves, always lost, must be bought; hats and coats. The stove must be put up in the living room next to the kitchen; it must be checked and kept filled. Money must be put aside for . . . the doctor."[71] All of Lucia Santa's decisions involve careful and pragmatic deliberations about what would be best for the family as a whole, rather than for individual members. Thus, when she tries to decide whether to take her psychotic husband out of Bellevue, she considers the possibility that his presence at home might force Octavia, the chief breadwinner, into an early marriage to escape her stepfa-

---

[68] Roche, "The Italian Girl," p. 108.
[69] Puzo, *The Fortunate Pilgrim*, p. 30.
[70] Ibid., p. 65.
[71] Ibid., p. 145, 146.

ther. She weighs against this possibility her fear of the deep and perhaps lasting anger of her younger children if she refuses to let him come home.[72]

It is interesting that Lucia Santa considers her obligations toward the children to be greater than her loyalties to her husband. Women bore the children, did most of the caring for them, and often only the mothers survived into old age with them. Parents hoped their adult children would assist them in their old age.[73] The preservation of the family through future generations depended on children's survival. And so it was for the sake of their offspring that Italian women—like most mothers—worked the long hours, scrimped, saved, and supervised. One widow in DiDonato's *Christ in Concrete*, despondent after hearing that her husband has been killed on a construction job, also wants to die. But "for them [her eight children] you must live," she is told, and she resolves to continue to "protect his [children] and mine."[74]

In protecting family interests Italian women could be as aggressive in confronting outsiders as they were among their own relatives. Even as they tended to steer away from activities in the public arena, Italian wives in New York learned how to manipulate and even to confront authorities openly when they believed public officials were threatening the family livelihood. For example, families set up elaborate systems to warn each other when city and state inspectors arrived at the tenements to investigate possible illegal homework. One violent incident occurred when the New York State Labor Department inspectors visited an Italian family in East Harlem to check on a report that a mother and her children were making baby clothes in their apartment, in violation of the homework law.

> At first [Mrs. DeToris] denied that she was doing any work at all and ordered us to leave her apartment. When I [the inspector] refused . . . she struck me and kicked me repeatedly. . . . Before I could seize [the baby clothes] Mrs. DeToris began screaming terribly and jumped on my back. Just then Mrs. D'Iorio [the landlady] rushed in and began also to kick and strike me. . . . They threw a milk bottle at me . . . Mrs. D'Iorio bit me

---

[72] Ibid., pp. 123–24.

[73] As Puzo writes, "Lurking behind this [Lucia Santa's sense of obligation to her children] was the primitive dread that parents have of their own fate when they are old and helpless and become their children's children, and in their turn seek mercy." Ibid., p. 124.

[74] DiDonato, *Christ in Concrete*, p. 63.

severely on the right hand and afterwards hit me on the head. . . . She also seized a carving knife and tried to stab me with it, but did not succeed in doing so. Finally, after about two hours, the policeman arrived . . . [he] endeavored to get her to tell him for whom she was working. She then admitted she was working for a factory but claimed she did not know where it was, as she said she got the work from her sister.[75]

"Implacable enemies of death," wrote Puzo about the Italian mothers of Tenth Avenue, ". . . ready to murder anyone who stood in the way of so much as a crust of bread for themselves or their children."[76] In all aspects of their lives, then, Italian wives struggled, as homeworkers, housekeepers, shopworkers, and mothers, to help keep their families and, if possible, to improve the quality of their existence.

Among the most important decisions Italian mothers, and fathers, had to make in looking out for their families was whether to send their children to school, and for how long. In the next chapter we examine the schooling opportunities of Italian daughters during the early decades of the twentieth century.

[75] New York State, Department of Labor, *Annual Report of the Industrial Commission, 1918* (Albany, N.Y.:, 1919), p. 39.
[76] Puzo, *The Fortunate Pilgrim*, p. 286.

ITALIAN FAMILIES, THEIR DAUGHTERS, AND SCHOOLING

Jennie Martini, a backward girl of fifteen was kept at home to work on feathers. The truant officer was sent after her, but could never find her. She was always "next door at her sister's," but by the time the officer had reached the sister's, Jennie had gone—presumably over the roof—and could not be caught. When she was finally summoned to court, her mother had lengthened her skirts and heightened her heels, put up her hair, and engaged her to be married to a boy of eighteen. The mother pleaded that she was too old for school, and that "her fellow didn't want her to go" and the judge dismissed the case. When we found Jennie, she was working on feathers. The "fellow" was sitting by, and the mother boasted that she had outwitted the authorities and that three other girls on the block had "got tired of school and had got fellows just like her."

—Elizabeth Sergeant, "Toilers of the Tenements"

Jennie Martini's story, reported by Elizabeth Sergeant as part of her investigation of homeworkers in 1910, illustrates the themes of this chapter.[1] Like leisure, schooling played a subsidiary role in the lives of Italian girls during the early decades of the twentieth century because time spent in school diminished the daughter's ability to contribute to the family. For Jennie Martini, as for so many Italian girls, time spent in the classroom could otherwise be spent making artificial feathers. For Mrs. Martini, like other Italian parents, the code of "proper behavior" for young women had to be flexible enough to meet that paramount goal—the social and

[1] Elizabeth Shipley Sergeant, "Toilers of the Tenements: Where the Beautiful Things of the Great Shops Are Made," *McClure's* 35 (July 1910). The quotation is from p. 242.

economic well-being of the family. To that end, Mrs. Martini took advantage of common perceptions about gender roles in the Italian community. Manipulating authorities, she invoked the patriarchal rights of males to dictate women's behavior when, clearly, she was in charge here. The judge's willingness to accept Mrs. Martini's argument at face value suggests the government's lack of enthusiasm for keeping these immigrant girls in school. In this chapter we see how the needs of Italian parents and the attitudes of state officials, together, resulted in the early drop-out rate of Italian daughters.

Schooling Patterns among Italian Children

Italian parents tended to take their children, particularly their daughters, out of school as early as possible. The census is a problematic source for information on school attendance because of parents' reluctance to admit to census takers that they were keeping children out of school in defiance of the law; nevertheless, it suggests general patterns. In samples from the 1905 New York State Manuscript Census 94 percent of the first-generation boys and 83 percent of the first-generation girls aged ten to thirteen were recorded as being in school, but only 41 percent of the boys and 26 percent of the girls aged fourteen and fifteen were so listed. In the second generation 94 percent of the ten-to-thirteen-year-old boys and 93 percent of the girls of the same age were in school; among fourteen- and fifteen-year-olds, 53 percent of the boys were listed in school and 36 percent of the girls.[2] After 1913 school attendance was compulsory in New York until students were fourteen years old and had finished eighth grade, or if fifteen, the sixth grade.[3] Analysis of schooling patterns of Italian neighborhoods

[2] New York State Manuscript Census, 1905, 5-percent sample, three Italian neighborhoods in Manhattan (see Appendix A for details about sampling method). The New York State Department of Labor estimated that 75.5 percent of all fourteen- and fifteen-year-olds in New York City were in school in 1910. See New York State, Department of Labor, *The Trend of Child Labor in New York State*, New York State Department of Labor Special Bulletin no. 122 (Albany, N.Y., 1923), p. 8.

[3] See Jeremy Felt, *Hostages of Fortune: Child Labor Reform in New York State* (Syracuse, N.Y.: Syracuse University Press, 1965), chap. 4.

in Manhattan and Brooklyn, based on information from the 1920 federal census for New York City, shows apparent compliance with the law. Of second-generation girls and boys, both, 93 percent were recorded attending school at age fourteen; however, by age fifteen attendance had dropped to only 61 percent of the boys and 54 percent of the girls.[4]

A retrospective study of first- and second-generation immigrants, published as part of the 1950 federal census, provides a more reliable estimate of the educational achievement of Italian Americans. By this period concealing illegal withdrawal from school was no longer critical.[5] Even if all New York Italians were enrolled in school through the legal age,

[4]In contrast, the New York Department of Labor estimated in 1920 that only 78 percent of New York City children aged fourteen and fifteen were in school. See *The Trend of Child Labor*, p. 5. Information on Italian schooling was taken from the U.S. federal census of 1920 and recorded for New York City by sanitary districts by Walter Laidlaw, in *Statistical Sources for the Demographic Study of Greater New York, 1920* (New York: New York City 1920 Census Committee, 1922). The sanitary districts included here are all areas where the population was at least 90 percent Italian. In Manhattan they are located in the heart of the Italian settlement, below Fourteenth Street and west of Broadway. Much of this area also has been included in the general sample taken from the 1905 New York State Manuscript Census. Since the area was identified with homework, there may be a bias in favor of child labor. Fortunately, information for Brooklyn is also available. Eight sanitary districts in Brooklyn were found to have at least 90 percent Italians living in the area; information on the school was recorded for all. Two included the Union, Lorimer, Driggs section recorded in 1910, and one included Nevins, First, and Fourth avenues. Three others were in the heavily Italian section around New Utrecht, Fourteenth and Sixteenth avenues; one was located at Canal, Neptune, West Fourteenth, and West Twelfth streets; and one included Lefferts, Albany, Midwood, and New York streets. Calculations were done for all children in these sanitary districts.

[5]The data recorded are for the New York metropolitan area, which includes the immediate surrounding urban and suburban areas in New York State and northeastern New Jersey. Hence, it can only be used to approximate the schooling patterns for New York City Italians. The results from this study are presented here because they offer the best available information on the educational achievements, by age cohorts, for two generations of Italian Americans. The federal manuscript census schedules after 1910 are unavailable to the public, and New York did not conduct a state census after 1925. Although Italians living in the suburban area are better off economically than those living in the city, it is most likely that in the older age cohorts the women grew up in New York or in other urban areas of the region. One could argue, indeed, that the area covered by this 1950 census report more accurately reflects the experience of New York Italians precisely because it includes suburban areas; thus, the data is not biased in favor of the poorer Italians who remained in the city at midcentury. It should also be noted that the data on education include, for the older groups, schooling received in Italy. Since most Italian immigrants came to the United States before the 1920s, only in the oldest group, among those men and women aged forty-five and older, would there be many who had come to the United States after they had reached age fourteen.

Table 7. The schooling of first- and second-generation Italian Americans of New York, by age and sex, 1950

	First generation				Second generation			
	Aged 25–44		Aged 45+		Aged 25–44		Aged 45+	
	M	F	M	F	M	F	M	F
Percentage completing 1 year or more in high school	36	27	12	7	60	55	29	20
Percentage completing 4 years or more in high school	21	14	8	5	31	29	16	10
Median school years completed	8.5	8.2	5.6	4.3	10.1	9.6	8.4	8.2
N (in thousands)	42.4	41.5	217.8	177.2	283.0	292.9	58.4	58.0

Source: U.S. Department of Commerce, Bureau of the Census, *U.S. Census of Population, 1950. Vol. IV, Part 3A: Special Reports, Nativity and Parentage* (Washington, D.C.: Government Printing Office, 1954), p. 284. See also this chapter, n. 5.

Note: M = male; F = female. Geographic area covered is the New York–New Jersey Standard Metropolitan Area

many, especially females, did not complete grammar school (see Table 7). The 1950 special report listed the educational achievement of two age cohorts each, for first- and second-generation Italian Americans. All four cohorts were at least age fifteen by 1940 and so are relevant for our discussion of education in the early decades of the century. In all the categories of women except the second generation, aged twenty-five to forty-four, the median number of school years completed by the groups was 8.2 or less. Among the first-generation women aged forty-five and over, only 7 percent had completed one year of high school. Among the first-generation women aged twenty-five to forty-four, 27 percent had completed at least the ninth grade and only 14 percent had completed at least the twelfth grade. Only among the second-generation women aged twenty-five to forty-four did median school years completed include a full year of high school. In this group 55 percent reported at least one year of high school and 29 percent graduated. These data also demonstrate that if Italian families invested in advanced schooling for their offspring at all, they were more likely to invest in the boys than the girls.

Educational achievement among Italians was especially low in comparison with that of other ethnic groups. A more detailed comparison of the Italians with their Jewish counterparts in New York is presented later in the chapter. Comparing Italians to all immigrant groups, one notes that in 1911, 63 percent of Italian-American children (both first- and second-generation) aged ten to twelve were below the proper grade for their age, a good 15 to 20 percent more than other immigrant groups surveyed. For all adults in New York City aged twenty-five and over (the breakdown by sex is not available), the 1950 federal census reported median school years completed as 9.1 but only 7.8 for first- and second-generation Italians.[6]

Educators, modern scholars, and Italians themselves often have remarked on the difficulties of school for Italians. Discussions have usually

[6] U.S. Congress, Senate, *Reports of the Immigration Commission*, vol. 30, *The Children of Immigrants in Schools*, vol. 4, S. Doc. 5874, 61st Cong., 2d sess. (Washington, D.C.: Government Printing Office, 1911), p. 614; Leonard Ayres, *Laggards in Our Schools* (New York: Russell Sage Foundation, 1909), p. 107. In his book on the Italian communities of Utica, Rochester, and Kansas City, John Briggs suggests that the discrepancy in educational achievement between Italians and other groups has been exaggerated because children of Italian households tended to begin school later than most children, at the legally required age of seven, rather than six, in accordance with southern Italian custom. Once they were in school, he argues, their attendance records were similar to other groups, but because they were over-age for their class, they, more often than other children, reached the age of fourteen without completing elementary school. See *An Italian Passage: Immigrants to Three American Cities, 1890–1920* (New Haven: Yale University Press, 1978), pp. 255–38. My analysis of the school attendance patterns of Italian and Jewish children in New York City suggests that the difference cannot be explained by the fact that Italian children tended to get a later start at school. Comparing the percentage of Italian and Jewish children in New York schools as recorded by the U.S. census of 1920, we find the differences for children age six to be quite small (less than 5 percent). Yet by age fourteen and fifteen, 10–15 percent more of the Jewish children were in school than was the case with Italians. Data taken from the information of Laidlaw, *Statistical Sources for the Demographic Study of Greater New York, 1920*, four census tracts for Manhattan, sixteen tracts for Brooklyn. See also Michael Olneck and Marvin Lazerson, "The School Achievement of Immigrant Children, 1900–1930," *History of Education Quarterly* 14 (Winter 1974): 454–82. For the 1950 figures see Welfare and Health Council of New York, Research Bureau, *Characteristics of the Population by Health Areas, New York City, 1950*, part 1 (New York: Research Bureau, 1953), p. xxxii (U.S. census data used).

focused on Mediterranean peasant cultures, which, like other premodern cultures, placed little value on investment for the future. "The labor of children," Moses Stambler wrote in 1968, "was a culture lag, or institutional carry-over from agricultural society into a new industrial framework."[7] Contemporary reformers emphasized the Italians' orientation toward the immediate needs of the family because they felt so strongly that such behavior was ill suited for economic advancement in this new world. To some reformers, it appeared to be an irrational strategy that contributed to the perpetuation of poverty in the ethnic community. For women activists, Italian behavior was particularly pernicious, one more example of patriarchal efforts to block new opportunities for women to contribute to the community. Sergeant sums up the feeling of many others of her day:

> The fact is, the immigrant woman does not realize the difference between conditions in New York and those in her pastoral town. A child may grow up in a Sicilian mountain village with no other education than that which cultivation of the soil itself gives and yet be equipped to live out her life usefully as a strong-armed water carrier and digger in the terraced fields. The community does not suffer from her ignorance. But a Sicilian, unable to read and write, unable even to tell time when they [*sic*] no longer hear the village church bell has a new status in society when she is transplanted to the teeming center of New York. Here, her life and her children's are interwoven with political and social issues and responsibilities.[8]

My analysis indicates, however, that during the early decades of the twentieth century Italians' beliefs about the education of their children made good sense. They were not merely a carryover of traditions; like their attitudes toward women's work, their attitudes about schooling reflected the efforts of Italian mothers and fathers to cope with the realities of their lives in America. Southern Italians came from a society in which,

---

[7] Moses Stambler, "The Effect of Compulsory Education and Child Labor Laws on High School Attendance in New York City, 1898–1917," *History of Education Quarterly* 8 (Summer 1968): 195. See also Olneck and Lazerson, "The School Achievement"; Caroline Ware, *Greenwich Village, 1920–1930* (Boston: Houghton Mifflin, 1935); Mary Van Kleeck, *Working Girls in Evening Schools* (New York: Russell Sage Foundation, Survey Associates, 1914); Louise C. Odencrantz, *Italian Women in Industry* (New York: Russell Sage Foundation, 1919), p. 255.

[8] Sergeant, "Toilers of the Tenements," p. 248. See also Ware, *Greenwich Village*.

given the social, demographic, and political conditions, schooling had little place; they thus arrived in New York with little appreciation of schooling. The economic and social circumstances they found in New York, however, reinforced these attitudes. Italian families adopted strategies in New York like those in Italy largely because the problems they faced were similar.[9]

Work, Population, and School

In New York, just as in Italy, time spent in school had negative consequences for the family because it diminished the child's ability to contribute badly needed labor or wages or both. Analysis of demographic facts about the New York Italian community reveals the Italians' use of strategies that actually reinforced negative attitudes about education.[10] The mortality rate of Italian children (the number of deaths of children under five per 1,000) in New York was considerably lower than in their native land, but the rate of 42.5 in 1915 was still high, and greater than that of any other ethnic group in the city.[11] Infant mortality (the numer of deaths of children under one) among Italians, although falling, was also high in comparison with that of other New Yorkers. For the period 1916–1920 the infant death rate of 138.1 in the Italian neighborhood of Mulberry was extremely high in the city, which had overall experienced a great reduction in infant mortality.[12]

[9] John Bodnar makes a similar point about the role of peasant traditions in Slavic-American communities. See "Immigration and Modernization: The Case of Slavic Peasants in Industrial America," *Journal of Social History* 10 (Fall 1976): 44–71.

[10] See Chapter 2. On the relationship between fertility and attitudes toward education, see Charles Tilly, "Population and Pedagogy in France," *History of Education Quarterly* 13 (1973): 113–28.

[11] In 1915 the mortality rates of children under five by national origin were as follows: Austrian-Hungarian, 26.3; German, 32.3; Irish, 36.8; Russian and Polish, 24.9; American (i.e., of native white or black parentage), 40.0; total Manhattan, 37.9. See New York City, Department of Health, *The Influence of Nationality upon the Mortality of a Community with Special Reference to the City of New York*, by William Guilfrey, M.D., New York City Department of Health Monograph Series no. 18 (New York, November 1917).

[12] John J. Gebhart, *The Health of a Neighborhood: A Social Study of the Mulberry District* (New York: New York Association for Improving the Condition of the Poor, 1924), p. 15.

High mortality reinforced the lessons of past experience, which prompted a strategy of relatively high fertility among immigrants. The consequences for individual families had not been severe in nineteenth-century Italy because of even higher child mortality. But as high as infant mortality was among Italian Americans, most families found that far more children were now surviving. Evidence points to a clear drop in infant mortality among Italians in New York as early as the 1920s, due in part to the early efforts of health service reformers.[13] The long-term effects of this drop are discussed in the next chapter, but here we note that the short-term strategy of high fertility meant that Italian-American families were quite large. The strain on family resources was enormous; consumers had to be turned into wage earners as soon as possible. In short, the economic and demographic pressures encouraged parents to view their offspring as workers rather than school children.

Evidence from the census, however limited, can suggest how opportunities for paid labor acted as incentives for parents to remove young adolescents from school, particularly among the first generation (see Table 8). Of first-generation fourteen- and fifteen-year-old boys sampled from the 1905 state census, more than three-quarters of those who were out of school were earning wages, about one-half in manufacturing jobs and one-half in street trades, a typical employment of immigrant boys. Many first-generation girls stayed at home, doing domestic chores and homework. But the supposed Italian conviction that daughters should be kept behind the protective walls of home did not prevent a strikingly high proportion of these young women (some 64 percent of those out of school) from earning wages outside.[14] Not surprisingly, the garment industry was the largest employer of the adolescent women working outside the home.[15] Although a large proportion of young girls out of school were also being sent to the factory, a comparison of the employment of first- and second-generation adolescents shows that, contrary to assumptions

[13] See East Harlem Health Center, *A Decade of District Health Center Pioneering* (New York: East Harlem Health Center, 1932); Savel Zimand, "District Health Administration in New York City," in *District Health Administration: A Study of Organization and Planning*, ed. Ira Hiscock (New York: Millbank Memorial Fund, 1936), p. 41.

[14] See, for example, Virginia Yans-McLaughlin, *Family and Community: Italian Immigrants in Buffalo, 1880–1930* (Ithaca, N.Y.: Cornell University Press, 1977), chap. 7.

[15] New York State Manuscript Census, 1905.

Table 8. The employment status of first- and second-generation fourteen- and fifteen-year-olds not in school, by sex, 1905 (percentage distribution)

	Males	Females
First generation		
Works	76.6	64.5
Works at home	0	9.6
Not at work or school	23.3	25.8
(Total N out of school)	(30)	(31)
Second generation		
Works	86.9	47.6
Not at work or school	12.0	52.3
(Total N out of school)	(23)	(21)

Source: New York State, Manuscript Census, 1905.

about Italian attitudes toward female work outside the home, the more "Americanized" families of the second-generation children (all these parents had to be U.S. residents at least fourteen years) kept their daughters at home. The small numbers in this sample make definitive analysis impossible, but it may be that, like the more prosperous families in southern Italy, the more settled families in New York could behave according to stricter norms defining proper female behavior.[16]

While the Italians' willingness to put young adolescent girls to work, both in the home and outside, is clear, the way variations in family resources affected the work patterns of the fourteen- and fifteen-year-olds is not. Differences in the earning capacities of fathers, as measured by their occupational status, were not associated with variations in daughters' employment status (as shown also in Chapter 2 for older daughters). Our ability to establish any pattern is hampered by the fact that few children were recorded in the census as being out of school and by the problems in using occupational categories to indicate earning capacity.[17] Scattered evi-

[16] In the case of the boys (see Table 8) a greater percentage of first-generation than second-generation males were neither at home or work. This seems puzzling since, presumably, for boys not at school in the newly arrived families, work would be the first priority. The apparent anomaly may be due to the greater opportunity for boys among the second-generation to find more steady employment.

[17] The household ratio of wage earners to consumers in the case of the younger adolescents revealed the opposite trend than was revealed with the older daughters; the households

dence suggests the ways that economic considerations affected parents' willingness to send their girls of any age to school. Lillian Wald's study of schooling patterns among Italian homeworker families of East Harlem revealed that of a group of 100 children doing homework, each child had been absent, an average, 29.5 out of 89 school days in the year. "There was never a day when all of the children of school age were in school," reported a social worker living among Italians in the Mulberry Street area. "It was a fight to get the little ones in school," she noted, "a fight to keep them there."[18] By contrast, in neighborhoods dominated by skilled workers where mothers were not taking in work, officials found that Italian families were sending their children more regularly to school.[19]

The decision to put young adolescents to work was not only a response to the individual ups and downs of any one family; it also reflected a norm, which made sense given the realities of life in New York's Little Italy. On the basis of one's experience of one's own family and one's neighbors, Italians knew that the labor of children as well as adults was a means of surviving, even improving, one's standard of living. "The Italian," reported Harriet Daniels in 1914, "seeing that his neighbors' children work and seeing the economic value of the procedure, is ready to take his daughter from school and put her to work at the earliest possible moment." "Without exception," another study reported, "girls are kept home to work."[20] The Italians' determination to send daughters to work in the factory as well, even when families were not in the most dire straits, produced some perplexing cases for social workers and others trying to

---

having a higher ratio of earners to consumers were more likely to send their fourteen- and fifteen-year-olds to work. Perhaps they were households that were family enterprises such as tailoring shops or stores that depended on the labor of close relatives. Or it might be that in families poor enough to put fourteen- and fifteen-year-olds to work, more than one adult or older child also had to work. See Chapters 2 and 3 on the difficulties of using occupational categories.

[18] Lillian Betts, "The Italians in New York," *University Settlement Studies* 1 (October 1905–January 1906): 99.

[19] New York State, Factory Investigating Commission, *Public Hearings in New York City, Second Series* (reprint from the *Preliminary Report of the New York Factory Investigating Commission*; Albany, N.Y.: J. B. Lyon, October 1911), pp. 1739–40.

[20] Harriet Daniels, *The Girl and Her Chance: A Study of the Conditions Surrounding the Young Girl Between Fourteen and Eighteen Years in New York City* (New York: Fleming H. Revell, 1914), p. 18; Elisabeth Irwin, *Truancy: A Study of the Mental, Physical, and Social Factors of the Problem of Non-Attendance at School* (New York: Public Education Association of the City of New York, 1910), p. 26.

keep the girls in school. One Italian father complained to the Board of Health in 1913 because his fifteen-year-old daughter, having failed to write a simple English sentence, was refused working papers and told to remain in school until she was sixteen. The social worker reporting on the case was very much bothered because this family was not destitute. The mother was dead, but the father and older children all had employment. Such work patterns were perceived as evidence of backward values, which were marked by a lack of appreciation for schooling. The father, like Mrs. Martini, tried to manipulate common perceptions about Italians, telling the authorities that work was actually the more attractive prospect for his daughter; school hours were not long enough, he reported, and the child would therefore be home alone and might wander about the streets. The social worker this time was skeptical. "Whether the father's sentiment (the lack of supervision for his daughter after school) was true or not, without much question this child will never go regularly to school again, if she goes at all—in spite of school attendance officers and all."[21]

Social reformers notwithstanding, Italian attitudes toward schooling were quite strategic. In the early grades children were taught to read, write, and speak English, and to do simple arithmetic, useful skills for the Italian community. Families sacrificed little in terms of wages by sending the young ones to school, at least for a good part of the year, because full-time employment was not available to the young. Thus, whether or not they finished grammar school, the majority of young children obtained some schooling. But for Italian adolescents, schooling was hardly more valuable in New York than it was in southern Italy because the occupations that were available to them required little education. If the family could afford to forgo their wages, schooling beyond the elementary grades could be beneficial for boys. Vocational training in secondary school enabled some males, though not many, to enter skilled jobs. And by the 1920s, as shown earlier, a small number of second-generation Italian males were obtaining white-collar work that required some formal education. From the perspective of Italian families the circumstances for females, however, still rendered schooling for them less valuable than it was for males. With the skills they learned from kin, girls were fully

[21] Eleanor Hope Johnson, "Social Service and the Public Schools," *The Survey* 30 (May 3, 1913): 177.

prepared to contribute to the family, either within the home or outside. Schooling was simply not very helpful in enabling them to secure better paying, less dangerous, or more stable work.[22] Reformers often lamented the lack of ambition on the part of Italian girls, who seemed uninterested in furthering their education so that they might gain better positions. They had to concede, however, that most often Italian women had to take what they could get, regardless of training.[23]

The State, the Reformers, and the Schools

If schooling had little to offer most Italian families, it is also true that in New York, just as in southern Italy, immigrant families had little to fear from government authorities if they kept their daughters or sons away from school. In order to understand the behavior of Italian families, we must appreciate not only the needs of the immigrants but the role of local and state government, including the school system, with respect to child labor and school attendance. Women's and family historians have become increasingly convinced that an understanding of everyday life must take into account the connections between public institutions and private lives. Federal, state, and local government initiatives affected children in New York City; furthermore, they affected girls differently than boys.[24] Laws on compulsory education and child labor, for example, had a greater impact on Italian girls because unskilled factory work in New York was so heavily dominated by young women. If such laws were enforced, families would face severe constraints whenever they had to put their daughters to work. During the early decades of the twentieth century, however, legislation was not enforced, and Italian families could operate with relative impunity. To understand the environment in which Italian families made decisions about their daughters, we shift the focus from the ethnic com-

---

[22] See Daniels, *The Girl and Her Chance*, p. 37.

[23] Odencrantz, *Italian Women in Industry*, p. 225.

[24] For some preliminary discussions on the way in which the development of the welfare state affected women and men differently, see the articles in the special issue on women and the welfare state, *American Historical Review* 95 (October 1990). See also the articles in Linda Gordon, ed., *Women, the State, and Welfare* (Madison: University of Wisconsin Press, 1990).

munity to the reformers, educators, government officials, and New York manufacturers, all of whom had a role in determining the work and school patterns of Italian women.

Progressive reformers interested in the welfare of Italian girls were committed to keeping them in school and away from paid employment. From the point of view of reformers, Italian families, like other poor New Yorkers, needed the rigorous protection of the state, and whether immigrants wanted it or not, sweated labor had to be eliminated. The growing literature on the history of women and the welfare state gives us a sense that the motivations, priorities, and strategies of the fight for special protective legislation is quite complex. Many reformers undoubtedly crusaded against homework because it was perceived as a threat to middle-class notions of domesticity, that is, a domicile freed of paid production, and where only adult men earned wages.[25] Yet the imposition of traditional gender roles was not the whole or even the most important point, for many activists. The eradication of homework was also part of efforts of trade unionists and their sympathizers to eliminate sweated labor of all kinds.[26] At any rate, for reformers, whether or not Italian families wished to keep girls away from school was beside the point.

[25] For an analysis of the crusade against homework as an effort to impose middle-class notions of domesticity, see Cynthia Daniels, "Between Home and Family: Homeworkers and the State," in Eileen Boris and Cynthia Daniels, eds., *Homework: Historical and Contemporary Perspectives on Paid Labor at Home* (Urbana: University of Illinois Press, 1987), pp. 13–32. On the concern for the family wage on the part of reformers, see also Martha May, "The Historical Problem of the Family Wage: The Ford Motor Company and the Five Dollar Day," *Feminist Studies* 8 (Summer 1982): 55–77.

[26] Linda Gordon has recently pointed out the dangers in assuming that the development of welfare policies reflects only efforts at social control, which kept women dependent. See "The New Feminist Scholarship on the Welfare State," in Gordon, ed., *Women, the State and Welfare*, pp. 9–35. How activists in the United States have used the politics of gender to advance class issues is discussed in Kathyrn Sklar, "Florence Kelley: Resources and Achievements," paper delivered at the Berkshire Conference on the History of Women, Vassar College, June 1981; Sklar, "Explaining the Power of Women's Political Culture in the Creation of the American Welfare State, 1890–1930," forthcoming in *Gender and the Origins of Welfare States in Western Europe and North America*, ed. Seth Koven and Sonya Michel (Routledge). See also Miriam Cohen and Michael P. Hanagan, "The Politics of Gender and the Making of the Welfare State in England, France and the United States," *Journal of Social History* 24 (Spring 1991): 469–84; Joan G. Zimmerman, "The Jurisprudence of Equality: The Women's Minimum Wage, the First Equal Rights Amendment, and Adkins v. Children's Hospital, 1905–1923," *Journal of American History* 78 (June 1991): 188–215.

Paraphrasing the then recent U.S. Supreme Court decision in *Muller v. Oregon*, which upheld the constitutionality of state legislation limiting women's work hours, Sergeant addressed the issue of Italians and home-work, from the point of view of her fellow activists, quite succinctly: "The health of the worker and that of the community are intimately re-lated, and the police power of the state, may, in the interest of the general good, be invoked to protect the worker against herself and those who profit by her exploitation."[27]

Others more powerful than reformers, however, had different views about what constituted the general good. Like the Italian families, school and government officials and manufacturers often were at cross-purposes with reformers, but unlike the immigrants, their ability to influence the state was considerable. Where there was general agreement among school officials, manufacturers, and government officials, reformers had suc-cess. The use of child labor in factories was one good example. After 1910, when New York children were legally required to attend school between the ages of seven and fourteen, any employer who hired children under fourteen to do factory work was subject to penalty. With the in-creasing use of machinery in garment shops and the need to maintain production at a fast pace, such prohibition against employing young chil-dren made sense, not only from the point of view of dedicated reformers, but from that of manufacturers as well. There were some violations of the law, but as factory size increased and factories modernized, the number of young children employed in industry diminished.[28] The question of ado-lescent labor was more complicated. Young teenagers could easily be put to work in factories—girls as clothing finishers, box packers and folders, or candy wrappers; boys as machine helpers, carriers, runners—in major New York industries dependent on cheap labor. Thus, although New York State boasted some of the most progressive school and child-labor legislation in the country, state and local institutions did very little to block the efforts of immigrant parents to send their children out to work.

Propelled by the efforts of welfare reformers, the New York State legis-lature passed a series of laws to ensure that only young adolescents who were both minimally educated and healthy could leave school to seek em-

---

[27] Sergeant, "Toilers of the Tenements," p. 248.

[28] See Jeremy Felt, *Hostages of Fortune*, chap. 4. See also Walter J. Trattner, *Crusade for the Children* (Chicago: Quadrangle Books, 1970), p. 159.

ployment. Yet, neither the city health department, the schools, nor the courts were willing to enforce the regulations. A fourteen- or fifteen-year-old wishing to leave school was supposed to obtain authorization from the school stating that he or she could read and write; after 1913 a fourteen-year-old pupil was required to complete the eighth grade, or else remain in school until fifteen and had completed the sixth grade. After presenting proof of age and a school record to the New York City Department of Health and being certified as healthy, the child would be issued an employment certificate. Each year from 1910 to 1922 the Department of Health issued between 30,000 and 50,000 certificates. But a large proportion of those issued employment certificates had not actually met the requirements of the law, and thousands of additional children quit school without any papers whatsoever.[29] False papers certifying a child's age were easily obtained in immigrant neighborhoods; physical examinations given by the Health Department were most often cursory, if given at all.[30]

The schools, responsible for certifying the child's educational achievement, were the weakest institutional link in the process of regulating child labor. Revisionist historians of education have emphasized that elites wished to keep immigrants in school so that they could be taught American values. Equally true, however, was the fact that large segments of the educational bureaucracy itself, from administrators to teachers, wanted to be *rid* of as many immigrant pupils as soon as possible, because they viewed the students as unruly and uneducable. Reformers were often dismayed when they actually confronted the attitudes of many teachers toward their immigrant pupils. Adele Marie Shaw reported in her study of the New York City schools in 1903 that in the majority of schools she visited, she was "continually embarrassed by the discourtesy with which the children were addressed or ignored. . . . [Teachers] would talk in front of them as if they [the students] cannot understand them. . . . One

---

[29] See Felt, *Hostages of Fortunte*, chap. 5, esp. p. 108. Also see New York City Department of Education, *Fourteenth Annual Report of the City Superintendent of Schools* (New York: Department of Education, 1912); New York State, Department of Labor, *The Health of the Working Child*, New York State Department of Labor Special Bulletin no. 134 (Albany, N.Y.: 1924). From 1913 to 1923 approximately, 2,000 children were found annually working in factories without any employment papers. See New York State, Department of Labor, *The Trend of Child Labor in New York State, Supplementary Report for 1923*, New York State Department of Labor Special Bulletin no. 132 (Albany, N.Y., 1924), p. 23.

[30] Felt, *Hostages of Fortune*, pp. 100, 108.

teacher was seen removing children in her way by any portion of the body that comes in handy."[31]

Even those in the educational bureaucracy who expressed sympathy for the problems of immigrant students shared many of the negative attitudes of their colleagues. Albert Shiels, director of the Division of Reference and Research for the New York City Department of Education, for example, explained in 1915 why native-born Americans might be prejudiced toward immigrants: "We are apt to confound the accidental and temporary with the fundamental and permanent. An immigrant may be unclean in his habits and apparently content to live under oppressive conditions. Yet in such matters he may in many cases be a creature of circumstance. . . . The real questions are whether he is inherently vicious, criminal or indolent, and on the other hand, whether he may not under favorable conditions develop into a desirable citizen."[32] Apparently many teachers and administrators were not so convinced that their hard work could turn the "vicious, unclean and repellent" into "desirable citizens," or that it was worth the effort to find out; many felt that the easiest course was to let the children seek employment. Hence, school officials at the local level regularly certified students they knew to be functionally illiterate, failing, and even under age. During the progressive era Superintendent of New York City Schools William Maxwell, a strong advocate of child welfare reform himself, was constantly having to crack down on "the attempts of his principals to hurry children into the labor market," and he conceded that his efforts were meeting with little success.[33]

In truth, as Maxwell himself stated, the New York City school system had no idea how many fourteen- and fifteen-year-olds lived in the city and belonged in school. This was a particularly vexing problem during the years of mass immigration when hundreds of children were pouring into the city almost daily. In 1915 one report estimated that some 13,000 to 20,000 immigrant children moved into New York City annually. This,

[31] Adele Marie Shaw, "The True Character of New York Public Schools," *World's Work* 7 (December 1903): 4217, 4215.

[32] New York City, Department of Education, Division of Reference and Research, *The School and the Immigrant*, Publication no. 11 (New York: Department of Education of the City of New York, 1915), p. 8.

[33] See Felt, *Hostages of Fortune*, p. 100. Also see New York City Department of Education, *First Annual Report of the Director of Attendance for the Year ending July 31, 1915* (New York: Department of Education, 1916).

along with the number of school transfers that occurred every year as families moved about the city (some 175,000), meant that keeping track of students was virtually impossible.[34] A census bureau did exist for the purpose of tracing all New York City children of school age; after 1914 the Bureau of Attendance was established to coordinate the enforcement of compulsory school laws and to take the census. The unit was severely understaffed and insufficiently funded to do its job, however.[35]

During the progressive years efforts were made to provide some evening schooling for those young adolescents who had left regular school for the factory. By 1924 state law required fourteen- to eighteen-year-old workers without high school degrees to attend four hours of class a week, between the hours of 8:00 A.M. and 5:00 P.M. Though many New York children attended these continuation schools, this law, too, was impossible to enforce, and the instruction offered in these classes was minimal. As one New York City school teacher put it, "Among the teaching fraternity, they are a joke."[36]

If schools were not following laws about permitting youngsters to work, manufacturers, for their part, although theoretically liable for hiring children without proper papers, had little to fear. The number of factory inspectors in New York was far too small to enforce regulations. In 1903 Florence Kelley estimated that about two hundred state factory inspectors for the Empire City alone would be necessary; at the time the state Labor Commission employed thirty-seven inspectors for the entire state. The results of such meager efforts were predictable. In 1904 there were only forty-nine prosecutions for violations of any aspect of the factory law including child labor violations; of those, twenty-five convictions were obtained for a total fine of $630! Although the number of inspectors and prosecutions increased after the Triangle Shirtwaist fire of 1911, their numbers were still inadequate to address the problem.[37] Finally, the courts regularly refused to fine parents for allowing children

---

[34] Paul Klepper, *The Bureau of Attendance and Child Welfare of the New York City School System*, reprinted in *Education Review*, November 1915 (originally, New York: New York Attendance Bureau, 1915), p. 379.

[35] Felt, *Hostages of Fortune;* New York City, Department of Education, *First Annual Report of the Director of Attendance*.

[36] Felt, *Hostages of Fortune*, p. 119; New York State, Department of Labor, *The Health of the Working Child*.

[37] Felt, *Hostages of Fortune*, chap. 4.

over fourteen to remain out of school, even if they had failed to obtain the proper certifications. Magistrates were generally hostile to compulsory school attendance laws, believing that they interfered with parental authority.[38] The judge who granted Mrs. Martini the right to keep her daughter out of school was probably a case in point. In response to complaints from the superintendent of schools, who was criticizing the courts for failing to fine parents of a child at work illegally, one judge admitted, "I have no hesitation in stating that it would be a very aggravated case before I should . . . fine a poor parent five dollars."[39]

Although reformers found it difficult to enforce laws regarding the employment of adolescents in factories, regulating the labor of young children in homework operations was next to impossible, and it remained so until the 1930s. Hence, like the attempts to combat the high drop-out rate, the battle to combat absenteeism among the younger pupils was also futile. "If, as I hope you will, recommend a thorough investigation of this [homework] problem," Lillian Wald told the New York State Factory Investigating Commission at its public hearings in 1911, "you will find that our desire to have the children educated for citizenship is nullified to a great extent among the [very] children whom we greatly desire to have all the advantages of their few years of schooling."[40] Repeatedly, reformers found Italian families in neighborhoods where homework flourished keeping children out of school for two or three days a week, or permitting children to attend school for half-days only.[41] Not only were Italian children doing homework during school hours, those children attending school during the day were often required to help in homework operations at night; this was particularly true for girls. Louise Odencrantz in her study of Italian working women found that of 504 of them who had previously attended school in New York City, 42 percent had been required to

[38] Stambler, "The Effect," p. 202; Felt, *Hostages of Fortune*, chap. 5; New York City, Department of Education, *First Annual Report of the Director of Attendance*.

[39] Letter to District Superintendent Stewart, October 3, 1905, quoted in Stambler, "The Effect," p. 202.

[40] New York State, Factory Investigatng Commission, *Public Hearings*, p. 1740.

[41] See U.S. Congress, Senate, *Report on Condition of Woman and Child Wage Earners*, vol. 2: *Men's Ready-Made Clothing*, S. Doc. 645, 61st Cong., 2d sess. (Washington, D.C.: Government Printing Office, 1911), pp. 234–39; Odencrantz, *Italian Women in Industry*, p. 239.

do homework after school hours.[42] Reformers were particularly concerned because children who did homework during the day, or after school, were often exhausted when they came to school in the mornings; they had a difficult time doing their classroom work and would inevitably drop out. "These children [who] go to school in the morning are heavy, dull and tired," Dr. F. Josephine Baker, director of the Division of Child Hygiene of the New York City Department of Health, told the New York State Factory Investigating Commission in 1913. "They are not able to study. They suffer from headaches and most of them are anemic."[43]

Child welfare advocates knew that in order for these immigrant children to benefit from schooling, opportunities for youngsters to do homework had to be eliminated. We must "compel the child's return to school," wrote Mary Van Kleeck in a 1909 report on the Italian girls she found working in the artificial flower industry as homeworkers, "by preventing effectively the work which was the most important cause of their absence."[44] This the progressive activists were never able to do. By the turn of the century, as indicated earlier, homework operations in New York State had come under some regulation—but not enough to change behavior. Despite a 1903 law mandating that buildings housing homework operations be licensed, thousands of buildings remained unlicensed. After 1913 tenement manufacture of such items as food, dolls, doll clothing, and children's wear was prohibited, but many women—the knife-wielding Mrs. DeToris of the preceding chapter is but one example—were at work in these illegal operations.

The same year, 1913, to the delight of New York child labor reformers, the employment of children under the age of fourteen in tenement manufacture was to have been eliminated by law. The new statute required that the manufacturer keep accurate lists of homeworkers; this way he could be held liable for illegal child labor. But enforcement, in the words of the New York State Factory Investigating Commission, "was a hopeless task" and "the increase in the number of inspectors will help but

<hr />

[42] See Odencrantz, *Italian Women in Industry*, p. 259. Also see Felt, *Hostages of Fortune*, p. 142.

[43] New York State, Factory Investigating Commission, *Second Report of the Factory Investigating Commission*, vol. 3 (Albany, N.Y.: J. B. Lyon, 1913), p. 106.

[44] Mary Van Kleeck, "Child Labor in New York City Tenements," *Charities and the Commons* 19 (18 January 1908): 6.

little." When it conducted an investigation of garment manufacturers to determine the extent of compliance with the new law, the commission found that 80 percent of the homeworkers' addresses furnished them by the manufacturers were incorrect. Either the families had never lived at the addresses provided, or they had moved without notifying the factory.[45] The law stated that a manufacturer was liable only if it could be proved that he actually knew of illegal child labor being used in his homework. Since this was almost impossible to prove, manufacturers had little to fear. During the years 1919 and 1920, for example, only 6 cases among the 635 alleged violations of the child labor homework provisions, came to trial. And parents of the young homeworkers could not be prosecuted either, because they were not the employers of the child.[46]

With very little muscle behind the labor law, homework and the employment of children in homework continued to flourish. Between 1910 and 1913 several agreements between the International Ladies Garment Workers Union and the Coat, Suit and Slack Manufacturers Association eliminated some homework in the industry, but it continued on a very large scale, to the distress of both the men's and women's garment unions.[47] In 1924, in response to the pleas of groups such as the Child Labor Committee and the Consumer's League, the New York State legislature appointed a committee to study homework operations. Their report concluded that "in the ten years since the [Factory] Commission report . . . practically nothing has been done towards the solution of the problem." Bowing to the realities of economic life in New York, they concluded that "this system has become so entrenched in our industrial life that its very involvement is the only reason that can be given for not recommending the immediate complete prohibition of homework in tenements." The committee recommended that the list of prohibited articles be extended, but such efforts were quashed in 1924, and again in 1925 and 1928.[48]

[45] New York State, Factory Investigating Commission, *Preliminary Report of the New York State Factory Investigating Commission*, vol. 1 (Albany, N.Y.: J. B. Lyon, 1912), p. 86; New York State, Factory Investigating Commission, *Second Report*, p. 101.

[46] See Felt, *Hostages of Fortune*, pp. 149–50. See also Cynthia Daniels, "Between Home and Family."

[47] See Felt, *Hostages of Fortunte*, p. 147. Also see Lazar Teper and Nathan Weinberg, "Aspects of Industrial Homework in the Apparel Trades," ILGWU research paper (July 1941), located in the Russell Sage Collection, Cohen Library, City College of New York.

[48] Quoted in *Hostages of Fortune*, pp. 150, 151.

As long as homework was available for their children, Italian parents refused to cooperate with social workers and factory inspectors who attempted to get the youngsters into school. They shoved the clothing goods into drawers or under beds when inspectors arrived, or they refused to answer questions.[49] Often, families did not bother to conceal the work from social investigators because they knew that despite their zeal, the reformers were not really able to shut off this source of employment for Italian children. Reporting on its investigations of Italian flower makers, one settlement house concluded in 1916 that "although a house would be visited and work stopped for a time, it was only a matter of months until a family would secure flowers from another factory. So well aware of this were most families that in the majority of cases, they made no attempt to hide the flowers."[50]

School officials were no more helpful in supporting reformers' crusades against absenteeism than they were in the campaigns to lower the drop-out rate. Since many principals and teachers wanted to be rid of the difficult students, they made little effort to force truant students back into class.[51] Moreover, there were never enough truant officers available to return absentee children to class, and they were notoriously lax about rounding up children in immigrant neighborhoods.[52] One of the reasons for the low number of truant officers was the school system's inability to recruit people for a job to which the general public was so hostile. "When a man working alone attempts to arrest a persistent violator," the associate superintendent of schools noted, "he is usually surrounded by a mob."[53] The situation often never came to the confrontation point. "Italian mothers could easily evade the compulsory education law by keeping the children home intermittently, since a child was not pursued until he/she was absent five consecutive days."[54]

[49] Also see New York State, Factory Investigating Commission, *Second Report*, pp. 104–8; Felt, *Hostages of Fortune*, pp. 149, 150. Also see Chapter 3 of this work.

[50] Greenwich House, *Annual Report* (1916), p. 25.

[51] On the attitudes of school principals and teachers, see, among others, Betts, *Italians in New York*; Felt, *Hostages of Fortune*, p. 42.

[52] See New York State, Factory Investigating Commission, *Public Hearings*, testimony of Lillian Wald, p. 1739; Felt, *Hostages of Fortune*; New York City, Department of Education, *First Annual Report of the Director of Attendance*.

[53] Letter, 28 January 1909, quoted in Stambler, "The Effect," p. 203.

[54] Sergeant, "Toilers of the Tenements," p. 248.

In truth, adequate enforcement of child labor and compulsory school laws would not only have had severe repercussions for New York's "industrial life," as the Factory Commission put it — it would also have had disastrous consequences for the schools. The New York City school system, although large in comparison with others in the country, was not adequate to accommodate all of the children in the rapidly growing metropolis. After visiting every school in one immigrant neighborhood Adele Shaw estimated that "to do what needs to be done," five times the money then allocated was needed. "There is not room for them in the schools," Lillian Betts wrote of the truant Italian children in the Mulberry District. "I saw 117 boys brought into school in this region as a result of a truancy raid. There were 8 vacant seats in the whole building that morning. . . . What a farce!"[55] To meet the crisis, New York maintained a building-expansion program but also permitted thousands of "surplus" youths to enter the labor market.[56]

Italian parents found themselves in an environment in which the economy needed child labor and the political institutions were unwilling to eradicate the practice. The elders faced few sanctions against keeping children out of school. Given the motive, and opportunity, particularly for daughters who could work both at home and at the factory, Italian parents drastically limited female education in favor of work and domestic responsibilities.

Italian Students and the Schools

It is not surprising that many Italian children were less than eager students. As some teachers and judges knew, they were happy to leave school for the responsibilities of work. In the early decades of the century the overwhelming majority of Italian children attended public school; Catholic parochial schools were still for the Irish and other immigrants

---

[55] Shaw, "The True Character," p. 4206; Betts, "The Italians in New York," p. 100.

[56] See Felt, *Hostages of Fortune*, chap. 5. Also see New York State, Factory Investigating Commission, *Public Hearings*, testimony of Lillian Wald, pp. 1735–46; and Betts, "The Italians in New York," p. 95.

who had a much closer relationship with the church hierarchy.[57] The fact that Italians attended schools that had important connections to the Protestant establishment only heightened the Italians' sense of disjunction between the world of school and home. And like other immigrant children, young Italians often kept their parents as far away from school as possible because they were ashamed of the foreign ways of their elders.[58] A vicious cycle developed in the relations between school personnel and the children. Teachers often presented materials that students could not comprehend. Students who were sleepy from a night of homework—not the academic kind—could not pay attention. Their poor health not only made it difficult for them to concentrate in class, it also contributed to their absenteeism.[59]

The continuation schools and special classes, supposedly oriented toward the vocational needs of working-class immigrants, offered little to females, who usually were not hired for skilled jobs.[60] And in all classes, in special programs or part of a general education, the emphasis on disciplining the immigrants, well documented by historians of immigrant education, dominated the Italian experience. "If a boy or girl is to become an industrious, efficient and contented worker or citizen," noted one report on the continuation schools in the early years of the Depression, "he must be taught habits of thrift. In the continuation schools, every opportunity is seized to inculcate habits of thrift, whether it's to eliminate waste, economize on time, save money." In one regular school a visitor reported that teachers expended tremendous effort at "keeping children still, so that, indeed, they do not move a foot—pencils, elbows, placement of hands

---

[57] See Paula Fass, *Outside In: Minorities and the Transformation of American Higher Education* (New York: Oxford University Press, 1989), pp. 222–24. As Fass notes, it was not until the mid-1950s that many of the new ethnics of the early twentieth century began sending their children to Catholic schools, no longer as a reflection of ethnicity, but as "an expression of Catholic middle-class identification" (p. 225).

[58] It was estimated that less than 1 percent of Italian school children were enrolled in parochial schools in 1911. See Albert Perceroni, "The Italians in the United States," *Forum* 45 (January 1911): 15–59. On the shame Italian children felt about the foreign ways of their parents, see Leonard Covello, *The Heart Is the Teacher* (New York: McGraw-Hill, 1958), p. 47.

[59] On the relationship between the poor health of immigrants and absenteeism, see Ian Davey, "The Rhythm of Work and Rhythm of School, Hamilton, Ontario in the Nineteenth Century" (unpublished paper, 1977 [?]).

[60] See Daniels, *The Girl and Her Chance*, p. 36.

Taking the Pledge of Allegiance at the Mott Street School, Little Italy, New York City, 1892. (Photograph by Jacob Riis, courtesy of the Library of Congress.)

insured." An Italian recalled of his early days at school that "the constant drilling and pressure of memorization, the homework and detention raised havoc with many students."[61] The dissatisfaction cut across gender lines. "I do not want to go to school," reported one girl applying for working papers; "they scold me all the time." A social worker described this girl as "undoubtedly dull and unambitious." One might well ask, ambitious for what?[62]

The Italians' attitudes about school stood in marked contrast to those of their New York neighbors, eastern European Jews. Both groups were recent arrivals, poor, clustered to some extent in similar occupations, yet immigrant Jews were willing to invest in education. The Jewish interest in educating children was a source of admiration to many middle-class reformers. As one report noted, Jewish parents wanted their children, especially the males, to become "doctors, lawyers, teachers and merchants," wheras "the Italian parent is satisfied if a child can just read or write."[63] Like most Americans, Jews pulled daughters out of school before sons; nevertheless, Jewish girls as well as boys received more education than Italian girls and boys. "Jewish parents expected their daughters to work [but] they realize the value of education and a vast number of Jews were found in the higher institutions of learning."[64]

Many Jewish children were not much interested in school or very good at it. Nevertheless, the contrast between Italians and Jews reported by contemporaries during the early decades of the century can be confirmed by the U.S. Census Bureau retrospective survey of 1950 on ethnic groups in American cities. The differences cut across age and gender, and are true for both first- and second-generation immigrants. Two times the percentage of Jewish men, in comparison with the Italian men, had com-

[61] New York City, Board of Education, *Youth in School and Industry: The Continuation Schools and Their Problems*, Special Report Submitted with the 36th Annual Report of the Superintendent of Schools (New York: Board of Education, 1934), p. 56; Shaw, "The True Character," p. 4213; Covello, *The Heart*, p. 177.

[62] Johnson, "Social Service and the Public Schools," p. 177. See also Odencrantz, *Italian Women in Industry*.

[63] Kelly Durand and Louis Sessa, "The Italian Invasion of the Ghetto" (New York: n.p. [1909?]), p. 10 (reprint in the New York City Public Library). See also J. B. Maller, "Vital Indices and Their Relation to Psychological and Social Factors," *Human Biology* 5 (February 1933): 94–121.

[64] Daniels, *The Girl and Her Chance*, p. 19. See also Van Kleeck, *Working Girls in Evening Schools*.

pleted high school; in the second generation almost three times the proportion had completed high school (see Table 9). The educational achievement of foreign-born women of both groups was consistently below that of the men; nevertheless, in both the first and second generations more than two times the percentage of Jewish women than Italian women completed high school (see Table 10).

In accounting for these patterns, contemporary and latter-day scholars have emphasized differences in the world views of southern Italians and eastern European Jews. Jewish culture, the argument goes, because of its appreciation of education, enabled these immigrants to benefit from American schools. Further, because of their commitment to upward mobility, Jewish immigrants were anxious to invest in the future of their children, so that they could take advantage of opportunities in America.[65] It is true Jewish families arrived in America better prepared to benefit from schooling. But their cultural traditions cannot be divorced from the particular social and economic history of the group. Vague explanations that dominate these ethnic histories obscure the fact that for both Italians and Jews parental attitudes were realistic approaches to the challenges they faced in New York City. By comparing family strategies with respect to daughters' education for both groups, we can gain insight into the way different conditions provide different opportunities and constraints for women's lives.

Though Jewish immigrants were poor, by and large they came from the ranks of artisans or small shopkeepers, literate segments of their community.[66] This was particularly true of the Jews who immigrated after 1900. Whereas 54 percent of the Italian immigrants between 1899 and 1910 told immigration officials when they arrived that they could neither read nor write, only 26 percent of the Jewish immigrants, a population that in-

---

[65] See, for example, Olneck and Lazerson, "The School Achievement." See also Alice Kessler-Harris and Virginia Yans-McLaughlin, "European Immigrant Groups," in *Essays and Data on American Ethnic Groups*, ed. Thomas Sowell with the assistance of Lynn D. Collins (Washington, D.C.: Urban Institute, 1978), pp. 107–37.

[66] See Thomas Kessner, *The Golden Door: Italian and Jewish Immigrant Mobility in New York City, 1880–1915* (New York: Oxford University Press, 1977); Moses Rischin, *The Promised Land: New York's Jews, 1870–1914* (Cambridge: Harvard University Press, 1962).

Table 9. Educational status of first- and second-generation Italian and Jewish men in New York, by age and ethnicity, 1950

	First generation						Second generation					
	Aged 25–44		Aged 45+		All ages		Aged 25–44		Aged 45+		All ages	
	I (N=42.4)	J (N=20.2)	I (N=217.8)	J (N=148.2)	I	J	I (N=283.0)	J (N=156.7)	I (N=58.4)	J (N=52.9)	I	J
Percentage completing 1 year or more in high school	36	61	12	28	24	44	60	88	29	63	44	75
Percentage completing 4 years in high school or more	21	44	8	20	14	32	31	72	16	47	23	59
Median number of school years completed	8.5	10.9	5.6	8.1	–	–	10.1	12.7	8.4	11.4	–	–

Source: U.S. Department of Commerce, Bureau of the Census, *U.S. Census of Population, 1950, Vol. IV, Part 34: Special Reports, Nativity and Parentage* (Washington, D.C.: Government Printing Office, 1954), pp. 283, 284.

Note: I = Italian; J = Jewish. N = total in population in thousands. The surveyed area is the New York–Northeastern New Jersey Standard Metropolitan Area. Many of the immigrants aged 45 and over were educated in Europe.

Table 10. Educational status of first- and second-generation Italian and Jewish women in New York, by age and ethnicity, 1950

| | First generation | | | | | | Second generation | | | | | |
| | Aged 25–44 | | Aged 45+ | | All ages | | Aged 25–44 | | Aged 45+ | | All ages | |
	I (N=41.5)	J (N=27.2)	I (N=117.2)	J (N=143.3)	I	J	I (N=292.9)	J (N=170.8)	I (N=58.0)	J (N=53.4)	I	J
Percentage completing 1 year or more in high school	27	54	7	18	17	36	55	87	20	59	37	73
Percentage completing 4 years in high school or more	14	36	5	12	9	24	29	69	10	40	19	54
Median number of school years completed	8.2	9.7	4.0	5.8	–	–	9.6	12.4	8.2	10.5	–	–

Source: U.S. Department of Commerce, Bureau of the Census, *U.S. Census of Population, 1950, Vol. IV, Part 3A: Special Reports, Nativity and Parentage* (Washington, D.C.: Government Printing Office, 1954), pp. 283, 284.

Note: I = Italian; J = Jewish. N = total in population in thousands. The surveyed area is the New York–Northeastern New Jersey Standard Metropolitan Area. Many of the immigrants aged 45 and over were educated in Europe.

cluded a higher proportion of women, stated that they were illiterate.[67] Jewish adults had for years used their literacy in their work lives, their leisure lives, and certainly in their political activities.[68] They expected their children would also acquire such skills and encouraged sons especially to attend school. Since foreign-born Jewish children arrived in New York with a reading and writing knowledge of one language, they could more easily learn to read and write English than could children who arrived with no such skills.[69]

Moreover, the newly arrived Jewish children continued the pattern of educational achievement because the social and economic conditions of the Jewish community in New York made it easier for them than for the Italians to be students rather than wage earners. We have seen that the Jewish immigrant population was better off economically than the Italian because there was a greater proportion of skilled workers among the Jews and because Jewish males in the late nineteenth century gained a foothold in the expanding garment industry *before* the bulk of the southern Italians arrived in the United States. With a background as small traders in Europe, they were better prepared than the Italians to take advantage of small-scale mercantile operations available in New York.[70] These more

[67] See U.S. Congress, Senate, *Reports of the Immigration Commission*, vol. 3, *Statistical Review of Immigration, 1819–1920—Distribution of Immigrants, 1850–1900*, S. Doc. 756, 61st Cong., 3d sess. (Washington, D.C.: Government Printing Office, 1911), p. 84. Thomas Kessner points out that the 26 percent figure for Jews probably represents the number of Jews who could neither read nor write Yiddish or Russian; almost all Jewish men could read Hebrew. See *The Golden Door*, p. 41. See also U.S. Congress, Senate, *Reports of the Immigration Commission*, vol. 26: *Immigrants in Cities*, S. Doc. 338, 61st Cong., 2d sess. (Washington, D.C.: Government Printing Office, 1911), 2: 328–31.

[68] Many people have written about the importance of education for the Jewish work life, leisure, and political life. See, for example, Irving Howe, *World of Our Fathers* (New York: Harcourt, Brace, Jovanovich, 1976). For a discussion of another immigrant group whose behavior is, in some ways, similar to that of Italians, see John Bodnar, "Materialism and Morality: Slavic-American Immigrants and Education, 1890–1940," *Journal of Ethnic Studies* 3 (Winter 1976): 1–19.

[69] See U.S. Congress, Senate, *Reports of the Immigration Commission*, vol. 26: *Immigrants in Cities*, 2: 329–31. See also Maller, "Vital Indices and Their Relation to Social Factors," p. 120; Katharine Murdoch, "A Study of Race Differences in New York City," *School and Society* 11 (31 January 1920): 147–50; Dorothy Wilson Seago and Theresa Shulkin Kolden, "A Comparative Study of the Mental Capacity of Sixth Grade Jewish and Italian Children," *School and Society* 22 (31 October 1925): 564–68.

[70] See Nathan Glazer and Daniel P. Moynihan, *Beyond the Melting Pot: The Negroes, Puerto Ricans, Jews, Italians, and Irish of New York City* (Cambridge, Mass.: M.I.T. Press, 1970), chap. 3; Kessner, *The Golden Door*, chaps. 2–4; and Chapter 3 of this book.

prosperous parents could forgo children's earnings. And, because more Jewish mothers could afford to do domestic chores full time, fewer daughters had to leave school to assist either in homework tasks or child care.[71]

Differences in family size also made it easier for Jewish families to give up the earnings of their children. In 1917, while Italians had the highest child mortality rate in New York City, the Russian Jewish rate of 24.9 was the lowest; along with the lower rate came greater pressures to control fertility.[72] Why the mortality rates of the two groups differed so greatly is not clear, because both lived in poor housing and highly congested neighborhoods. A more precise investigation of infant and child mortality rates in the two communities is beyond the scope of this study. One common assumption, that the Jewish diet was healthier, is questionable in the light of present knowledge about nutrition.[73] More important, perhaps Jewish families had greater access to modern medical care in the early years of the century, largely because health services were funded and serviced by the older German Jewish population; eastern European doctors were available to the community as well. By contrast, Italians in need of medical care had to seek help from persons outside their own ethnic community; hence, they tended to avoid these services.[74] Finally, by the second decade of the century, homework operations, with all their attendant health and safety hazards, were a less important source of employment in Jewish households. Before 1900 Jews dominated homework; by 1911 their numbers had shrunk to about one-third of the work force and continued to decline as the community prospered and strong unions developed in the women's clothing industry and cigar manufacturing, where most Jews worked. Most likely, fewer Jewish children were exposed to the unhealthy particles of material that filled the air in poorly ventilated tenements.[75]

---

[71] See Chapter 3. Also, the U.S. Immigration Commission reported that among the Russian Jewish households it surveyed, 17 percent of the wives reported that they were at work, compared with 30 percent of the southern Italians. See U.S. Congress, Senate, *Reports of the Immigration Commission*, vol. 26: *Immigrants in Cities*, p. 228.

[72] New York City, Department of Health, *Influence of Nationality*.

[73] On American Jews and diet, see Rischin, *The Promised Land*, p. 87.

[74] On Jews and health services, see ibid., especially chap. 6. On the difficulties of getting Italians to take advantage of the medical services offered by New York philanthropists, see, for example, Lucy Gillett, *Adapting Nutrition Work to a Community* (New York: New York Association for Improving the Condition of the Poor, 1923).

[75] On the decline of Jewish participation in homework, see Felt, *Hostages of Fortune*, p.

Although the connection between lower infant and child mortality and lower fertility patterns is a hotly debated topic among historical demographers, there is evidence that both trends were occurring among American Jews during the early decades of their settlement. One detailed study of New York Italians and Jews in the first three decades of the century found lower infant mortality rates and lower birth rates for Jewish neighborhoods, along with greater school achievement.[76] With fewer youngsters to support, these families could more easily afford to invest in the next generation.

Although among Jewish immigrants advanced schooling always was considered more appropriate for sons, increased education became attractive for Jewish daughters as well — for very practical reasons. In the early decades of the century Jewish girls were already finding jobs in the white-collar sector, for which high school training was essential. Large corporations seldom hired southern European ethnics for office work before World War II, especially the foreign born. Jewish women, however, often worked as secretaries and bookkeepers in small-scale Jewish businesses that abounded in the early decades of the twentieth century. Even before

---

141; Van Kleeck, "Child Labor in New York City Tenements"; New York State, Department of Labor, *Homework in Men's Clothing Industry in New York and Rochester*, New York State Department of Labor Special Bulletin no. 147 (Albany, N.Y., 1926). It was not only the presence of strong unions that led to the earlier elimination of homework in the Jewish branches of the industry; because Jewish families were less dependent on the earnings of women and children in homework, it was also easier to organize the community to fight homework. This possibility is worth further study.

[76]Maller, "Vital Indices and Their Relation to Social Factors," pp. 119–21. For the country as a whole, a U.S. report on the fertility of immigrant women indicated that Jewish women had fewer children than did their Italian counterparts during the first three decades of the twentieth century. The number of children ever born per 1000 ever-married Russian and Polish Jewish immigrant woman, as recorded in 1940, was 4.8 for women aged sixty-five to seventy-four, 3.7 for women aged fifty-five to sixty-four, and 2.9 for women aged forty-five to fifty-four. All of these women, except for the last group, had passed their peak child bearing years (to age forty-four) by 1930. For ever-married Italian immigrant women, the figures are as follows: for women aged sixty-five to seventy-four in 1940, 5.4; for women aged fifty-five, 5.2; for women aged forty-five to fifty-four, 4.7. See U.S. Department of Commerce, Bureau of the Census, *Census of Population, 1940: Differential Fertility, 1940 and 1910* (Washington, D.C.: Government Printing Office, 1942), table 40. Also see Ira Rosenwaike, "Two Generations of Italians in America: Their Fertility Experience," *International Migration Review* 7 (Fall 1973): 273.

World War I some social investigators began to understand how changing employment opportunities for working-class women would be linked with changing educational strategies for the new immigrants. "Office work," wrote Harriet Daniels in 1914, "pays better in the end . . . but there is need of preparation." In this area of employment, she added, "it is interesting to note that the Jewish girl is to be found in office work and stenography while the Italian girl is found in factories."[77] Summarizing a group of private and governmental studies done in the second decade of the century, Daniels showed the differences between the occupational patterns and educational achievement of Jewish and Italian girls. Among Jewish girls fourteen to sixteen years old, only 5 percent were in factory work, 10 percent in office work, and 75 percent in public and trade schools, the highest proportion in school of all groups surveyed. The way employment opportunities acted as incentives to keep Jewish girls in school was suggested by a group of sixteen- to eighteen-year-olds, many of whom were already holding jobs: 20 percent were in school, only 28 percent in factory work (the lowest of any group studied), while 38 percent were found in offices, the *highest* among the groups surveyed.[78] The data about the Italians provide a stark contrast and suggest why schooling had so little meaning for them: Among fourteen- to sixteen-year-old girls, 43 percent were in school, 40 percent in factories, only 1 percent in offices. Only 2 percent of the older girls were in school, more than 71 percent were in manufacturing (the highest of all the groups studied), and 14.5 percent were in office work (the lowest of any group).[79]

The situation for Italian girls was to change toward the end of the Great Depression. Their work and school patterns would begin to parallel those of their Jewish counterparts, rather than offer such a contrast. During the early decades of the twentieth century Italian families faced pressures to turn children into wage earners as soon as possible; it was easy to keep

---

[77] Daniels, *The Girl and Her Chance*, p. 58.

[78] Ibid., pp. 58–61. Of the fourteen- to sixteen-year-olds 5 percent were in stores; 3.7 percent, in domestic service or at home. Of the sixteen- to eighteen-year-olds, 6.5 percent were in stores, 7.4 percent, in domestic service or at home.

[79] Ibid. Of the younger Italian girls, 3 percent were in stores, 6.4 percent at home. Among the sixteen- to eighteen-year-olds, less than 1 percent were in stores, and 11.3 percent were at home or in domestic service.

daughters out of school, and parents saw little benefit in educating women. The social conditions of the Italian community, the economic circumstances of those living in the city, and the role of the government all changed during the New Deal years and beyond. Employment opportunities for Italian women also changed. These developments shaped the work and school experiences of Italian-American women in new and important ways.

ITALIAN WOMEN
AND THE EMERGENCE OF
THE WHITE-COLLAR ECONOMY

Mary Capio, Captain, G.O. Representative, Personality Representative
"A girl who likes to dance, a secretary-to-be
We hope she gets that certain 'he.' "

Angela Rodino
"She has her fellow on a string
You can hear her heart go ding-aling-aling."
[Career Goals] Secretary and Model

—Julia Richman High School, *Spotlight*, Class of 1949

Mary Capio and Angela Rodino, Italian-American graduates of New York's Julia Richman High School, class of 1949, like their classmate Marie Conti, encountered in the introduction of this book, lived very different lives than the majority of Italian women only a decade or so before them.[1] The entries under their graduation pictures in the school's yearbook tell us something about the differences. Work chores and domestic tasks had dominated the lives of Italian girls during the early years of settlement in this country, but the girls of the class of 1949 spent their adolescence in school and in extracurricular interests. Those who planned to work expected to hold jobs quite different than those held by their mothers or even their older sisters and cousins.

[1] All names for students at Julia Richman High School are fictional. A discussion of the use of records at Richman appears later in the chapter.

Toward the end of the Great Depression young Italian women began attending school more regularly and staying on into the high school years. Why did the increase in schooling take place at this time? After decades of failure, had reformers finally convinced Italians that educating women was worthwhile?[2] What conditions made Italians "ripe" for the message that education was the key to social and economic achievement in the late 1930s, when they had not been not interested in such notions earlier? We have seen how demographic and social circumstances shaped earlier attitudes about work and school. When these conditions changed during the New Deal years, Italian family strategies changed; the community was now in a position to change attitudes about how daughters might best use their time.

Commitment to the well-being of the family remained the paramount goal for Italians throughout the period under study. Italian families made significant economic gains from 1900 to 1950; nonetheless, most remained working class and continued to rely on the wage work of several household members. During the Depression, moreover, many Italian families were hit quite hard; the acute economic problems of the early 1930s lasted throughout the decade. In 1940 eight Italian neighborhoods in Brooklyn and Manhattan reported that almost one-quarter of household heads were unemployed or on "work relief," and some areas reported more than one-third.[3] Under these circumstances, in this population middle-class values emphasizing the individual expectations of children had little resonance. Parents were no more interested in female autonomy than their elders before them; they still expected daughters to contribute to the

---

[2] For this argument, see Caroline Ware, *Greenwich Village, 1920–1930* (Boston: Houghton Mifflin, 1935), pp. 152–202; and Leonard Covello, *The Social Background of the Italo-American School Child* (Totowa, N.J.: Rowman and Littlefield, 1972).

[3] These unemployment and work-relief figures were tabulated by health area (H.A.), which are subunits of the city's neighborhood health districts. Areas were chosen in which at least 80 percent of the inhabitants are first- or second-generation Italians. There are two areas in the Lower West Side Mulberry neighborhood, three in East Harlem; in Brooklyn, one area in Fort Greene and two in Red Hook–Gowanus. The exact unemployment percentages are Lower West Side H.A. 68: 21.1%, H.A. 69: 34.6%; East Harlem H.A. 21: 41.9%, H.A. 22: 34.5%, H.A. 26: 34.7%; Fort Greene H.A. 11: 27.3%; Red Hook–Gowanus H.A. 40: 26.5%, 41: 24.6%. See New York City, Committee on Neighborhood Health Development, *Statistical Reference Data, Ten Year Period, 1930–1940*, comp. Marjorie Bellows, Godias, J. Drolet, and Harry Groble, 4th ed. (New York: Department of Health, 1944), pp. 73, 87, 149, 157.

welfare of the family. One Depression-era survey of Italian families in East Harlem found that one-half the boys but the majority of girls contributed their entire earnings to the family. The majority of families in the study still believed children owed absolute obedience to parents, that the needs of the family came first.[4]

But, as always, within the parameters of these familial goals, Italians were pragmatic in their efforts to adapt to American life. If they were flexible in their approach to women's work, so, too, were they flexible in their attitudes about schooling. Demographic changes, even in the poorest Italian communities, and changes in the employment structure of New York profoundly affected the educational and work patterns of Italian-American women who approached adulthood by midcentury.

Demographic Changes: Italian Families and Education

The demographic changes affecting Italian communities were striking. Infant and child mortality among Italian families declined almost as soon as they arrived in the United States, but as we have seen, in comparison with the rest of New York City, the rates were nonetheless high. By the 1920s a substantial fall in these rates was apparent, in part a result of the sharply lower mortality from diphtheria, measles, and scarlet fever.[5] During the 1930s, while all New York neighborhoods reported a continuing decrease in infant and child mortality, the decline in most Italian-dominated areas were proportionately greater.[6] The mortality declines (see Table 11) are particularly striking because they occurred in Italian neigh-

---

[4]Marie J. Concistre, "Adult Education in a Local Area: A Study of a Decade in the Life and Education of the Adult Italian Immigrant in East Harlem, New York City" (Ph.D. diss., New York University, 1943), pp. 55, 339, 341, 348.

[5]See East Harlem Health Center, *A Decade of District Health Center Pioneering* (New York: East Harlem Health Center, 1932), pp. 114, 116, 117. See also Mary Simkovitch, "Twenty Five Years of Greenwich House, 1902–1927" (available in the Russell Sage Collection, City College of New York).

[6]The Committee on Neighborhood Health Development collected and recorded data by health districts and the subunits, or health areas, only. Those areas that were at least 80 percent Italian are used for analysis here. Naturally, these are areas in the heart of New York City and do not give us a picture of the more prosperous Italians who by 1940 had

Table 11. Infant mortality rates in four Italian neighborhoods and in New York City, 1929–1940

Health district	1929– 1933	1931– 1935	% change 1929–1935	1936– 1940	% change 1931–1940
Lower West Side					
Health Area 68[a]	64	62	3.1	42	32.2
Health Area 69	67	63	4.4	26	58.7
East Harlem					
Health Area 21[a]	60	60	0	55	8.3
Health Area 22[a]	60	57	5.0	42	26.3
Health Area 26	68	61	10.2	61	0
Red Hook–Gowanus					
Health Area 40 (Brooklyn)	66	54	18.0	40	25.0
Health Area 41	73	61	16.0	44	27.0
Fort Greene					
Health Area 11 (Brooklyn)	[b]	77	–	45	41.0
New York City, all neighborhoods	55	52	5.4	40	15.3

Sources: New York City, Committee on Neighborhood Health Development, "Health Center Districts," in *New York City Handbook: Statistical Reference Data, Five Year Period of 1929–1933*, comp. Godias J. Drolet, Marguerite P. Potter, Kenneth O. Widener (New York: Committee on Neighborhood Health Development, 1935), pp. 97, 103, 115, 109; idem, *Statistical Reference Data, Ten Year Period, 1930–1940*, comp. Margorie Bellows, Giodias J. Drolet, and Harry Groble, 4th ed. (New York: Department of Health, 1944), pp. 75, 91, 150, 151.

Note: Information recorded by health areas where population is 80 percent Italian-born or second generation. Dates are those used by the committee.

[a]Includes areas sampled from 1905 and 1925 New York State, Manuscript Census. See chapters 2–4.

[b]Fort Greene Health Area 11 was not yet 80 percent Italian in 1929–1933, so data are not used here.

moved to the perimeter. These figures are used because they are the best demographic information available by ethnicity in New York for these years when manuscript census schedules are closed. A discussion of the health center system and the committee follows in the text.

borhoods that were experiencing special hardships during the Depression years. Comprehensive figures for the Italian population of the city are unavailable; but we know that although the infant mortality rate among Italians in the United States was above average in 1920, by the mid-1930s it was almost identical to that for all Americans.[7]

What caused this decline in infant and child mortality among Italians? Nutritionists of the day pointed to improvements in diet, especially for infants.[8] More importantly, the increasing availability of modern medical care in New York, a service virtually beyond the reach of southern Italians in Europe, ultimately had its effects on even this reluctant immigrant community. The spread of public health care in New York City during the Depression illustrates again how state policy redounded on family life. Community health services such as health centers and local branches of the Health Department had existed in certain needy areas of New York since World War I, and some child and baby stations even earlier.[9] However, efforts at citywide coordination and expansion of programs began in earnest in 1929, with the establishment of the Committee on Neighborhood Health Development. The committee, composed of medical professionals and representatives from health and welfare organizations, worked closely with the New York City Department of Health to promote public health in the city, especially in those areas of greatest need.[10]

By 1934, under the vigorous leadership of Mayor Fiorello LaGuardia, the district health center program had been developed on a wide scale; what had once been a system of health care facilities partly public and

[7]In 1926 the rate of deaths per 1,000 infants of Italian mothers was 75.6; for white American mothers, 66.7. In 1932 the figure was 53.4 for Italians, 52.5 for all white Americans. See Massimo Livi-Bacci, *L'Immigrazione et l'Assimilazione degli Italiani negli, Stati Uniti* (Milan: Dot. A. Giuffrè, 1961), p. 86.

[8]See Dorothy L. Bovee and Jean Downes, "The Influence of Nutrition Education on Families of the Mulberry Area of New York City," *Milbank Memorial Fund Quarterly* 19 (1941): 121–46.

[9]The East Harlem and Mulberry District Health centers, for example, did serve many Italians by the late 1920s.

[10]See Savel Zimand, "District Health Administration in New York City," in *District Health Administration: A Study of Organization and Planning*, ed. Ira Hiscock (New York: Milbank Memorial Fund, 1936), p. 35; New York City, Committee on Neighborhood Health Development, *Vital Statistics in the Development of Neighborhood Health Centers in New York City*, by Godias J. Drolet and Louis Weiner (New York: Department of Health, 1932).

partly private became the responsibility of the city's Department of Health. The East Harlem Health Center, already operating as a demonstration facility, became the first of the administrative health centers in 1929. Full-time district administrators were assigned to East Harlem, the Lower West Side, Red Hook, and Gowanus, all areas heavily populated by Italians, along with several other areas of great need. With the help of federal funding, new child health stations and baby stations were built or renovated. As of 1939 the entire city had been brought into the system, and nine new district health buildings had been constructed by the federal Public Works Administration; five new ones were underway.[11] In 1942 the East Harlem Health Center operated three child health stations, dental clinics, chest units, a social hygiene clinic, a massive program to immunize children against diphtheria, and a health education program to reduce infant mortality.[12] Referring to the nursing and health programs of East Harlem from 1928 to 1942, one woman who had grown up in the community and had studied it during the Depression years concluded: "thousands of babies, mothers and young children in East Harlem owe their health and perhaps their lives to the direct ministry of this institution."[13]

Among the most important programs conducted or assisted by the district centers were education and health examination projects in the schools. Programs to teach children about preventing disease epidemics and examinations of New York City students go back to the early decades

[11] See Zimand, "District Health Administration"; New York City, Neighborhood Health Development, Inc., "Health Planning for the Future through District Health Center Development," by John L. Rice, M.D., Commissioner of Health (New York, 1939); New York City, Committee on Neighborhood Health Development, *A Survey of Child Health Facilities and Recommendations to the Department of Health for the Development of a More Adequate Service* (New York: Department of Health, Child Health Care Services, September 1938). Naturally, government appointees tend to exaggerate the progress made during their administration, and these sources probably do that, but the general improvements made in the 1930s are corroborated by other materials, as shown below.

[12] See also New York City, Neighborhood Health Development, "Health Planning"; Concistre, "Adult Education," pp. 122–27.

[13] Concistre, "Adult Education," p. 117; also p. 447. See also Charles Boulduan, Louis Weiner, and Marguerite P. Potter, "Some Special Health Problems of Italians in New York City, A Preliminary Survey," *Quarterly Bulletin* 11 (Department of Health, 1934), in Francesco Cordasco, ed., *Italians in the City: Health and Related Social Problems* (New York: Arno Press, 1975).

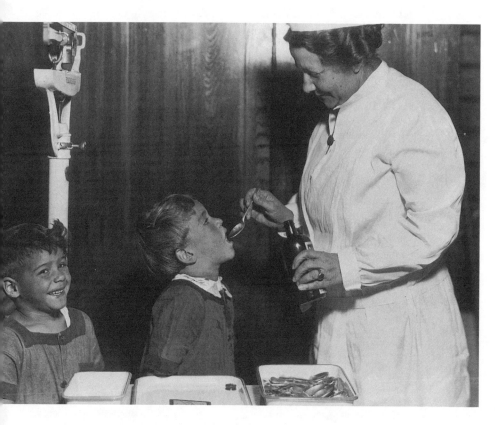

School nurse with an immigrant kindergarten class, New York City, 1920. (Photograph by Lewis W. Hine, courtesy of the New York Public Library.)

of the century, but they were accelerated during the Depression in conjunction with the development of the district health system.[14] Finally, better economic conditions—however limited—over the course of three decades and the relief programs of the New Deal contributed to improved health for Italians, young and old.[15]

The complex reasons for the decline in child mortality rates require further analysis, but certainly the overall improvement in the health of children meant less absenteeism and often better school performance. And, as more children survived, parents became more receptive to notions about the value of education.[16] At the same time, growing numbers of surviving children increased the economic burden of the family, and pressures to decrease fertility began to take effect. Changed fertility strategy in turn had spiraling consequences. With fewer children to support, it made more sense for families to invest more of their resources in the education of their children. One good way to marshal resources was to have still fewer children.[17]

---

[14] See, for example, reports of health and educational officers in New York State, Factory Investigating Commission, *Second Report of the Factory Investigating Commission*, vol. 3 (Albany, N.Y.: J. B. Lyon, 1913), pp. 106, 107. See also *Physical Defects: The Pathway to Correction* (New York: American Child Health Association, 1934), Appendix A, "School Health Organization and Procedure in the Elementary Schools of New York City"; New York City, Department of Education, *Elementary Schools of the City of New York, Their Problems and the Efforts Being Made to Solve These Problems*, part of the *Annual Reports to the Superintendent of Schools for the School Year, 1933–34* (New York: Department of Education, 1934), p. 40.

[15] On occupational mobility for Italian males, see Chapter 2.

[16] As noted in Chapter 4, Ian Davey has analyzed the relationship between changes in health conditions and school attendance, "The Rhythm of Work and Rhythm of School, Hamilton, Ontario in the Nineteenth Century" (unpublished paper, 1977 [?]).

[17] This draws on arguments presented in Charles Tilly, "Population and Pedagogy in France," *History of Education Quarterly* 13 (1973): 113–28. See also Charles Tilly, ed., "The Historical Study of Vital Processes," in Charles Tilly, ed., *Historical Studies of Changing Fertility*, pp. 3–55 (Princeton: Princeton University Press, 1978); E. A. Wrigley, "Fertility Strategy for the Individual and the Group," pp. 135–54, in ibid.; J. A. Banks, *Prosperity and Parenthood: A Study of Family Planning among the Victorian Middle Classes* (London: Routledge and Paul, 1954); Mary Ryan, *Cradle of the Middle Class: The Family in Oneida County, NY, 1790–1865* (New York: Cambridge University Press, 1981). Among the poorest families, of course, there were fewer resources available for child care, and infant mortality continued to be high. These families had less incentive to reduce fertility. High fertility rates among these poorer households and the consequent numerous children posed severe problems for families in the second quarter of the twentieth century,

Comparable fertility data for Italians in New York after 1925 are unavailable, but information for the same Italian-dominated neighborhoods in New York and for Italians in the United States as a whole indicates a sharp decline in fertility at the end of the 1930s. Fertility decline was common in all white American groups during the Great Depression, as families tried to conserve resources during hard times, but the drop for Italians was particularly striking. Age-specific fertility data for all Italians in the United States show that their fertility, already on the decline prior to the mid-1920s, fell sharply at the end of that decade and further in the 1930s. Italian fertility dropped at a faster rate than that of the population as a whole. Thus, for example, among all Italian women aged twenty-five to twenty-nine, completed fertility (for married women) was 2.2 in 1926, 1.5 in 1931, and 1.2 in 1936; for native white Americans, it was 1.4 in 1926, 1.2 in 1931, 1.1 in 1936, hardly lower than the Italians.[18] Second-generation Italian women shared in the post–World War II baby boom: women who entered their peak child-bearing years at that time were the first to show higher rather than lower rates of fertility in comparison with older cohorts, but in comparison with other American females, their fertility remained low. Ever-married Italian-American women born between 1915 and 1925 reported an average of 2.2 children; all white women, an average of 2.3.[19]

Clearly, Italian families were choosing to concentrate their resources on fewer children. Both boys and girls were affected by the change, but for daughters, a decrease in family size may have had a particularly important effect. Fewer children meant that mothers' child-care burdens were lightened; since their daughters could more easily be spared away from home, parents were more likely to allow them to attend school.

---

however, because legal prohibitions against child labor in factories were being enforced more stringently. Thus, these families also felt the need to limit the number of offspring.

[18] Livi-Bacci, *L'Immigrazione et l'Assimilazione*, pp. 65, 67. It is not clear if Livi-Bacci has used ever-married Italian women in determining fertility, or only married women living with spouses. He estimated the population of Italian women on the basis of annual regions of immigration adjusted by annual mortality calculated from life tables. See his discussion in ibid., pp. 62, 63, and app. B.

[19] See Ira Rosenwaike, "Two Generations of Italians in America: Their Fertility Experience," *International Migration Review* 7 (Fall 1973): 276. For the other cohort of women, born between 1905 and 1915, the figures were 2.1 for Italian, 2.0 for all white ever-married women.

A New Deal for Child Labor and the Schools

Even as demographic change encouraged Italian parents to invest in the education of their children, changes in employment opportunities for youngsters in New York during the Depression removed one of the most important incentives for their families to keep them out of school. Job possibilities for youth in New York City, particularly for females, shifted dramatically in the 1930s. The changes resulted partly from market forces — in this case, the collapse of the economy — but they were also a result of important transformations in public policy. To understand the shifts in Italian family strategies, we move the focus away from the Italian community to the political arena.

Some fifteen years after Mary Van Kleeck had called for the abolition of all industrial child labor as the first crucial step in dealing with truancy, federal and state governments took the necessary steps to abolish child labor in all areas of manufacturing. As part of this effort, the New Deal governments of President Franklin D. Roosevelt and New York Governor Herbert Lehman set out to eliminate homework completely. This move was partly a response to increased agitation by the garment unions.[20] Government officials also believed that homework was unacceptable because they were convinced that all sweated labor, which depended on the cheap and irregular labor of women and children, was an obstacle to New Deal plans for recovery.[21]

The first federal attempts to eliminate homework began as early as 1933 with the passage of the federal National Industrial Recovery Act. In accordance with National Recovery Administration (NRA) stipulations, the garment manufacturers and the unions drew up industrywide codes for the regulation of wages, prices, and hours of work; homework operations were specifically prohibited.[22] The NRA program eliminated many

[20] On the New Deal coalition, see Sam Lubell, *The Future of American Politics* (New York: Harper, 1942); Arthur Schlesinger, Jr., *The Age of Roosevelt*, vol. 3: *The Politics of Upheaval* (Boston: Houghton Mifflin, 1960); William E. Leuchtenburg, *Franklin D. Roosevelt and the New Deal* (New York: Harper and Row, 1963), chaps. 3 and 8.

[21] Leuchtenburg, *Franklin D. Roosevelt and the New Deal*, chap. 4, remains one of the finest summaries of the economic strategies of the Roosevelt administration.

[22] See Jeremy Felt, *Hostages of Fortune: Child Labor Reform in New York State* (Syracuse, N.Y.: Syracuse University Press, 1965), p. 151; Lazar Teper and Nathan Weinberg,

but not all homework practices. As New Deal historians have long pointed out, employers were notorious for violating NRA codes in many industries operating under the program.[23] Also, there was substantial protest in local communities because the new prohibition of homework eliminated work opportunities that for some people were the only ones available in New York during the early years of the Depression.[24] In 1935, when the National Industrial Recovery Act was declared unconstitutional, the volume of homework increased sharply.[25] But the efforts to eliminate homework in New York were by no means over. In 1934 a revised state statute made it easier to prosecute garment manufacturers for the use of child labor in production. The New York State Department of Labor was committed to the elimination of homework, and between 1936 and 1938 Labor Commissioner Elmer F. Andrews issued orders eliminating homework in the artificial flower and feather industry, the men's and boys' outer clothing industry, and the men's and boys' neckware industry.[26]

Since these industries were the largest employers of homeworkers in the 1930s, the new laws, combined with important union gains in the garment and artificial flower industries, had far-reaching effects on homework operations in the Italian community. Between 1933 and 1937 Italian women had become the dominant group in the New York City chapter of the Amalgamated Clothing Workers of America (ACWA), makers of men's clothing. More than 80 percent of the women had joined in those five years. "By far the largest proportion of this group," the union noted, "consists of finishers and fellers pursuing tasks within the shops

---

"Aspects of Industrial Homework in the Apparel Trades," International Ladies Garment Workers Union research paper (July 1941), p. 16; New York State, Department of Labor, *Homework in the Artificial Flower and Feather Industry*, in New York State, Part III, New York State Department of Labor Special Bulletin no. 199 (Albany, N.Y., 1938), pp. 16, 17; Donald Martha, "Wage, Hour and Child Labor Legislation in the Roosevelt Administration," *Lawyers Guild Review* 5 (1945): 185–91.

[23] See, for example, Leuchtenburg, *Franklin D. Roosevelt and the New Deal*.

[24] In May 1934, for example, President Roosevelt issued an order exempting disabled persons from the homework prohibition. The situation became extremely confused with "inspectors going back and forth, telling people they could and could not do homework." Felt, *Hostages of Fortune*, p. 151.

[25] See Teper and Weinberg, "Aspects of Industrial Homework," p. 34; New York State, Department of Labor, *Homework in the Artificial Flower and Feather Industry*.

[26] See Felt, *Hostages of Fortune*, pp. 151, 152.

that had formerly been accomplished in slum tenement flats as home-work."[27]

On the federal level the Roosevelt administration finally succeeded in abolishing homework almost entirely in major industries through the enactment of federal minimum-wage standards provided by the Fair Labor Standards Act of 1938. Since the act applied to labor done in the home as well as in the factory, it destroyed one of the strongest incentives for employing homeworkers. Because the act set national standards, it removed incentives for manufacturers in those states with homework laws, like New York, to operate illegally in order to compete with manufacturers operating in states without laws. Violations of the law continued, to be sure, and final assurance of the constitutionality of homework restrictions did not come until 1945, when the U.S. Supreme Court affirmed the judgment of a lower tribunal.[28] Although homework was not totally eliminated, the number of homeworkers declined sharply; in 1955 the state of New York issued only 5,616 licenses for legal homework operations, compared with 52,026 in 1937.[29] Once work was removed from the home, an important outlet for young Italian girls' wage labor virtually disappeared; so, too, did one of the most important factors that accounted for their chronic absence from school.

By the mid-1930s, in addition, it was no longer possible for fourteen- and fifteen-year-olds to obtain factory employment. There had been widespread discussion in New York ever since the onset of the Depression about the importance of keeping young adolescents out of the labor mar-

[27] Jacob Loft, "Jewish Workers in the New York City Men's Clothing Industry," *Jewish Social Studies* 2 (January 1940): 61–77.

[28] See Felt, *Hostages of Fortune*, p. 152; Martha, "Wage, Hour and Child Labor Legislation," p. 190. The ILGWU, it should be noted, was concerned that the Fair Labor Standards Act (FLSA) would not completely eliminate homework, for unlike the NRA, it did not completely prohibit the operation, but, rather, made state wage, hour, and child labor legislation mandatory. See Teper and Weinberg, "Aspects of Industrial Homework." By 1945, apparently, thanks to better enforcement of New York State law and federal enforcement of the FLSA homework was ended in the garment industry, according to Martha. See also Russell Lindquist and Donald D. Smith, "Industrial Homework," *Minnesota Law Review* 29 (1944–45): 295–317; Eileen Boris, "Homework and Women's Rights: The Case of the Vermont Knitters, 1980–1985," pp. 234–35, in Eileen Boris and Cynthia Daniels, eds., *Homework: Historical and Contemporary Perspectives on Paid Labor at Home* (Urbana: University of Illinois Press, 1987).

[29] Felt, *Hostages of Fortune*, p. 153.

ket so that they would not compete with their elders for the few available jobs. In 1931 Lieutenant Governor Herbert Lehman, a strong advocate of raising the school-leaving age, put the issue this way: "What would it mean this winter to many discouraged and thinly-clad breadliners, sometimes only a few years beyond school age, if these [employed] boys and girls had remained in school and left the jobs for their elders to fill?"[30]

At first, New Dealers and other reformers faced opposition from parents who needed the earnings of their children to the idea of raising the mandatory school-age requirement; formidable opposition also came from the Catholic church.[31] By the middle of the 1930s, however, voters in the state of New York were ready to accept a change in the school law. The imposition of the NRA codes in 1934 had virtually established sixteen years as the minimum age for all workers in New York industries engaged in interstate commerce. Keeping children in school was one good way to occupy their time. In 1935 the New York State legislature passed a new school-attendance law requiring New York children, with some exceptions, to remain in school until age sixteen; the law went into effect in September 1936.[32]

Committed to keeping children out of an economy that now had no room for them, New York officials—in contrast to earlier practice—enforced the new law. School principals, teachers, and staff cooperated with attendance officers, and the budget of the Bureau of Attendance was increased; rules and regulations that permitted underage children to leave the classroom were rigorously applied. New schools were built throughout the city to house the enlarged student population.[33] There were now so

[30] Quoted in ibid., p. 121.

[31] At the time, the church did not have a massive high school program; in 1920 there were only thirty-five diocesean high schools in the country. Thus, in the short run the church was in no position to accommodate an increased school population. In the long run the church reaped "the benefits of changes in the school law and increased enforcement in child labor laws," as Fass points out, as well as "the increased prosperity of German and Irish Catholics, and, increasingly, the newer immigrants"; the result was an expansion of the parochial high school system. See Paula S. Fass, *Outside In: Minorities and the Transformation of American Education* (New York: Oxford University Press, 1989), pp. 195-96.

[32] Felt, *Hostages of Fortune*, p. 126.

[33] Ibid., pp. 126, 127. See also Works Progress Administration, Historical Records Survey, Population file, Municipal Archives, New York City; and New York City, Board of Education, *Thirty-Seventh Annual Report of the City Superintendent of Schools for the School Year 1934-35* (New York: Board of Education, 1936), p. 85.

many youngsters who earlier would have been working part time but now could not find jobs, and so many high school drop-outs who could not find work, that the old continuation school program became a full-time vocational school system. Parochial schools, though still relatively less important for Italians, were also built to fill the need in Italian and other ethnic communities across the city, and school curricula were revised to encourage school attendance.[34] One Italian, writing for the federal Writers' Program of the Works Progress Administration on Italian life in New York City in 1939, succinctly summarized the changes:

> It must be admitted that (earlier) New York's truant officers did not always display the greatest zeal for gathering Italian children of school age. Politics may or may not have been responsible, but the fact is, most public schools in these (neighborhoods) were filled to overflowing. . . . The Catholic Church stepped in and set up parochial schools. . . . In recent years a number of public grammar and high schools, especially in the Italian neighborhoods have added courses in Italian.[35]

Italian Women and the Incentive for Schooling

By the mid-1930s Italian families were confronting a different situation than they had found when they arrived in New York City. Although factory jobs for older adolescents during the Depression were scarce, younger boys could still do street jobs. There was very little that younger girls could do, however, because homework was eliminated. Furthermore, the state was now enforcing the law to keep adolescents in school as long as possible. In sum, the economic advantage in keeping girls away from

[34] Felt, *Hostages of Fortune*, pp. 126, 127; New York City, Board of Education, *Youth in School and Industry: The Continuation Schools and Their Problems*. Special Report Submitted with the 36th Annual Report of the Superintendent of Schools (New York: Board of Education, 1934); Works Progress Administration, Historical Records Survey, New York City Guide Files, Catalogue no. 3561, "Italians," article 16, "Schools and Education," 1939, pp. 2, 3, Municipal Archives, New York City.

[35] Works Progress Administration, Historical Records Survey, New York City Guide Files, Catalogue no. 3561, "Italians," pp. 2, 3. See also Leonard Covello, *The Heart Is the Teacher* (New York: McGraw-Hill, 1958).

school had practically been eliminated, and legal sanctions prohibiting that behavior were greater than ever before.

The lack of available alternatives and the threat of legal sanctions alone do not fully explain why Italian families began allowing daughters to remain in school, especially beyond the legal age of sixteen. Today, for example, despite the existence of legal sanctions against truants, there is widespread absenteeism among poor, newly migrated populations in the United States. The question, then, is why Italian families, during the last years of the Depression and in the 1940s, came to see a positive value in schooling for their daughters and decided to keep daughters in school, often beyond the legal age. What did schooling have to offer?

During the early years of the century schooling did little to prepare Italian girls for adult life. Toward mid-century, major shifts in the female employment structure of New York City strikingly altered that situation. New York had been a center for the production of consumer goods, but as the century progressed, the tertiary sector of the economy (which encompasses services of all kinds), rather than manufacturing, grew more rapidly. As the scale of business and distribution increased, so, too, did the number of clerical jobs for women. The communications industry and retail commerce also developed rapidly, providing other "women's" jobs.

Manufacturing had dominated the female employment structure in New York at the turn of the century, but by 1930 clerical work was the largest single job category for women, occupying 30 percent of the city's female labor force. Daughters of small entrepreneurs, farmers, and skilled workers had been moving into clerical jobs since the late nineteenth century.[36] The very rapid growth of white-collar work in twentieth-century New York offered opportunities for women of the new immigrant communities as well. In 1930 in New York the proportion of all female workers who were employed in the clerical sector was almost two times that of the country as a whole. Office work was becoming an increasingly important part of the job market in the nation's largest city, now the headquarters for business and sales operations of many major corporations. The change was very important for the city's women; by 1950 clerical and communications work in New York accounted for 35 percent of the fe-

---

[36] See Ileen A. DeVault, *Sons and Daughters of Labor: Class and Clerical Work in Turn-of-the-Century Pittsburgh* (Ithaca, N.Y.: Cornell University Press, 1990).

male work force and sales another 6 percent; manufacturing accounted for only about 25 percent.[37] New York was still a large manufacturing center, but the dominance of the white-collar sector is clear.

To be a clerical worker or a salesperson, one has to know at least how to read and write English readily and to be competent at simple arithmetic. The impact of clerical work on mass education was substantial. By 1940 a high school diploma had become the standard prerequisite for most secretarial or bookkeeping jobs. New York high schools had for years been offering courses in clerical training. To meet the growing demand, almost all high schools by the 1930s offered courses in typing, shorthand, and bookkeeping, and a number of schools provided complete commercial preparation.[38]

Clerical jobs were attractive to working-class women for several reasons. White-collar work offered women cleaner working conditions and better hours; in some cases, but by no means all, it also offered better pay. Perhaps the most important advantage of white-collar employment was that it was more secure than factory work, less subject to seasonal fluctuation and often less vulnerable to downturns in the business cycle. During the Depression unemployment hit factory workers first and hardest; clerical workers felt the impact of the Depression later and with less severity. In 1930, 10 percent of women in manufacturing in New York City were unemployed, but only 5 percent of female clerical workers were unemployed.[39]

New York officials understood that white-collar employees suffered less than industrial workers during the Depression; they also knew that,

[37] See Personnel Research Federation, *Occupational Trends in New York City: Changes in the Distribution of Gainful Workers, 1900–1930* (New York: National Occupational Conference, 1933), charts 1 and 2; U.S. Department of Commerce, Bureau of the Census, *Census of Population, 1950, Vol. II: Characteristics of the Population, Part 32: New York State* (Washington, D.C.: Government Printing Office, 1952), pp. 266–75. (Figures quoted in the text are for New York City proper; for the New York–Northeastern New Jersey Standard Metropolitan Area, 34 percent of female workers were clericals, while 24 percent were operatives.)

[38] Randolph C. Wilson, *Office Work as an Occupation* (New York: New York Board of Education in cooperation with the Federal Works Progress Administration for the City of New York, 1940).

[39] See Personnel Research Federation, *Occupational Trends in New York City,* index, citing the *Fifteenth Census of the United States,* vol. 2. Women as a group fared somewhat better in terms of unemployment during the Depression, particularly in the early years,

regardless of the specific effects of the Depression, in the long run job opportunities in the manufacturing sector were shrinking because of structural changes in the economy. By the end of the 1930s the New York superintendent of schools was calling for curriculum modification to deal with these changes. For years, he noted in his annual report of 1937–1938, evening school programs had trained young working-class adults to fill manufacturing jobs. But that was no longer a viable strategy, for "the unemployed were those who fit the old order of things." A broader vocational training program would be the solution to the problem. As a consequence, he reported, the New York evening schools were becoming more like the general high schools, "replacing the more obvious subjects usually associated with evening schools with English, Journalism, Math and French." In this way, he hoped that students would acquire more flexible job skills that would better fit the demands of the job market.[40]

The Italian Response to the Economic and Social Changes

Did Italian families grasp these changes and see a new need to educate their daughters? Italians could observe, on the basis of their own experience, the advantage of clerical work. During the Depression they saw that the clerical workers in their own communities were better able to withstand the effects of the economic crisis than were the factory workers. In one Italian neighborhood in 1930, for example, where the level of unem-

---

because of their greater concentration in clerical, sales, and trade occupations. See Iva Peters and Lorine Pruette, *Women Workers through the Depression* (New York: Macmillan, 1934); Susan Ware, *Holding Their Own: American Women in the 1930's* (Boston: Twayne Publishers, 1982), chap. 2; and Ruth Milkman, "Women's Work and Economic Crisis: Some Lessons from the Great Depression," in Nancy F. Cott and Elizabeth H. Pleck, eds., *A Heritage of Her Own: Toward a New Social History of American Women* (New York: Simon and Schuster, 1979), pp. 507–41.

[40] Works Progress Administration, Historical Records Survey, no. 3597, article 19, p. 19, *Thirty-Ninth Annual Report of the Superintendent of Schools* quoted. See also Personnel Research Federation, *Occupational Trends in New York City*, p. xii.

ployment was high for all female workers, two times the percentage of clerical workers as factory workers were employed full time. In 1932 three times the percentage of clerical workers as factory workers were employed full time. In a community so heavily dominated by blue-collar workers, the favorable position of white-collar employees must have been striking.[41] No wonder one Depression-era study of East Harlem reported that the overwhelming majority of the families surveyed listed office work as the most desired occupation for their children. Furthermore, 81 percent of the Italian parents surveyed expressed the wish that daughters at least complete high school, almost identical to the 83 percent of parents who expressed such a desire for their sons.[42]

Italian families were now in a position to appreciate the value of high school for their daughters because, in contrast to earlier years, white-collar jobs were opening up for Italian women in New York. Native-born offspring had a better chance of being hired for office work than did foreign-born women, if only because they spoke English without accents and because they looked and behaved more like native-stock Americans. Unlike most factory work, white-collar work involves mingling across class and gender lines. American male executives were more comfortable working with the more acculturated second-generation females.[43] White-collar work also involved interacting with the public in reception offices, in service agencies, and in stores. In the words of the 1937 annual report of the superintendent of schools, "the rising incidence and social need of

[41] Gwendolyn H. Berry, *Idleness and the Health of a Neighborhood* (New York: New York Association for Improving the Condition of the Poor, 1933), p. 80.

[42] Concistre, "Adult Education," pp. 353, 356. Concistre's purpose was to study the impact of adult education on the behavior and attitudes of Italians. To that end, she surveyed a group of fifty families in which one parent had attended adult education classes and a group of fifty families in which no adult attended such classes. The results of the survey of all the families are reported here because the group of fifty that contained an adult student did not, as might be expected, bias the population in favor of education. It seems that there are no significant differences between the two groups in any area. In this case, a higher percentage of families in the group with *no* adults in class favored high school education for their children.

[43] On the importance of appropriate personality characteristics and office decorum for female white-collar workers, see Wilson, *Office Work as an Occupation*. See also Anne Valles, "Miss America Takes Shorthand: Job Manuals and the Changing World of Women and Work, 1900–55" (Senior thesis, Vassar College, 1979); Cindy Sondik Aron, *Ladies and Gentleman of the Civil Service: Middle-Class Workers in the Victorian Era* (New York: Oxford University Press, 1987), part 3.

'distribution' and services, as types of occupations has [*sic*] emphasized the importance of correct speech, poise, attractive appearance . . . [because] customers buy kind words, a pleasing voice, harmonious colors . . . along with their commodities and services."[44] Such characteristics were not perceived as attributes of foreign-born women, but since the native born could acquire them, they were the people thought to be potentially the most suitable for office work.

Further, as second-generation Italian men began organizing their own small businesses, it became easier for Italian women to obtain white-collar jobs. We have noted that a substantial number of Jewish women had already worked in office jobs within their own community. By midcentury Italian women as well were able to find jobs in businesses owned and run by Italians.[45] During the New Deal years federal, state, and local government bureaucracies grew enormously, becoming huge employers of ethnic women. This was a particularly important development in New York City, where ethnic voters were such an important element in local political coalitions. After World War II, as the tertiary sector of the economy expanded even further, it became easier for ethnic women to obtain jobs even in the large corporations. Employers could no longer afford to act on lingering prejudices against ethnic women because the number of native-stock American women available in New York was insufficient to fill these posts.[46]

By 1950 Italian women had entered the ranks of white-collar workers in large numbers. The U.S. Census Bureau reported that although only 8 percent of first-generation women workers were employed in clerical

[44] New York City, Board of Education, *The Thirty-Eighth Annual Report of the Superintendent of Schools of New York for the School Year 1935–36*, part 2 (New York: Board of Education, 1937), p. 89.

[45] On the growth of small-scale Italian businesses, see Nathan Glazer and Daniel P. Moynihan, *Beyond the Melting Pot: The Negroes, Puerto Ricans, Jews, Italians, and Irish of New York City* (Cambridge, Mass.: M.I.T. Press, 1970), pp. 206, 207. Glazer and Moynihan note that Italian businesses experienced a period of growth a generation later than was the case of New York Jews but had nonetheless made gains by midcentury.

[46] On the enormous growth in demand for female clerical and sales workers in the twentieth century and its effects on the attitudes of employers, see Valerie Kincaid Oppenheimer, "Demographic Influence on Female Employment and the Status of Women," *American Journal of Sociology* 78 (1973): 946–61. Also see Valerie Kincaid Oppenheimer, *The Female Labor Force in the United States*, Population Monograph Series no. 5 (Westport, Conn.: Greenwood Press, 1970).

work, 40 percent of the second generation were employed in those occupations (see Table 12). Among the youngest second-generation workers, females born between 1926 and 1936, 58 percent were employed in clerical occupations. The shift in the female employment pattern was more rapid and more pervasive than the shift in the employment structure of Italian-American males. Although Italian males had, by 1950, moved into the ranks of stable wage earners, a breakdown of occupations by categories shows that more than 50 percent of the second-generation males still worked in blue-collar jobs, as craftsmen, operatives, or laborers. Only 17 percent of the males were employed in clerical jobs; adding those who were professionals, managers, and proprietors gives 33 percent of the second-generation males in white-collar jobs, as opposed to 47 percent of the females. Among workers aged fourteen to twenty-four, more than 50 percent of the males were still working in blue-collar jobs; only 31 percent of males as opposed to 62 percent of females had white-collar jobs.

A comparison of the educational achievements of Italian American men and women who were in the prime of their working lives in 1950 offers insight into how the shifts in the employment structure affected Italian family behavior with respect to children and education. Among the tiny population in all age groups that went to college, more men than women graduated. And for both first-generation and second-generation Italian Americans who were between the ages of twenty-five and forty-four in 1950 (born between 1906 and 1925), the percentage completing high school was higher among the males than the females. In younger cohorts, however, the gaps between the educational achievements of the men and women is less pronounced, and the pattern is even reversed for second-generation Italian Americans aged fourteen to twenty-four in 1950 (born between 1926 and 1936). In this cohort a higher percentage of females than males either completed some high school or graduated (see Table 14).

If changes in school patterns among Italian men and women reflected the adoption of modern attitudes, these results would be puzzling. Although one might expect that the level of female educational achievement would rise as Italians became "Americanized," it seems unlikely that a culture that presumably was so prejudiced against the idea of female education per se would, in a matter of decades, *reverse* its age-old conviction and allow women to equal and even surpass the achievement of their

Table 14. The educational status of young first- and second-generation Italians in New York, by age and gender, 1950

	First generation				Second generation			
	Aged 14–24		Aged 25–44		Aged 14–24		Aged 25–44	
	M (N=5.9)	F (N=6.7)	M (N=42.4)	F (N=41.5)	M (N=119.3)	F (N=126.3)	M (N=283.0)	F (N=292.9)
Percentage completing 1 year or more	52	54	36	27	75	80	60	55

Table 12. Occupations of first- and second-generation Italian women, 1950 (percentage distribution)

	First generation				Second generation			
	Age group				Age group			
Occupations	All (N=51.7)	14–24 (N=3.2)	25–44 (N=14.9)	45+ (N=33.5)	All (N=177.2)	14–24 (N=64.3)	25–44 (N=97.9)	45+ (N=14.9)
Professional workers	2	3	4	2	5	4	5	4
Managers and proprietors	4	1	3	4	2	–	3	5
Clerical and sales workers	8	28	12	4	40	58	31	19
Craftspeople	2	1	2	3	2	1	3	3
Operatives	77	63	73	80	44	31	51	58
Private household workers	1	–	–	1	–	–	–	1
Service workers	4	2	3	4	4	3	4	7
Laborers	–	1	–	–	–	–	–	–
Not reported	1	1	1	1	1	1	1	1

Source: U.S. Department of Commerce Bureau of the Census, *U.S. Census of Population, 1950, Vol. IV, Part 3A: Special Reports, Nativity and Parentage* (Washington, D.C.: Government Printing Office, 1954), p. 234.

Note: N = total number employed, in thousands. Amounts constituting less than 1 percent are not reported. Numbers and percentages are rounded to the nearest hundred. Farming occupations are not included, as these account for well under 1 percent of the population. The area surveyed is the New York–Northeastern New Jersey Standard Metropolitan Area, 1950.

Table 13. Occupations of first- and second-generation Italian men, 1950 (percentage distribution)

Occupations	First generation				Second generation			
	All (N=196.7)	Age group			All (N=369.4)	Age group		
		14-24 (N=3.9)	25-44 (N=39.4)	45+ (N=153.4)		14-24 (N=65.4)	25-44 (N=254.5)	45+ (N=49.6)

brothers. If, however, Italian behavior and attitudes with respect to proper roles for girls and boys are seen as inextricably intertwined with familial needs throughout the period under study, the pattern is understandable. Italian parents were pragmatic about schooling throughout the first half of the century. When schooling was of little value to this working-class community, parents kept the children away; when schooling became essential for training girls to meet the needs of a changing job market, they were sent to school. The families faced a contrasting situation for their sons: many more manufacturing jobs were available for working-class males, and after the Depression men could earn relatively good wages, particularly if they were skilled laborers and worked in strongly unionized industries. As a consequence, completing high school was less critical for boys.[47]

That Italian women high school students were already focused on careers in office work is suggested by information about the 1944 and 1949 graduates of Julia Richman High School for girls in Manhattan. Like most high schools in New York City that drew students from a wide area, Richman drew young women from all over Manhattan and from several ethnic groups. Richman was chosen for this study partly because of the willingness of school administrators to provide access to their historical materials, but also because it was a general high school, offering both college preparatory programs and commercial courses; one can, therefore, analyze career choice by ethnic group.[48] All school records for such recent graduates are closed; however, the yearbooks for two classes in the 1940s provide helpful information on high school life by midcentury.

Richman's fourteen academic departments offered classes ranging from business, accounting, and secretarial studies to Latin, modern languages, and textile arts. The postgraduation plans listed by graduates in the annual yearbook reflect the breadth of the school's curriculum. Approximately 17 percent of the class of 1944 could be identified as of Italian origin; most likely they were second-generation girls, born in the mid- to late

[47] Craft work, operative jobs, and laboring jobs accounted for 45 percent of the male work force in the New York–Northeastern New Jersey area as a whole, compared with 24 percent for females. See U.S. Bureau of the Census, *Census of Population, 1950, Vol. II: Characteristics of the Population, Part 32*, pp. 266–45.

[48] Also important for this study, Richman had a significant number of both Jewish and Italian girls.

Table 15. Postgraduation plans of members of the class of 1944, Julia Richman High
School (percentage distribution)

	Italians (N = 109)	All graduates (N = 676)
Office work[a]	50.0	28.8
Business school[b]	3.6	3.6
Profession (requiring college degree)	5.5	6.6
College	11.0	22.0
Nursing	6.4	6.6
Arts[c]	6.4	3.6
Garment professions[d]	2.7	2.5
Marriage[e]	4.5	2.9
Miscellaneous[f]	9.1	22.9

Source: Julia Richman High School, *Spotlight* (1944).
[a]Includes bookkeeper, clerk, office worker, secretary, stenographer.
[b]Includes court-reporting school.
[c]Includes performing and visual arts.
[d]Buyers, designers.
[e]Includes only those students who listed marriage as a career choice.
[f]Scattered choices that did not require college degrees, such as lab technician, dental
hygienist, stewardess.

1920s.[49] In 1944, 50 percent of the Italian graduates whose plans were
reported in the yearbook listed some type of office job, such as secretary,
stenographer, or bookkeeper (see Table 15).

Another 3.6 percent listed business school, which in those years
meant, in the case of women, commercial training; another 11 percent
listed college, along with 5 percent who listed professions that required a
college degree. Only 4.5 percent listed marriage as their only goal. The
graduating class of Julia Richman as a whole reported 28.8 percent looking forward to office work, with 3.6 percent listing business school; 22
percent, college; and another 6.6 percent, professions requiring college.
In 1949 34.6 percent of Italian graduates who reported their plans listed
clerical work; 19.1 percent listed college or collegiate professions (see
Table 16). The drop in clerical work between 1944 and 1949 can be accounted for partly by increases in the choice of college and professional

[49]The ethnicity of students was determined by the last name; unclear cases were dropped.

Table 16. Postgraduation plans of Italian-American members of the class of 1949, Julia Richman High School (percentage distribution)

	(N=53)
Office work[a]	34.6
Business school[b]	1.9
College	3.8
Professions	15.3
Nurse	4.3
Arts[c]	11.3
Garment professions[d]	1.9
Marriage[e]	15.0
Miscellaneous[f]	13.4

Source: Julia Richman High School, *Spotlight* (1949).
[a]Includes bookkeeper, clerk, office worker, secretary, stenographer.
[b]Includes court-reporting school.
[c]Includes performing and visual arts.
[d]Buyers, designers.
[e]Includes only those students who listed marriage as a career choice.
[f]Scattered choices that did not require college degrees, such as lab technicians, dental hygienist, stewardess.

careers as well as the arts. The greatest difference is in the percentage reporting marriage as their most immediate expectation; this, perhaps, is a reflection of the increased marriage rate of all American women in the postwar years.[50]

The extent to which the growth of white-collar jobs for women affected educational trends across ethnic backgrounds is suggested by again a comparative look at what was happening among New York's Jews. Although Jewish women and men maintained higher achievement levels

[50]Of the 1944 graduates identified as Italian, 6 percent did not list career plans and were not included in the study. Although it may be that they were all planning careers or college but just did not respond to the yearbook's query, many may actually have been planning to marry and not to take jobs. Of the total graduating class of 703, 4 percent listed no plans. In 1949 close to one-third of the students identified as Italian listed no career goal at all, perhaps indicating an increase in the proportion planning to marry immediately after graduation. It also should be noted that because Julia Richman was a general high school, students often chose it precisely because it did offer collegiate preparation; hence, the proportion of Italian girls here who planned on college may well be higher than in the Italian population at large.

than did Italians, by 1950 a similar pattern of gender differences had emerged in both groups. Among the older cohorts, those born between 1905 and 1925, men showed greater educational achievements than women. Among the younger group of native-born Jewish Americans born between 1926 and 1936, although a larger proportion of men than women completed college, more *women* (67 percent) than men (61 percent) remained at least through high school (see Table 17).[51] How might we account for this shift? In contrast to the Italian community, in the Jewish community there were many white-collar workers among the men (see Tables 18 and 19). However, many of the large number of white-collar Jewish males in 1950 were small entrepreneurs, an occupation that did not require formal education. Among second-generation Jewish male workers, 27 percent were listed as managers and proprietors, whereas only 19 percent were professionals and another 28 percent were clerical workers. In the case of second-generation females, however, 63 percent were clerical workers and another 16 percent were listed as professionals. Among the younger women, 89 percent were clerical workers or professionals; in the case of males, 55 percent were clerical workers or professionals. Thus, it is not surprising to find the same pattern seen in the Italian community: in 1950 more Jewish women than Jewish men aged fourteen to twenty-four held high school diplomas. These figures only suggest the ways that structural changes in the economy influence the educational patterns of both men and women, whatever the ethnic community. We know, however, that it was common in the Jewish community for women to help out in the family business by working as a bookkeeper or secretary, and for women to marry businessmen who were wealthier but less educated than themselves.[52]

Gender differences in educational strategies among the new immigrants of the twentieth century, with girls surpassing boys by midcentury, reflected patterns already set by older immigrant, working-class groups in the late nineteenth century. The greater achievement among girls in the American working class suggests that historians of education need to re-

[51] U.S. Department of Commerce, Bureau of the Census, *U.S. Census of Population, 1950, Vol. IV, Part 3A: Special Reports, Nativity and Parentage* (Washington, D.C.: Government Printing Office, 1954), p. 283.

[52] See Charlotte Baum, Paula Hyman, and Sonya Michel, *The Jewish Woman in America* (New York: Dial Press, 1976).

Table 17. The educational status of young first- and second-generation Jews in New York, by age and gender, 1950

| | First generation[a] | | Second generation | | | |
| | Aged 25–44 | | Aged 14–24 | | Aged 25–44 | |
	M (N=20.2)	F (N=27.2)	M (N=50.9)	F (N=52.7)	M (N=156.7)	F (N=170.8)
Percentage completing 1 year or more in high school	61	54	89	91	88	87
Percentage completing 4 years of high school or more	44	36	61	67	72	69
Median number of school years completed	10.9	9.7	12.4	12.4	12.7	12.4

Source: U.S. Department of Commerce, Bureau of the Census, *U.S. Census of Population, 1950, Vol. IV, Part 3A: Special Reports, Nativity and Parentage* (Washington, D.C.: Government Printing Office, 1954), p. 283.

Note: M = male; F = female. N = total in population in thousands. The surveyed area is the New York–Northeastern New Jersey Standard Metropolitan Area.

[a]Fewer than 500 males and 500 females who were foreign born and aged 14–24 were counted, so this cohort is not included. It was small because the 1930s was a time of lower fertility and, more importantly, because after the mid-1920s the quota restrictions were extremely severe, almost barring southern and eastern European immigrants.

Table 18. Occupations of first- and second-generation Jewish women, 1950 (percentage distribution)

Occupations	First generation				Second generation			
	All (N=30.4)	Age group			All (N=80.8)	Age group		
		14-24 (N=-)	25-44 (N=7.8)	45+ (N=22.3)		14-24 (N=22.4)	25-44 (N=45.3)	45+ (N=13.0)
Professional workers	8	–	11	7	16	12	17	16
Managers and proprietors	12	–	9	13	8	3	8	14
Clerical	28	–	37	24	63	77	59	50
Crafts	2	–	2	2	1	–	1	2
Operative	40	–	33	43	8	4	9	11
Private household	2	–	1	2	–	–	–	–
Service	4	–	4	6	3	2	3	3
Laboring	–	–	–	–	–	–	–	–
Not reported	1	–	1	2	1	–	–	2

Source: U.S. Department of Commerce, Bureau of the Census, *U.S. Census of Population, 1950, Vol. IV, Part 3A: Special Reports, Nativity and Parentage* (Washington, D.C.: Government Printing Office, 1954), p. 283.

Note: N = total number employed, in thousands. Amounts constituting less than 1 percent are not reported. Numbers and percentages are rounded to nearest hundred. Farming occupations are not included, as these account for well under 1 percent of the population. Foreign-born Jews aged 14–24 are too few to enumerate (see notes to Table 17). The area surveyed is the New York–Northeastern New Jersey Standard Metropolitan Area.

Table 19. Occupations of first- and second-generation Jewish men, 1950 (percentage distribution)

Occupations	First generation				Second generation			
	All (N=130.4)	Age group			All (N=216.5)	Age group		
		14-24 (N=—)	25-44 (N=18.9)	45+ (N=111.2)		14-24 (N=22.7)	25-44 (N=146.0)	45+ (N=42.7)
Professional	9	—	13	8	19	14	20	16
Managerial and proprietary	32	—	31	32	27	10	27	34
Clerical	14	—	19	13	28	41	26	27
Crafts	16	—	14	17	10	11	11	8
Operative	23	—	17	24	12	15	12	10
Private household	—	—	—	—	—	—	—	—
Service	4	—	3	4	3	3	3	3
Laboring	2	—	1	2	1	3	1	1
Not reported	1	—	—	—	1	1	1	1

Source: U.S. Department of Commerce, Bureau of the Census, *U.S. Census of Population, 1950, Vol. IV, Part 3A: Special Reports, Nativity and Parentage* (Washington, D.C.: Government Printing Office, 1954), p. 283.

Note: N = total number employed, in thousands. Amounts constituting less than 1 percent are not reported. Numbers and percentages are rounded to nearest hundred. Farming occupations are not included, as these account for well under 1 percent of the population. Foreign-born Jews aged 14–24 are too few to enumerate (see notes to Table 17). The area surveyed is the New York–Northeastern New Jersey Standard Metropolitan Area.

think the meaning of high school for the American working class. Revisionists have long noted that high school had little practical value for the working class as industrial work in the late nineteenth and twentieth century became increasingly less skilled.[53] Even if that was true for males, however, high school was a practical necessity for females. This may be one reason why girls were less alienated from the classroom. One study of a working-class high school in the early 1960s is significant. Sociologist Arthur Stinchcombe attributed the rebellious behavior among the boys to the fact that boys saw little relationship between school tasks and their own futures; the girls, on the other hand, tended to view high school training as an entry to white-collar jobs.[54]

By midcentury the high school years, both inside and outside of the classroom, had assumed a new importance in the lives of Italian females. They gave girls time and space before they took up the responsibilities of work and marriage. School, work, and marriage are the subject of the next, and last, chapter.

---

[53] See Samuel Bowles and Herbert Gintis, *Schooling in Capitalist America* (New York: Basic Books, 1976); Christopher Jencks, *Inequality: A Reassessment of the Effects of Family and Schooling in America* (New York: Basic Books, 1972).

[54] Arthur I. Stinchcombe, *Rebellion in a High School* (Chicago: Quadrangle Books, 1964), chaps. 4 and 5. According to Stinchcombe, those girls who did not succeed in school oriented themselves toward marriage.

CHAPTER SIX

WORK, SCHOOL, AND ITALIAN-AMERICAN FAMILIES AT MIDCENTURY

Jeannie Marlino, Mimeograph Squad, Secretary, Bank Representative

"Jeannie with her chestnut hair,
Known to her friends as 'slim,'
Among her many interests,
Top rating goes to 'him' "

[Career Goal] Marriage

—Julia Richman High School, *Spotlight*, Class of 1949

For Jeannie Marlino and her classmates, going to high school opened up new possibilities. Nevertheless, the limits were very real and apparent to the students. The changes and continuities that Italian females shared with the generation before are the subject of this final chapter. If Italian parents sent daughters to school to train for white-collar working-class jobs, the high schools, for their part, did what they could to orient the young women toward such work and not beyond. One recent oral history study of second-generation Italian women in Providence, Rhode Island, reports that not one woman interviewed said that she had been encouraged to attend college; in 1953 the class valedictorian graduated from high school to become a bank teller.[1] The information from the Julia

[1] Sharon Hartman Strom, "Italian American Women and Their Daughters in Rhode Is-

Richman *Spotlight* suggests that for at least one group of Italian women, the situation was beginning to change, with 19 percent of the Italians graduating in 1949 planning to attend college. The large majority, however, had no such plan. Just as schools tried to discipline an earlier generation of students, especially males, who took up manual labor, the commercial curriculum now taught subordinate roles appropriate to low-level white-collar work. Proper appearance, good character, good habits, "a pleasing personality" as the school superintendent's annual report put it in 1937, along with vocational skills, became important for a new generation of female workers who would have closer working relationships with their employers. And since girls were expected to work only a short time before marriage, the schools expanded courses in various aspects of home economics.[2]

If high school did not offer Italian adolescent girls much opportunity to cultivate and ultimately fulfill personal ambition, it did mean that they had more free time than had earlier generations. Their mothers and older sisters had spent day and night working and helping at home with domestic chores and homework. They had largely missed out on the world of working-class leisure that caught the attention of both contemporary observers and modern scholars. In contrast, the Italian-American women who were adolescents in the late 1930s and 1940s had opportunity for sociability; the high school was the focal point for these activities. In the mid-1930s and again in early 1940s East Harlemites reported that there was still a great deal of family unity and that children expressed affection for their parents. They also reported, however, a marked tendency for second-generation children to spend more recreational time away from home, particularly by the early 1940s.[3] At Julia Richman High School,

---

land: The Adolescents of Two Generations, 1900–1950" (unpublished paper, Providence, 1977).

[2] See New York City, Board of Education, *Thirty-Seventh Annual Report of the City Superintendent of Schools for the School Year 1934–35* (New York: Board of Education, 1936), p. 89; Works Progress Administration, Historical Records Survey, Catalogue no. 3597, article 19; New York City, Board of Education, *Youth in School and Industry: The Continuation Schools and Their Problems*, Special Report submitted with the 36th Annual Report of the Superintendent of Schools (New York: Board of Education, 1934).

[3] Marie Concistre, "Adult Education in a Local Area: A Study of a Decade in the Life and Education of the Adult Italian Immigrant in East Harlem, New York City" (Ph.D. diss.,

Italian girls participated in sports, in clubs, and in student government. With fewer work chores, they could pursue hobbies; they partied and they spent time with boyfriends. Angela Carbone, for example, a member of the class of 1949, was a school captain, a representative to the student government, and must have had a serious boyfriend, perhaps in the air force. "A girl who's true to the sky / Therefore she wants to fly," declared the *Spotlight* under her photograph. "She's going to rocket to the moon / With a pilot very soon." Rosalie Petrullo was secretary of the Leaders' Club and a representative to student government. "She likes to sew, knit and bake. And everyone likes her tasty cake," reported the *Spotlight*. Catherine Giordano, who hoped to be a writer, was vice-president of the senior class, a Personality Representative, a member of the Sound Squad and of Arista, the honor society. "Full of Fun," the *Spotlight* described her, "yet a willing helper. Next to dancing, she likes watching the Yankees win." When Nancy Campanella "learns to drive a car," the *Spotlight* noted under her picture, "she will have achieved her ambition." Louise Bagele was "just wild about Vic Damone records."[4] The small group of Italian girls who attended high school in earlier decades had undoubtedly participated in similar activities; the point is not that life in high school was so different, but that now, more and more Italians could share the experience.

In making the most of their adolescent years, these Italians, more than their elders before them, attended the movies, window shopped, read popular magazines. Increased exposure to the popular media helped second-generation women to acculturate into mainstream society, that is, to take on the speech patterns, the habits, and the tastes of the dominant culture.[5] Young Italian-American women, like their elders, enjoyed the movies, radio, and popular fiction because they could fantasize about the characters in the stories. Stars like Katharine Hepburn or Rosalind Russell may have enhanced the attractiveness of office work, but expectations

---

New York University, 1943), pp. 343, 363. Concistre admits that since the information comes from the parents and not the children, there may well be a tendency to idealize the state of family harmony, but she notes that the evaluation by the parents is consonant with what she knows, sees, and has experienced in the community.

[4] The information on Julia Richman students comes from *Spotlight* (1944), pp. 40, 52, 24, 17.

[5] On acculturation as a process distinct from assimilation, see Milton Gordon, *Assimilation in American Life* (New York: Free Press, 1965).

continued to be informed by the girls' own experience and that of the people around them. A few, inspired by Hollywood actresses, must have gone off to seek their fortunes independently of their families, or to better themselves through education.[6] Most knew, as the information from Julia Richman's *Spotlight* indicates, that they would become typists, stenographers, or salesgirls for New York businesses, or telephone operators, nurses, laboratory technicians, and dental hygienists.

A series of interviews with first- and second-generation Italian women in Providence reveal occupational patterns similar to those of the New York females; they underscore the finite quality of the adolescent experience, the limits of their own expectations. Most of the Providence women born between 1918 and 1934 had at least some high school experience. The women had fond memories of school sports such as swimming, volley ball, soccer; others talked about school plays. But in the end, one Italian woman from Providence put the situation succinctly when she noted: "She had wanted to be a secretary . . . practically all the girls in school took clerical courses and very few went to college *or even* considered the thought."[7]

Italian girls made the most of their high school years by having fun. There is some evidence that girls who planned to go to college used their extracurricular time differently. At Julia Richman more than half of the Jewish girls from the classes of 1944 and 1949 stated that they intended to go to college or pursue collegiate careers. They also enjoyed many of the leisure pastimes pursued by the Italians, but Jewish girls dominated such extracurricular activities as the school newspaper, yearbook, and literary magazine.[8] Having fun in high school was time well spent for Italians,

[6] For a discussion of women who acted on such impulses in an earlier era, leaving home to live as single women in Chicago, see Joanne Meyerowitz, *Women Adrift: Independent Wage Earners in Chicago, 1800–1930* (Chicago: University of Chicago Press, 1988).

[7] Strom, "Italian-American Women and Their Daughters," p. 11. On the importance of high school life for Italian-American families at midcentury, see also Theresa Woods, "Family and Community, Kingston, New York" (term paper, Vassar College, 1978).

[8] A total of 120 girls were identified as being Jewish in 1944; 111 listed postgraduation plans. In 1949, of 190 who were listed as Jewish, 75 listed career goals. Leslie Woodcock Tentler has made the point that working-class girls use the high school years as a period of freedom before taking on adult responsibilities, whereas middle-class girls use college this way (lecture given at the University of Michigan, 1971). Paula Fass found that although a number of Italian women participated in academic extracurricular clubs, Jewish women

because by the age of eighteen or so, most took up the responsibilities of work and then marriage.

When School Days Were Over

Italian women coming of age after the Depression could look forward to working in jobs that were cleaner, safer, and often less tiring than the jobs in garment factories. Though much of the clerical work available to ethnic women was relatively poorly paid, monotonous, and rigidly super- vised, some jobs, particularly in smaller offices, provided women the freedom to pace their work and socialize on the job. In most settings, whether an office, department store, or service work such as waiting on tables, women depended on one another for support in dealing with day- to-day difficulties that arose at the workplace and for advice on personal matters. Single women shared news about boyfriends and engagements. They joined in the preparation for upcoming weddings among coworkers. Where women were able to exercise personal judgment in their work, they took pride in their accomplishment; those in the highest level as administrative assistants enjoyed the challenge.[9]

Most white-collar work for women, however, offered little opportunity to exercise autonomy. The jobs required the ability to respond well to authority, the willingness, above all, to cooperate. Job manuals written during the years of expansion in clerical work, like the commercial cur- riculum in New York City public schools, emphasized discipline rather than creativity. Potential employees who wanted to know what office work would entail learned from one New York City manual that "accuracy . . . courtesy, honesty . . . loyalty, order, punctuality, speed and tact were ideal."[10] Another warned women about the reasons they might fail. "Often

---

were much more likely to be involved in literary activities. See *Outside In: Minorities and the Transformation of American Education* (New York: Oxford University Press, 1989), chap. 3.

[9] On the variety of experiences in office work, see, for example, Barbara Garson, *All the Livelong Day: The Meaning and Demeaning of Routine Work* (New York: Doubleday, 1975).

[10] Randolph C. Wilson, *Office Work as an Occupation* (New York: Board of Education of the City of New York in cooperation with the Federal Works Progress Administration for the City of New York, 1940), p. 15.

Students preparing for jobs as office workers at Brooklyn Girls Commercial High School, circa 1930s. (Courtesy Brooklyn Historical Society.)

the trouble seems to be the girl's inability to adapt herself to her employer's wishes or to the routine of the office. It is alright [*sic*] to be an individualist, *if you can afford to* [italics mine], but big business must be carried on along routine lines."[11] The majority of Italian women in 1950 could not afford to pursue individual aspirations through careers.

Because few single women were paid enough to live independently of their families, they continued living with their parents. Like the women of the earlier generation, Italians contributed to the family income, some by turning over their entire wages excepting an allowance, others most likely by paying a portion of their earnings to cover room and board.[12] For single working-class young adults, to live at home while they worked made sense, not only from the parents' point of view but from the children's perspective as well. Italian daughters, for example, could rely on their mothers to do their cooking, cleaning, and perhaps sewing for them. Such services were more cheaply obtained at home than anywhere else and provided daughters with free time for socializing with friends after work and on weekends.[13] Single Italian-American women in the postwar years, more so than their predecessors, worked regular hours. They were not obliged to juggle employment inside the home as well as out. Much more so than Italian-American women in the early decades, these workers used newly acquired free time for shopping, going to the movies, and dating.

Living at home also meant that daughters were still subject to parental discretion, to rules and regulations regarding their after-work activities. "Only at her place of work," one young East Harlem Italian noted in the early 1940s, "is [she] freer from the vigilance of her parents, her brothers or relatives." The stories of constant supervision are undoubtedly exag-

[11] Anne Valles, "Miss America Takes Shorthand: Job Manuals and the Changing World of Women and Work, 1900–55" (Senior thesis, Vassar College, 1979), p. 20, quoting Hazel Cades, *Jobs for Girls* (New York: Harcourt Brace, 1930), pp. 20–22. See also Margery Davies, *Woman's Place Is at the Typewriter: Office Work and Office Workers, 1870–1930* (Philadelphia: Temple University Press, 1982).

[12] See Strom, "Italian American Women and Their Daughters," pp. 11, 12. Also see Elinor Langer, "Inside the New York Telephone Company," p. 338, in *Women at Work*, ed. William O'Neill (Chicago: Quadrangle Books, 1972).

[13] For a further discussion of family strategies with respect to working-class daughters, see Louise Tilly, "Individual Lives and Family Strategies in the French Proletariat," *Journal of Family History* 4 (Summer 1979): 137–52.

Students preparing for jobs in the fashion industry at Brooklyn Girls Commercial High
School, circa 1930s. (Courtesy Brooklyn Historical Society.)

gerated. If it was difficult to supervise daughters in the early decades, in post–World War II America it was impossible. Nevertheless, as before, the daughter, unlike the son, was expected to maintain kin ties, assist in domestic chores, help with finances, and take care of parents in their old age.[14]

Parental expectations sometimes were the cause of struggles within Italian-American families, as in others. Daughters fought over issues of dating, school, work, and engagement or wedding plans.[15] Boys struggled with parents, but like males of earlier times, they could free themselves of overly burdensome families through their ability to support themselves; some could use the army as an avenue of escape.[16] Single women remained tied to families and, above all, familial obligations.

Marriage at Midcentury

Given prevailing assumptions about gender and the sex segregation of the labor market, which provided mostly lower-level jobs for females, the anthropologist Micaela di Leonardo's observations of second-generation Italian Americans in San Francisco are relevant to New Yorkers as well. "Marriage and family was still what [they] took seriously and invested effort in."[17] Captions from the Richman *Spotlight* suggested how important marriage was to the New York girls, even for those who were known for their artistic talents or hobbies, and for those who knew exactly what kinds of jobs they planned to obtain after graduation. Of Rosalie Petrullo, class of 1949, it was said that "the second interest in her life / Is to become a loyal wife." For Anna Guernari, school captain, marshall, and typist, "Her main ambition in this life / A trip to the altar 'as his wife.' "[18]

---

[14] Concistre, "Adult Education." See also Micaela di Leonardo, *The Varieties of Ethnic Experience: Kinship, Class, and Gender among California Italian-Americans* (Ithaca, N.Y.: Cornell University Press, 1984), chap. 6.

[15] Concistre, "Adult Education"; di Leonardo, *Varieties*.

[16] In Mario Puzo's autobiographical novel *The Fortunate Pilgrim* (New York: Atheneum, 1965), one of his brothers does use the army to escape what he feels is a too-burdensome family. See also Robert Anthony Orsi, *The Madonna of 115th Street: Faith and Community in Italian Harlem, 1880–1950* (New Haven: Yale University Press, 1988), chap. 5.

[17] di Leonardo, *The Varieties*, p. 199.

[18] Julia Richman *Spotlight* (1949), pp. 52, 15, 43.

During the prosperous postwar years the vast majority of Italian Americans, like American women in general, eventually married. The 1950 U.S. census recorded that 90 percent of first-generation Italian women in New York City and 82 percent of second-generation women aged twenty-five to forty-four were married, or had been married. The majority of second-generation Italian women in the United States married Italians; those who did not usually married other Catholics.[19] The increase in marriages outside the ethnic group suggests that within the limits of class and religion, Italian daughters had a larger choice of potential marriage partners and were exercising even greater discretion than before.

Even among women preparing for professional careers, marriage was an overwhelmingly popular choice in those years; that decision for most women meant giving up other ambitions. Eighty-nine percent of first-generation New York Jewish women and 86 percent of the second generation aged twenty-five to forty-four were or had been married.[20] The evidence from the Richman yearbooks of the 1940s indicates the importance of marriage for Jewish girls as well as the Italians. Some of the Jews, like the Italians, were planning to devote themselves to marriage immediately. Thus, of Amy Cohen, a school captain, aide, and secretary, who listed marriage as her goal, it was written, as it had been of Anna Guernari, "Her main ambition in this life / A trip to the altar as David's Wife." Other Jewish women listed marriage as a second occupation along with such things as composing and modeling.[21] But even the girls who had very ambitious ideas about their future roles in the public world probably understood that marriage was going to be their most important career. Ruth Goldblum, class of 1949, a reporter for the Richman *News*, a captain, and marshall, must have made quite an impression on her classmates as a most talented young woman. But the *Spotlight* at midcentury vividly acknowledged the disjunction between the capabilities of some of the women and the reality of opportunity in a whimsical comment about

---

[19] On Italian marriage patterns, see U.S. Department of Commerce, Bureau of the Census, *Census of Population, 1950, Vol. IV, Part 3A: Special Reports, Nativity and Parentage* (Washington, D.C.: Government Printing Office, 1954), p. 284. On marriage and intermarriage patterns of second-generation Italians, see Gordon, *Assimilation in American Life*, pp. 205, 206.

[20] U.S. Department of Commerce, Bureau of the Census, *Census of Population, 1950, Vol. IV, Part 3A: Special Reports, Nativity and Parentage*, p. 284.

[21] *Spotlight* (1944) and *Spotlight* (1949).

Ruth: "If she doesn't succeed in becoming President of the United States," the yearbook noted, "she'll settle for being a housewife."[22]

Once married, the young Italian, like most women, shifted her responsibilities to her new household. These women, like their older counterparts, made taking care of their families their highest priority; this meant raising the children, caring for the home, and, when necessary, taking on paid employment. Yet despite the continuity in goals between the generations, the lives of Italian-American mothers had changed by midcentury in several ways. First, those women who became mothers after World War II, although many had more children than women did during the Depression, still had fewer offspring than did women during the early decades of the century. Fewer children meant that they spent less time caring for babies. Second, because husbands were generally earning stable, although seldom high, incomes, married women were not obliged to do paid labor when they had preschoolers, as had been common in the earlier period. They could devote full time to their domestic responsibilities. For many, this meant tending to the first real house that the family had enjoyed in America, usually in the outer boroughs or immediate suburbs of New York. "Just keep wishing on that lucky star," the *Spotlight* wrote underneath Catherine Antonozzi's senior picture in 1949, "and you will get that dream house you've been yearning for."[23] Indeed, the opportunity to own a home was a dream come true for many Italian women and men at midcentury. Along with marriage, Concistre noted about East Harlem's second generation in the mid-1930s and early 1940s, came the move to the Bronx or Queens. Those who moved out of Lower Manhattan tended to go to Queens, Brooklyn, Staten Island, or New Jersey.[24]

With fewer children, greater certainty that they would survive, and more resources than their parents, Italian Americans were now positioned to adopt higher standards of domesticity. Thus, young Italian-American wives joined other American women in the growing consumerism surrounding home and child care. The daily chores were not as physically taxing as they had been; nevertheless, family responsibility kept women very busy. Sewing, cooking, fixing up one's house, involvement with

[22] *Spotlight* (1949), p. 30.
[23] Ibid., p. 45.
[24] Concistre, "Adult Education," p. 38.

neighborhood and school activities were both work and leisure for many women. Married Italian women also spent time reading, visiting friends, and going to the movies, particularly those wives not engaged in paid labor.[25] Home, however, remained the main focus; the free time available to adolescents at midcentury was not shared by married women.

Devotion to domesticity on the part of married Italian women at midcentury seldom bred the kinds of discontents that were to emerge among more prosperous women. Many college-educated women in postwar America resided in bedroom communities, cut off from relatives and associates from their younger years in the work force. Overeducated for a lifetime of chauffeuring children and housework, many would be receptive to Betty Friedan's message about women's discontents put forth in *The Feminine Mystique*. The Jewish women profiled in these pages were more likely than Italian-American women to experience these problems. Fewer Italian women lived isolated in the suburbs; they could maintain attachments with kin around the city, even high school friends.[26] In addition, like other white working-class women, many Italian wives in 1950 found that they could not afford to devote themselves exclusively to domestic chores.

By 1950 a small house in the outlying boroughs, a car, proper clothes for school children, household appliances, and recreation were all associated with stable working-class and lower-middle-class life. But these expenses often stretched beyond the income of the Italian-American husband. Since children would not (and could not) be put to work until late adolescence, it was mothers who took a job to help pay for family expenses. Many second-generation families were now willing to invest even greater resources in the futures of their children; many hoped to send at least one child, if not more, to college, and extra income was needed to pay for tuition.[27] It was not difficult for married women to find

[25] Ibid., pp. 341, 356.

[26] See di Leonardo, *The Varieties*, chap. 6.

[27] On the desire of Italian and other working-class women to work in order to meet family expenses, see Langer, "Inside the New York Telephone Company," pp. 337, 338; William Chafe, *The American Woman: Her Changing Social, Economic, and Political Roles, 1920–1930* (New York: Oxford University Press, 1972). On the aspirations of second-generation Italian families in New York City to send children to college, see Richard Gambino, "La Famiglia: Four Generations of Italian-Americans," in Joseph A. Ryan, ed., *White Ethnics* (Englewood Cliffs, N.J.: Prentice-Hall, 1973), pp. 42–51.

work because the female tertiary sector was so large in New York City. While pay for women remained considerably lower than for men, demand for clericals drove up female wages. This made paid employment ever more attractive to married women who needed to add to family income.[28]

Exactly how many married Italian women were working in 1950 is not clear because the published census data on women's employment was not reported both by marital status and by ethnicity, but statistics available on the number of Italian-American female workers, and the number of Italians by age, sex, and marital status for the New York metropolitan area, offer rough estimates. If we assume that all single, widowed, and divorced women worked, we can calculate the percentage of married women who would have had to work in order to account for the full numbers of Italian-American women in the work force. Since all single and widowed women obviously did not work, these calculations provide the absolute minimum percentage of married women working in 1950. In the case of the very young adults, aged fourteen to twenty-four, and the older women, aged forty-five and older, there were enough single or widowed women to account for all Italian women in the work force. But for first-generation women aged twenty-five to forty-four, at least 26 percent of the wives were working; among the second generation, at least 18 percent were at work.[29] That more foreign-born than native-born married women were at work should, by now, not be surprising since so-called traditional attitudes about females' working never kept Italian women out of the work force when it was necessary, and foreign-born men were likely to earn less than native born men.

In the New York Jewish community, by contrast, with its greater education and prosperity, so-called traditional gender patterns with respect to work are quite evident. Although the proportion of married and single women was similar among Jews and Italians, there were enough single and widowed Jewish women to account for all the Jewish women in the

[28] Valerie Kincaid Oppenheimer, "Demographic Influence on Female Employment and the Status of Women," *American Journal of Sociology* 78 (1973): 947. On relatively high wages as a draw for married women's work, see Tamara K. Hareven and Maris A. Vinovskis, "Marital Fertility, Ethnicity and Occupations in Urban Families: An Analysis of South Boston and South End in 1880," *Journal of Social History* 8 (Spring 1975): 69–93.

[29] U.S. Department of Commerce, Bureau of the Census, *Census of Population, 1950, Vol. IV, Part 3A: Special Reports, Nativity and Parentage*, p. 284.

New York labor force.[30] The comparison between Italian and Jewish wives suggests that the participation of married women in the work force at midcentury had less to do with traditional ethnic notions about gender than with attitudes and behavior associated with class. Until the modern feminist movement, which took hold in the later 1960s, very few middle-class wives, especially those with children, had jobs. Working-class mothers, such as Italian-Americans in New York, also tried to avoid working outside the home, but after World War II, the need and the demand was such that many, like the very poorest of their ancestors a generation earlier, went out to work.

How much satisfaction Italian wives derived from their paid work varied, as it did for all women at midcentury. It depended on the nature of the job, the interpersonal dynamics of the work, the extent of supervision. Many white-collar jobs were, like factory work, rigidly supervised and subject to speed-ups; in such work settings informal interaction with peers was almost impossible. In others, work schedules were flexible, and women not only socialized on the job, they could swap work hours so that they could do family chores during the work day.[31] Studies of women and work by Susan Porter Benson, Patricia Cooper, and others have shown that even though men and women have dealt with the workplace in different ways, the job experience was an important aspect of their lives for both sexes.[32] But for Italian-American wives at midcentury, whether they worked outside the home or not, domestic responsibilities remained the chief concern. In interviewing Italian Americans in San Francisco, who were contemporaries of the Italians under discussion here, di Leonardo found that although the men spoke in great detail about their employment, the women talked in very general ways about their paid jobs, usually mentioning "factors of ambiance, whether it was an attractive place to work, or

[30] Ibid., p. 283. For a discussion of the decrease in the proportion of Jewish wives who worked as this population prospered, see Charlotte Baum, Paula Hyman, and Sonya Michel, *The Jewish Woman in America* (New York: Dial Press, 1976).

[31] See Garson, *All the Livelong Day*, chap. 3.

[32] Susan Porter Benson, *Counter Cultures: Saleswomen, Managers, and Customers in American Department Stores, 1890–1940* (Urbana: University of Illinois Press, 1986); Patricia Cooper, *Once a Cigarmaker: Men, Women and Work Culture in American Cigar Factories, 1900–1919* (Urbana: University of Illinois Press, 1987). See also Mary Blewett, *Men, Women and Work: Class, Gender and Protest in the New England Shoe Industry, 1780–1910* (Urbana: University of Illinois Press, 1988).

whether it was a friendly place." Women may have been more comfortable talking about family because it conformed with gender expectations, di Leonardo noted, but the greater involvement and "serious" attitude toward issues of kin rather than work reflected the fact that there were few jobs for women that could yield high pay, job security, or even a chance of promotion. The same was true for Italian women in New York.[33]

A detailed look at the decades of married life for the second generation who came of age during and after World War II is beyond the scope of this book, but I will conclude with a few general observations. Married life often meant hardships, conflicts with spouses and children, and sometimes disillusion. A group of middle-aged Italian women in Providence in the 1970s told their interviewers about regrets that they had not finished college, or had chosen poor husbands. As we have seen, Italian-American wives now were often more educated than their blue-collar husbands. On the job women came into contact with middle-class men who supervised them in the office; second-generation women sometimes found it hard to relate to their spouses.[34] Already in 1940 one East Harlem mother worried that if she sent her daughter to school, the daughter might "get funny ideas of looking down on the average young man," but she sent her to high school anyway.[35] Italian women who were middle aged in the 1970s were likely to live farther from their adult children than their parents had. With more free time, many women returned to or continued to work outside the home; they were also active in community and church affairs. During the height of feminist mobilization in the 1970s some Italian women in Brooklyn formed a consciousness-raising group.[36] The middle-aged and older women di Leonardo interviewed in the same years in San Francisco spent most of their time trying to keep families close,

---

[33] di Leonardo, *The Varieties*, p. 199. For a similar analysis of the meaning of work and family for modern working-class women who do factory work, see Sallie Westwood, *All Day, Every Day: Factory and Family in the Making of Women's Lives* (Urbana: University of Illinois Press, 1985).

[34] Strom, "Italian American Women and Their Daughters," p. 19. Although Strom and I come to different conclusions about the attitudes of second-generation Italian women, her paper on first- and second-generation Italians in Providence has helped me enormously in thinking about the differences in the lives of first- and second-generation women.

[35] East Harlem Italian mother quoted in Orsi, *The Madonna of 113th Street*, p. 141.

[36] See Susan Jacoby, "What Do I Do for the Next Twenty Years?" *New York Times Magazine*, 17 June 1973, p. 10.

Mrs. Rose Carrendeno and grandchild, with her niece in the background, Brooklyn, 1943. (Photograph by Gordon Parks, courtesy of the Library of Congress.)

working hard preparing holiday get-togethers; some even promoted marriages, friendships, careers for their children and grandchildren.[37]

Maintaining the burden of family responsibilities, often in conjunction with paid labor, meant that second-generation wives and mothers were still unequal beneficiaries of family strategies; yet they remained committed to familial responsibilities. By and large, these women were in no position to relinquish these obligations. Like the women before them, they were dependent on kin—spouses, and eventually on grown children—to maintain an adequate standard of living. Limited opportunities in the public world reinforced the assumptions of both the men and the women that the latter would carry the burden of family responsibilities.

The situation for the next generation, coming of age in the 1960s and 1970s, was different. Now there were even greater opportunities for daughters as well as sons, and many more attended college. Parents sent daughters to college for the same reason that most white American parents sent their girls—to train for suitable occupations, such as elementary and secondary school teaching, and to find an attractive marriage partner. Some Italians undoubtedly had even higher ambitions for their daughters. Familial responsibilities, though still important to the vast majority, now had to make room for personal aspirations. Modern feminism, committed both to enhancing women's individual aspirations as well as to political and social issues of women as a group, attracted many Italian women growing up in postwar America. College educated and oriented partly toward careers—for some, even beyond traditional female jobs like teaching—third-generation Italian women began reevaluating their positions within the family.[38] By contrast, however, life for most second-generation adult women in 1950 meant enjoying some newfound prosperity, caring for children and home, and coping with the many familial obligations in their lives.

Very important changes in the work and school patterns had occurred for Italian-American women by 1950, all of them linked to social and demographic changes. Unlike her mother, the woman who came of age at midcentury probably had some high school education, had enjoyed a

[37] Di Leonardo, *The Varieties*, p. 213.
[38] See Elizabeth Stone, "It's Still Hard to Grow Up Italian," *New York Times Magazine*, 17 December 1978, p. 42.

freer adolescence, and was likely to do white-collar work at some point in her life. As a mother, she would have had fewer children than women married before the Depression. She therefore had more time to spend on home care, individualized child care, even some leisure as her children grew up. But the occupational and educational changes, however real, were nonetheless limited for the majority of second-generation women. Given the lack of opportunity for them outside the family, adult Italian women in 1950 were still very much enmeshed in the obligations expected of female family members.

CONCLUSION

The social, demographic, and political conditions facing Italian-American women in New York City in the years from 1900 to 1950 defined both the opportunities and the constraints that shaped their lives. This study focuses on two important aspects — work and school — of the everyday life of single Italian girls and women and on the ways the married women balanced paid and unpaid work. In the home and outside it, at work or at school, familial goals prevailed. Modern, individualist values were not the reasons for changes in work and school patterns among first- and second-generation Italian women, yet far-reaching changes occurred.

In southern Italy and New York City, Italian households relied on the contributions of all members. To meet their families' needs, single women often worked outside the home even before coming to New York. Much rhetoric heard within the Italian community and outside insists that a patriarchal tradition proscribed women's work outside the home. But the Italian Americans had to be pragmatic and flexible regarding women's work; thus, the most newly arrived families, those most likely to be influenced by this so-called tradition, sent women to work in greater numbers than the more settled families, precisely because the economic needs of the newly arrived were greatest.

Paid labor itself was not new for southern Italian women living in New York, but first- and second-generation single women who worked in the garment industries during the first three decades of the century encountered new experiences. They made new friendships within the Italian community in a work environment away from the strict supervision of their mothers that was so characteristic of their labor in Italy. But the work experience provided little freedom on the job for Italian women or much leisure time after hours. The nature of the work, the location of the job, its hours and wages, plus familial responsibilities after work meant that women had little opportunity to develop a social life independent of the family or to participate in community and political organizations.

Within the context of their families, however, Italian daughters, contrary to the stereotype, were often quite assertive. Carole Turbin has recently argued about nineteenth-century collar workers in Troy, New York, "while hierarchy is fundamental to male-female relations, just as women in nineteenth century working class families were not always entirely powerless, men, in turn, were not all powerful. Nor were they powerful in the same way in all aspects of their daily life."[1] As for their lack of participation in political activities, my study shows that the concept of patriarchal norms is not very useful for explaining why Italian women were so uninvolved in union activities in the early years of settlement, but then became loyal union members a decade or so later. Comparison of Jewish and Italian women during the clothing strikes of turn-of-the-century New York suggests that the need for Italian factory workers to do paid and unpaid labor in the home meant that there was less time for them, in comparison with Jewish garment workers, to participate in political activities. The more meager resources of Italian households made striking even more difficult. Finally, the general politicization of the Jewish community, where jobs in the garment industry cut across gender within the household, meant that Jewish women participated in unions often in a family context, and as participants in their ethnic community.

Wage work and domestic tasks also dominated the lives of married Italian women during the early decades of settlement. Paid labor outside the home was particularly hard, because wives were expected to combine domestic responsibilities with paid employment. Italian patterns conformed to assumptions about gender roles shared by most white Americans. If husband and children could earn enough money to support the household, the wife did not do paid labor, but instead devoted herself full time to the care of what was usually a very large household. Those mothers who did have to work usually took in garment-finishing work to do at home, or they tended boarders. Nevertheless, when necessary, Ital-

---

[1] Carole Turbin, "Beyond Dichotomies: Interdependence in Mid-Nineteenth Century Working-Class Families in the United States," *Gender and History* 1 (Autumn 1989): 296.

ian wives and mothers, more than any other white ethnic group in New York, went into the garment shops. Whether at home or in a factory, the Italian working mother was overburdened. In order to earn any kind of meaningful income at all, the working women put in extremely long hours. The Italian mother had to rely on her children to help her complete her tasks. Young children were set to work stitching garments or assembling artificial flowers. Italian mothers relied on their older daughters even more heavily; the daughters often not only worked outside the home but helped in domestic tasks as well. Neither mothers nor daughters enjoyed much leisure; they spent most of their days and nights close to home, with their families, at work.

Only in the context of familial need and work opportunities for immigrant women can we understand Italian attitudes about girls' education. In the early decades Italian children, particularly the girls, needed little schooling for the jobs open to them. Daughters who remained at home could assist their mothers in earning extra income and in family domestic chores. Italian families risked little by violating New York school attendance laws. Since the economy of New York City prior to the Great Depression needed an abundance of unskilled workers, and since the schools were not equipped to handle the hundreds of thousands of immigrant children living in New York, city and school officials tended to look the other way when underage children stayed away from school. Sometimes, school officials even encouraged young children to leave the classroom for the labor market.

The structure of the New York economy and the structure of Italian families changed by the end of the 1930s. These developments, by altering family strategies, affected the school patterns and work experience of Italian girls and young women. The survival rate of Italian offspring increased, fertility declined, and the size of the Italian household decreased. Because families were burdened by fewer children, they could more easily sacrifice the labor of the older children to send them to school. By the end of the 1930s it also "cost" parents less, in terms of potential wages, to send their children to school. Thanks to the diligent efforts of the state and federal governments, irregular child labor, which had occupied so many young Italian women in the early years, was virtually eliminated. Finally, by the 1940s the prosperity of the war and postwar years meant that more families would delay their children's entry into the job market.

As the employment structure in New York changed, education took on a positive value for Italian women, to such an extent that the educational achievement of women overtook that of men. This was not because parents abandoned their expectations about the familial responsibilities of either their daughters or their sons. Although Italian families had moved into the ranks of the stable working class by midcentury, families still needed to rely on the earnings of all household members; they still expected sons and daughters to work. As the economy shifted away from manufacturing, however, second-generation Italian women were able to find clerical jobs in New York. More Italian women remained in secondary school to train for these jobs, since clerical work required a high school education. Most Italian men, by contrast, continued to work in the manufacturing sector of the economy. The high school diploma had less value for them; hence, in 1950 the educational achievement of young second-generation men was lower than that of young second-generation women.

Regular attendance at high school, which began during the latter decades of the Depression and continued in the 1940s, was very important to Italian women, most of whom were now of the second generation. Girls no longer had to assist their mothers in homework, and because they did not have to work until they were at least sixteen, or even older, they had more free time as adolescents than their mothers and older female kin before them. They used their high school years for fun as well as for job training. The jobs in the white-collar sector that awaited high school graduates were cleaner and safer than those held by earlier generations; single women workers had more time after work to socialize.

But neither high school attendance nor the experience of white-collar work offered the vast majority of working-class Italian women opportunities to redefine their roles within the family. Expectations that daughters would subsume individual desires to those of the group remained powerful. As wives and mothers at midcentury, Italian women continued the tradition of their mothers, orienting their lives toward the needs of the family. They concentrated on child rearing, housework, and, when necessary, they engaged in paid labor, in an effort to prepare the third generation so that they might succeed, even prosper, in the postindustrial world.

Circumstances of class, ethnicity, and gender all affected the ways Italians used their traditions and coped with change in twentieth-century New York. To the extent that New York City Italians remained largely working class, the benefits of schooling had to be balanced against lost wages if children were to be kept out of the work force. Permitting daughters to surpass sons in the amount of high school education, by midcentury Italian Americans were shifting strategies along with other white working-class families in the United States. At the end of the 1930s and in the early 1940s school officials became aware of the increased proportion of students from many ethnic communities remaining in school. They noted the impact of new labor laws and school attendance regulations as well as the lack of jobs available as a result of the Depression. During the early 1940s, however, many feared that as job opportunities increased, the drop-out rate might increase among the poorer population; by the mid-1940s, however, it was clear that the pattern begun in the Depression was continuing.[2] Increasing prosperity made it possible for more parents to keep children in school. But there was also a change in attitude, a new belief in the value of a high school education. As early as the 1930s observers noted parents' increasing demand for schooling as a result of "a new faith in the efficacy of school," in the words of one 1937 school report.[3]

How to instill a faith in schooling among poor Americans is a much discussed topic today. One of the assumptions pervading the discussion is that in the past, poor parents (many of whom were white ethnics) came to appreciate education because they understood it to be the means by which they could provide their children the opportunity to achieve their full potential. Once the new settlers of the urban North adopted this attitude, they were willing to invest in the future of their children through schooling. And with the investment in schooling came the ability to succeed in America.

The history of changing school patterns for Italians suggests that faith in education might better be understood in the context of the expanding opportunities available to white Americans in the first two-thirds of the twentieth century.[4] Despite the crisis of the Depression, the middle dec-

[2] New York City, Board of Education, *The Thirty-Eighth Annual Report of the Superintendent of Schools of New York for the School Year 1935–36*, part 2 (New York: Board of Education, 1937), p. 2.

[3] New York City, Board of Education, *The Forty-Sixth Annual Report of the Superintendent of Schools for the School Year 1944–45* (New York: Board of Education, 1946), p. 54. *The Thirty-Eighty Annual Report*, p. 89.

[4] For a similar argument see Colin Greer, *The Great School Legend: A Revisionist Interpretation of American Public Education* (New York: Basic Books, 1972), chap. 5.

ades of the twentieth century were a period in which white working-class families could find a niche in the expanding economy. Some groups, like American Jews, were already moving into the ranks of the middle class. For most white ethnics, only a small proportion of the children, usually boys, went to college and became professionals. The majority found security because the sons obtained relatively well-paying blue-collar jobs, and their daughters moved into lower level white-collar jobs, for which high school training was a prerequisite. Italian working-class families understood that education for their children did not guarantee equal opportunity. Italian girls, for one, were not encouraged by the schools to go on to college. For the majority of Italian parents, sending children to high school was therefore not a reflection of individualist aspirations for their offspring, a motive for middle-class families but less meaningful for this community. Once persuaded of the practical connection between schooling and jobs, however, Italians—like Poles, other Slavs, and the Irish, who had long been sending daughters to high school—invested in education for girls so they could train for clerical work.[5]

The reality of increasing opportunity as well as the limits of that opportunity shaped the behavior of Italians and other white ethnic Americans toward schooling. To understand the lack of interest in school on the part of many poor and minorities today, we also need to know how opportunity shapes attitudes. For example, within the black community girls have historically completed more schooling than boys because they have had more opportunities in white-collar jobs, in teaching, then nursing, and more recently in sales and clerical work.[6] But, in the late twentieth century, for both boys and girls, the possibilities for step-by-step mobility among both black girls and boys does not nearly match the opportunities enjoyed by

---

[5] See John K. Folger and Charles Nam, *Education of the American Population* (Washington, D.C.: Government Printing Office, 1962), pp. 144, 145. See also Margery Davies, *Woman's Place Is at the Typewriter: Office Work and Office Workers, 1870–1930* (Philadelphia: Temple University Press, 1982). On the relationship between occupations and schooling for working-class girls and boys, see Harvey Kantor and David B. Tyack, eds., *Work, Youth and Schooling* (Stanford, Calif.: Stanford University Press, 1982). See also Ileen A. DeVault, *Sons and Daughters of Labor: Class and Clerical Work in Turn-of-the-Century Pittsburgh* (Ithaca, N.Y.: Cornell University Press, 1990), chap. 2.

[6] See Jacqueline Jones, *Labor of Love, Labor of Sorrow: Black Women, Work and the Family from Slavery to the Present* (New York: Basic Books, 1985).

white ethnics earlier in the century; hence the continuing lack of faith in education in large segments of the black community.[7]

If class shaped Italian attitudes about work, school, and family responsibility, the particular ethnic experience was also important. We have seen that other groups—New York Jews was the example I used—relied on family strategies to succeed in their new homeland; each ethnic group brought with it different experiences and traditions that helped them cope with the hardships in the Old World. Both Jews and Italians were poor then they arrived in New York, and they coped by depending on kin. When the demand for female employment in the city was greatest, both Italian and Jewish women worked in large numbers. Both groups responded to the expansion of female white-collar work by sending daughters to school. But Jewish financial resources, though meager, were still better than those of Italians. The Jewish stronghold in the garment industry, a carryover of their work patterns in eastern Europe as well as a consequence of their earlier arrival in New York than Italians, contributed to their greater economic stability. Infant mortality and family size decreased among Jews more rapidly, easing some of the strain; perhaps the Jewish community was healthier because older German Jewish networks were already providing medical care to the new immigrants. Their particular economic and demographic circumstances gave Jewish daughters more free time to explore recreation, political activism, even education. Finally, political organizations already active in eastern Europe, which encouraged unionizing in the Jewish community and new public roles for women, were brought to New York's Lower East Side. Jewish women's activism was thus partly based on their ethnic backgrounds, and not simply on their class and gender.

Ethnic identity, a sense of connection with one's ethnic group, involves occupational, political, religious, and recreational ties, as well as a sense of connection with one's past. Such an identity was an important part of the lives of first- and second-generation Italians, and it remained relevant for many in the third generation.[8] The focus on how Italian family strate-

---

[7] On the problems for blacks in terms of the occupational structure of late-twentieth-century America, see William Julius Wilson, *The Truly Disadvantaged: The Inner City, the Underclass, and Public Policy* (Chicago: University of Chicago Press, 1987).

[8] See Micaela di Leonardo, *The Varieties of Ethnic Experience: Kinship, Class and Gender among California Italian-Americans* (Ithaca, N.Y.: Cornell University Press, 1984), esp. chap. 4.

gies both reinforced traditional expectations about female roles and created important changes, however, goes beyond discussions of whether immigrants successfully adapted to America by abandoning Old World, premodern traditions or, as historians have tended to emphasize in the past twenty years, by maintaining cultural traditions.[9] Both continuity and change were integral aspects of the history of Italian women and men over two generations. In coping with social and economic circumstances that confronted them in New York, Italians drew on their capacity for hard work and familialism. They adapted to changing conditions in New York – changes in the availability of jobs for children, the emergence of new types of work for women, increased prosperity in post–World War II America. The result was changed behavior.

The evolution in gender roles among first- and second-generation Italian Americans is one of the best examples of the ways in which both continuity and change played a role in the lives of one group. This book ends as it began, comparing the life of one maker of artificial flowers in 1913 with a graduate of the Julia Richman High School class of 1949. Boys still reaped the benefits in family strategy in the later period. Marie Conti, the secretary-to-be, of the class of 1949, might not have been directly paying for a brother's medical school, as had the flower maker in 1913, but as a high school graduate she might well have been in a family sending boys to college; she could have been supporting herself and contributing to household expenses so that her parents could educate their sons. In 1950 the realities of the sex-segregated occupational structure reinforced prevalent norms, that sons, rather than daughters, ought to prepare for professions.[10]

The early postwar years found Italian daughters preparing for marriage and Italian wives busy with child care, domestic tasks, and, to some extent, wage work. It would be another generation before large numbers of Italian women would be educated as teachers, social workers, or doctors and lawyers. Italian women's continuing focus on the familial had political implications for the women's movement as it evolved in the 1960s.

[9] For another critique of the debate over continuity and change, see Dino Cinel, *From Italy to San Francisco: The Immigrant Experience* (Stanford, Calif.: Stanford University Press, 1982), chap. 10.

[10] The way the advantages of investing in sons continues to reinforce traditional assumptions about proper roles for women is discussed in Amartya Sen, "Economics and the Family," *Asian Development Review* 1 (1983): 14–26.

Twentieth-century feminism has expressed a commitment to the individual aspirations of women as well as a sense of solidarity among women.[11] To the extent that feminism appealed to women in positions to consider the possibility of some autonomy from the family, feminism had a much more immediate appeal for more prosperous women in postwar society— for American Jews, for example—than it did for women in communities like the Italian American in New York City.

Feminism was by no means inherently antithetical to the concerns of working-class women. In the early decades of the century organizations such as the Women's Trade Union League or the Women's Union Card and Label League boasted a feminism that combined an interest in individual rights for women, gender rights, and class issues; for activists organizing ethnic working-class women, familial issues were also important.[12] But, as Maurine Greenwald has pointed out, the partnering of gender and class solidarity, which set working-class feminism apart from middle-class feminism, called for a reorganizing of the social order, a challenge to the marketplace. While something of a force at the turn of the century, this type of feminism declined significantly among activists after World War I.[13] Efforts to combine trade union militancy with feminist issues emerged again only after the latter-day feminist movement was well underway.[14] By the late 1970s the women's movement addressed is-

[11] Nancy Cott, *The Grounding of Modern Feminism* (New Haven: Yale University Press, 1987), chap. 1.

[12] See Nancy Schrom Dye, *As Equals and as Sisters: Feminism, the Labor Movement and the Women's Trade Union League of New York* (Columbia: University of Missouri Press, 1980); Maurine Weiner Greenwald, "Working Class Feminism and the Family Wage Ideal: The Seattle Debate on Married Women's Right to Work, 1914–1920," *Journal of American History* 76 (June 1989): 118–49.

[13] Greenwald, "Working Class Feminism," p. 148.

[14] In the middle decades of the century the efforts to unite working-class issues and feminism were difficult for several reasons; one was the general decline in social reform in the early post–World War I years. By the 1930s, of course, women's involvement in social reform had resumed, but those activists close to trade unions were in deep conflict with those who identified themselves as equal-rights feminists. As members of the National Woman's Party, they tended to be early advocates of the Equal Rights Amendment, which until the 1970s was opposed by both women social reformers and labor reformers because it threatened gender-specific protective legislation. There are many discussions of this history. See, for example, Nancy Cott, *The Grounding*, and William Chafe, *The American Woman: Her Changing Social, Economic, and Political Roles, 1920–30* (New York: Oxford University Press, 1972).

sues of pay equity, job discrimination, and redistribution of household chores, which could appeal to Italian-American women working in low-level white-collar jobs, including many who were married. The movement also attracted many third-generation females concerned about such issues as equal opportunity, sexuality, and reproductive rights. But in 1950 the opportunities and constraints that confronted Italian women reinforced expectations about the proper roles for men and women; as in most American families, Italian men remained the "chief" breadwinners, and Italian women had to fit their work and leisure activities around family tasks.

The continuity apparent over the fifty years should not obscure the significant changes for Italian-American women that took place over two generations. In 1913 the flower maker spent her entire adolescence working night and day to send her brother to school; she reaped the benefits of her sweated labor only vicariously. Marie Conti spent her teen years in the 1940s enjoying recreational activities and preparing for her own career as a secretary. The shift in a matter of decades suggests that behavior with respect to gender roles is malleable; such behavior changes, and will continue to change, as opportunities for women change. Such a recognition has relevance beyond our understanding of one group of immigrant women from the past.

In the 1980s the U.S. Equal Employment Opportunity Commission charged in federal court that Sears, Roebuck and Company had systematically underemployed women in their most lucrative commission sales jobs. In justifying its placing few women in commission sales, Sears argued that women were largely uninterested in such jobs, which were highly competitive, risky, and often involved selling male-oriented products. Among the strategies Sears used to prove its argument was historical evidence—that women's familial, domestic values had always made them reluctant to take on male occupations.[15] The history of Italian women in New York shows the extent to which state action and changes in employer behavior can change female work and school patterns. Local and federal governments decided in the New Deal years to eliminate irregular sweated labor and the employment of young adolescents, not only as a

---

[15] See Alice Kessler-Harris, "Equal Opportunity Employment Commission v. Sears, Roebuck and Company: A Personal Account," *Radical History Review* 35 (1986): 57–79.

strategy to pull the economy out of Depression but also in response to the pressure of strong trade unions. In doing so, they enacted laws that were upheld by the courts and duly enforced by state and local officials. Poor families could no longer rely on these irregular jobs, which had so often been the source of employment for girls. State action was thus to alter significantly the ways many girls spent their youth and adolescence. Furthermore, when American businesses in New York began systematically to hire ethnic women for white-collar jobs, Italians and others responded accordingly; families changed their assumptions about the value of female education. Parents' aspirations for their children and women's aspirations for themselves as well as their behavior are conditioned by perceptions of available opportunity, as Alice Kessler-Harris has reminded us.[16] Italian women long oriented their lives toward domestic concerns and subsumed their personal wishes to familial needs. However, like ethnic values, women's values are "rooted in experience and [are] continually modified and altered as circumstances made it possible to do so."[17]

From 1900 to 1950 family strategies determined much about the ways Italian-American females spent their time. To a large degree parents controlled what their children, especially the girls, did. But continuity in strategies did not mean that Italian women in New York City were bound by an inflexible code of female behavior. Tough and assertive, in the early years they "did whatever needed to be done," in the words of one southern Italian peasant woman. When better opportunities appeared in later years, women seized them. Italian women and their families in New York thus exemplify the ways ordinary people can be constrained by the circumstances confronting them and yet still act as agents of social change.

[16] Ibid., p. 71.
[17] Ibid., p. 72.

SAMPLE SELECTION, NEW YORK STATE MANUSCRIPT CENSUS 1905 AND 1925

Samples were drawn from blocks consisting of eight and a half square city blocks, as recorded by an enumerator's walk. These blocks were divided among three large Italian neighborhoods in Manhattan. The 5-percent sample yielded approximately one thousand households for each year.

Two settlements were located in downtown Manhattan, below Fourteenth Street and west of Broadway, the area where the majority of southern Italians settled. One of these settlements was just below Canal Street and was bounded by Mulberry, Mott, Bayard, and Canal streets as one square block; the adjacent square block, bounded by Mulberry, Bayard, Baxter, and Canal streets, was also sampled. Above Canal Street, in the heart of the largest and most famous Little Italy in New York, the following contiguous square blocks were sampled: those bounded by Mott, Prince, Elizabeth and Spring streets, by Mott, Prince, Mulberry, and Spring streets, and by Mott, Prince, Elizabeth, and East Houston streets. In this group of blocks both sides of Elizabeth Street were included. The third area sampled was in the heart of the East Harlem Italian neighborhood, uptown, on the Far East Side. The three contiguous square blocks sampled were bounded by 112th and 115th streets and First and Second avenues.

These three neighborhoods were sampled for both 1905 and 1925 on the basis of the following criteria:

1. The neighborhoods were known to be dominated by southern Italians, from Calabria, Basilicata, and from Sicily. (The smaller number of

northern Italians tended to settle in the west end of lower Greenwich Village, around Thompson, Jones, and Sullivan streets.)

2. The blocks sampled were chosen because they were areas for which other social survey material were available. Thus, the square blocks sampled in the heart of Little Italy contained a long stretch of Elizabeth Street, which the U.S. Immigration Commission surveyed for its study, *Immigrants in Cities*. The East Harlem area also contained the other Italian block survey by the Immigration Commission for the report. The information provided in the survey adds to our knowledge of the families and serves as a check for the reliability of the census data.

3. Finally, there was a concern that the sample not contain an overwhelming proportion of families from the poorest, most densely populated areas. Preliminary calculations were done to confirm that the East Harlem area tended to attract slightly more prosperous families. My own calculations and those of Thomas Kessner indicate that the occupational status of male family heads, as a group, was higher than in the downtown areas.[1] I attempted to equalize the number of families from the downtown neighborhoods and from East Harlem. The number of blocks chosen in each area was calculated so that a 5-percent sample of households in East Harlem would amount to approximately the same number of households sampled in the downtown areas. A 5-percent sample in the downtown areas yielded 420 families in 1905; in East Harlem the number was 465. In 1925 the population in the downtown areas decreased, and thus there was a greater imbalance, with approximately 272 families from downtown sampled, compared with 382 families in East Harlem, but such an imbalance approximates the actual conditions in the Italian community as a whole by 1925.

To test whether or not different ethnic backgrounds were good predictors for women's work patterns, I drew another sample in an area populated by both Jews and Italians. I selected one or two blocks populated by both groups in hopes that I could find households with similar economic characteristics. Such an area was extremely difficult to find because most blocks were heavily dominated, if not exclusively populated, by one or the other immigrant group. Moreover, a block that may have been ethni-

[1] See Thomas Kessner, *The Golden Door: Italian and Jewish Immigrant Mobility in New York City, 1880–1915* (New York: Oxford University Press, 1977), p. 183.

cally mixed in 1905 was almost certainly in a transitional stage, soon to be dominated by one group in 1925. Only one square block proved to be at all satisfactory: that bounded by Stanton, Forsyth, E. Houston, and Eldridge streets in Manhattan's Lower East Side. For the comparison of Italians and Jews on the Lower East Side, I used a 1-percent sample of Jews for 1905 and a 2-percent sample of Italians.

The sample drawn in all areas was of the households of 5 percent of the people found in these blocks, rather than 5 percent of the households. This was done so that individuals in small households would have no greater chance of being included than persons in large households.

Information was gathered for everyone in the household. Unless otherwise indicated, the information recorded is based on the analysis of primary nuclear families. A *nuclear family* consists of a married couple, a married couple with offspring, or a widowed person with offspring. Hence, a married child living with a spouse and one or more parents is in two nuclear families. A *primary nuclear family* is the married couple that includes the household head and their offspring, or a widowed person with offspring if the widowed person is designated the household head. A *secondary nuclear family* is another family living in the same household with the primary family.

The codebook used was a variation of the codebooks designed by Louise Tilly and Leslie P. Moch for their studies of nineteenth-century European families. I am particularly grateful to Charles Tilly for the enormous amount of time and effort in helping me to devise a sampling procedure.

A P P E N D I X B

OCCUPATIONAL CATEGORIES

The occupational designations used for this analysis are a slightly modified version of the rankings used by Louise Tilly for her study of women's
work in nineteenth-century England and France. Each individual occupation was recorded and given a separate number. Each occupation was
given a sector number, representing the sector of the economy in which
the individual was employed. Finally, each occupation was given a status
number, representing a rank ordering of jobs.

The full titles of the occupational statuses are as follows, with the highest ranking listed first:

High professional, owner-entrepreneurs, high commercial, high indus-
   trial, rentiers
Subprofessional, submanagerials
Shopkeepers and small industrials
Employees and clericals
Skilled laborers
Semi-skilled laborers
Unskilled laborers

In several calculations the categories of high professional et al. and
subprofessional et al. were combined.

APPENDIX C

HOUSEHOLDS IN THE
MEN'S GARMENT INDUSTRY,
1910

Household data on 606 single women and 107 children was gathered by
the U.S. Bureau of Labor for its report on the men's garment industry.
The women and children were selected on the basis of payroll lists in the
men's garment industry in New York. Some households selected contained more than one employed child or woman; therefore, the number of
single women and children selected for investigation exceeded the number of households. Analysis was also done on the mothers in those households, comparing those who were employed in paid labor with those who
were not. The women and children investigated represented 10 percent of
the females employed in 88 men's garment shops surveyed by the bureau.
(See U.S. Congress, Senate, Bureau of Labor, *Report on Condition of
Woman and Child Wage Earners*, vol. 2: *Men's Ready-Made Clothing*, S.
Doc. 645, 61st Cong., 2d sess. [Washington, D.C.: Government Printing
Office, 1911], pp. 715, 716, 750, 751.)

Household data on 549 married women working in New York City was
also gathered by the U.S. Bureau of Labor in 1909 and 1910. The married
women were selected on the basis of payroll lists in the men's clothing
industry in New York. All families selected had at least one child or
female adult working for the men's clothing shop. The number of females
and children investigated represented 10 percent of the women and children employed in 88 garment shops in New York. (See *Report on Condition of Woman and Child Wage Earners*, vol. 2: *Men's Ready-Made
Clothing*, pp. 832–34, 852–53.)

SELECTED BIBLIOGRAPHY

Archives

Amalgamated Clothing Workers of America Archives. Amalgamated Clothing Workers of America Headquarters, New York City. Now at the New York State School of Industrial and Labor Relations, Cornell University, Ithaca, New York.

Julia Richman High School. *Spotlight.* 1944 and 1949. Julia Richman Library Archives, New York City.

New York State. Manuscript Census, 1905, 1925. New York County Clerk's Office, New York City.

Russell Sage Collection. Cohen Library. City College of New York.

Works Progress Administration. Historical Records Survey. Municipal Archives, New York City.

Federal Documents

U.S. Bureau of Labor Statistics. *Wages and Hours of Labor in the Men's Clothing Industry, 1911–1930.* Bureau of Labor Statistics Special Bulletin no. 557. Washington, D.C.: Government Printing Office, 1932.

U.S. Congress. Senate. *Report on Condition of Woman and Child Wage Earners,* vol. 2: *Men's Ready-Made Clothing.* S. Doc. 645, 61st Cong., 2d sess. Washington, D.C.: Government Printing Office, 1911.

——. *Reports of the Immigration Commission,* vol. 3: *Statistical Review of Immigration, 1819–1920 — Distribution of Immigrants, 1850–1900.* S. Doc. 756, 61st Cong., 3d sess. Washington, D.C.: Government Printing Office, 1911.

——. *Reports of the Immigration Commission*, vol. 11: *Immigrants in Industries, Part 6: Clothing Manufacturing*. S. Doc. 633, 61st Cong., 2d sess. Washington, D.C.: Government Printing Office, 1911.

——. *Reports of the Immigration Commission*, vol. 26: *Immigrants in Cities*, vols. 1 and 2. S. Doc. 338, 61st Cong., 2d sess. Washington, D.C.: Government Printing Office, 1911.

——. *Reports of the Immigration Commission*, vol. 30: *The Children of Immigrants in Schools*, vol. 4. S. Doc. 5874, 61st Cong., 2d sess. Washington, D.C.: Government Printing Office, 1911.

U.S. Department of Commerce. Bureau of the Census. *Census of Population, 1940: Differential Fertility, 1940 and 1910*. Washington, D.C.: Government Printing Office, 1942.

——. *Census of Population, 1950, Vol. II: Characteristics of the Population, Part 32: New York State*. Washington, D.C.: Government Printing Office, 1952.

——. *Census of Population, 1950, Vol. IV, Part 3A: Special Reports, Nativity and Parentage*. Washington, D.C.: Government Printing Office, 1954.

——. *Fifteenth Census of the United States, 1930: Special Report on Foreign-Born White Families*. Washington, D.C.: Government Printing Office, 1933.

——. *Women in Gainful Occupations, 1870–1920*, by Joseph A. Hill. Census Monographs no. 9. Washington, D.C.: Government Printing Office, 1929.

U.S. Department of the Interior. Office of Education. *Compulsory School Attendance Laws and Their Administration*. Bulletin no. 4. Washington, D.C.: Government Printing Office, 1935.

State and Local Documents

New York State. Department of Labor. *Annual Report of the Industrial Commission, 1918*. Albany, N.Y., 1919.

——. *Annual Report of the Industrial Commission, 1919*. Albany, N.Y., 1920.

——. *The Earnings of Women in Five Industries*. New York State Department of Labor Special Bulletin no. 121. Albany, N.Y., 1923.

——. *The Health of the Working Child*. New York State Department of Labor Special Bulletin no. 134. Albany, N.Y., 1924.

——. *Homework in the Artificial Flower and Feather Industry*, in *New York State*, Part II, New York State Department of Labor Special Bulletin no. 199. Albany, N.Y., 1938.

——. *Homework in the Men's Clothing Industry in New York and Rochester*. New York State Department of Labor Special Bulletin no. 147. Albany, N.Y., 1926.

——. *The Trend of Child Labor in New York State*. New York State Department of Labor Special Bulletin no. 122. Albany, N.Y., 1923.

——. *The Trend of Child Labor in New York State, Supplementary Report for 1923*. New York State Department of Labor Special Bulletin no. 132. Albany, N.Y., 1924.

——. *The Trend of Employment in New York State from 1914–1929.* New York State Department of Labor Special Bulletin no. 206. Albany, N.Y., 1930.

——. *Women Who Work.* New York State Department of Labor Special Bulletin no. 110. Albany, N.Y., 1922.

New York State. Factory Investigating Commission. *Fourth Report of the Factory Investigating Commission*, vol. 4. Albany, N.Y.: J. B. Lyon, 1915.

——. *Preliminary Report of the New York State Factory Investigating Commission*, vol. 1. Albany, N.Y.: J. B. Lyon, 1912.

——. *Public Hearings in New York City, Second Series.* Reprint from the *Preliminary Report of the New York State Factory Investigating Commission.* Albany, N.Y.: J. B. Lyon, October, 1912.

——. *Second Report of the Factory Investigating Commission*, vol. 3. Albany, N.Y.: J. B. Lyon, 1913.

——. *Third Report of the Factory Investigating Commission*, Albany, N.Y.: J. B. Lyon, 1914.

New York City. Board of Education. *Thirty-Seventh Annual Report of the City Superintendent of Schools for the School Year 1934–35.* New York: Board of Education, 1936.

——. *The Thirty-Eighth Annual Report of the Superintendent of Schools of New York for the School Year 1935–36*, part 2. New York: Board of Education, 1937.

——. *The Forty-Sixth Annual Report of the Superintendent of Schools for the School Year 1944–45.* New York: Board of Education, 1946.

——. *Youth in School and Industry: The Continuation Schools and Their Problems*, Special Report Submitted with the 36th Annual Report of the Superintendent of Schools. New York: Board of Education, 1934.

New York City. Committee on Neighborhood Health Development. *New York City Handbook: Statistical Reference Data, Five Year Period of 1929–1933*, comp. by Godias J. Drolet, Marguerite P. Potter, Kenneth O. Widener. New York: Committee on Neighborhood Health Development, 1935.

——. *Statistical Reference Data, Ten Year Period, 1930–1940*, compiled by Margorie Bellows, Godias J. Drolet, and Harry Groble. 4th ed. New York: Department of Health, 1944.

——. *A Survey of Child Health Facilities and Recommendations to the Department of Health for the Development of a More Adequate Service.* New York: Department of Health, Child Health Care Services, September 1938.

——. *Vital Statistics on the Development of the Neighborhood Health Centers in New York City*, by Godias J. Drolet and Louis Weiner. New York: Department of Health, 1932.

New York City. Department of Education. *Elementary Schools of the City of New York, Their Problems and the Efforts Being Made to Solve These Problems.* Part of the *Annual Reports to the Superintendent of Schools for the School Year 1933–34.* New York: Department of Education, 1934.

——. *First Annual Report of the Director of Attendance for the Year ending July*

31, 1915. New York: Department of Education, 1916.

——. *Fourteenth Annual Report of the City Superintendent of Schools.* New York: Department of Education, 1912.

——. Division of Reference and Research. *The School and the Immigrant.* Publication no. 11. New York: Department of Education of the City of New York, 1915.

New York City. Department of Health. *Analysis of Mortality Returns,* by William H. Guilfry, M.D., Shirley Wynne, M.D. New York: Department of Health, 1915.

——. *Influence of Nationality upon the Mortality of a Community with Special References to the City of New York,* by William Guilfry, M.D. New York City Department of Health Monograph Series no. 18. New York, November 1917.

New York City. Neighborhood Health Development, Inc. "Health Planning for the Future through District Health Center Development." John L. Rice M.D., Commissioner of Health. New York, 1939.

New York City. Welfare and Health Council of New York. Research Bureau. *Characteristics of the Population by Health Areas, New York City, 1950,* part 1. New York: Research Bureau, 1953.

Wilson, Randolph C. *Office Work as an Occupation.* New York: Board of Education of the City of New York and Federal Works Progress Administration for the City of New York, 1940.

Charity and Private Reports

Alesandre, John J. *Occupational Trends of Italians in New York City.* Casa Italiana Educational Bureau, Bulletin no. 6. New York: Columbia University, 1935.

Ayres, Leonard. *Laggards in Our Schools.* New York: Russell Sage Foundation, 1909.

Berry, Gwendolyn H. *Idleness and the Health of a Neighborhood.* New York: New York Association for Improving the Condition of the Poor, 1933.

Best, Harry. *The Men's Garment Industry in New York and the Strike of 1913.* University Settlement Studies. New York: University Settlement Society, 1914.

Betts, Lillian. "The Italians in New York." *University Settlement Studies* 1 (October 1905–January 1906): 90–105.

Bovee, Dorothy L., and Jean Downes. "The Influence of Nutrition Education on Families of the Mulberry Area of New York." *Milbank Memorial Fund Quarterly* 19 (1941): 121–46.

Brandt, Lillian. "A Transplanted Birthright." *Charities* 12 (1904): 494–99.

Chapin, Robert Coit. *The Standard of Living among Workingmen's Families in New York City.* New York: Russell Sage Foundation, 1909.

Durand, Kelly, and Louis Sessa. "The Italian Invasion of the Ghetto." New York: n.p. [1909?]. Reprint in the New York Public Library.

East Harlem Health Center. *A Decade of District Health Center Pioneering*. New York: East Harlem Health Center, 1932.

———. *Why East Harlem Needs Health Service*. New York: East Harlem Health Center, 1924.

Fred J. Lavenberg Foundation, Hamilton House. "What happened to 236 families who were compelled to vacate their dwellings for a large housing project." New York, 1933. [Reprint in the New York City Public Library Collection.]

Gebhardt, John J. *The Health of a Neighborhood: A Social Study of the Mulberry District*. New York: New York Association for Improving the Condition of the Poor, 1924.

Gillett, Lucy. *Adapting Nutrition Work to a Community*. New York: New York Association for Improving the Condition of the Poor, 1923.

Greenwich House. *Annual Reports* [title varies]. N.p.: n.p., 1900–1935. [In the Russell Sage Collection, Cohen Library, City College of New York.]

Harlem House. *Annual Reports* [title varies]. N.p.: n.p. 1912–1941. [Named Home Garden of NewYork City Settlement until 1915.]

Irwin, Elisabeth. *Truancy: A Study of the Mental, Physical, and Social Factors of the Problem of Non-Attendance at School*. New York: Public Education Association of the City of New York, 1910.

Johnson, Harriet M. "The Visiting Teacher in New York City." New York: Public Education Association, 1916.

Joint Board of Sanitary Control in the Cloak, Suit and Skirt Industries. *Tenth Annual Report*. New York: n.p., 1911.

Joint Board of Sanitary Control in the Cloak, Suit, Skirt, Dress and Waist Industries. *Monthly Bulletin* 1 (October 1919): 7–8.

Laidlaw, Walter. *Statistical Sources for the Demographic Study of Greater New York, 1920*. New York: New York City 1920 Census Committee, 1922.

Odencrantz, Louise C. *Italian Women in Industry*. New York: Russell Sage Foundation, 1919.

Personnel Research Federation. *Occupational Trends in New York City: Changes in the Distribution of Gainful Workers, 1900–1930*. New York: National Occupational Conference, 1933.

Roche, Josephine. "The Italian Girl." In *The Neglected Girl*. West Side Studies. New York: Russell Sage Foundation, Survey Associates, 1914.

Speranza, Gino. "The Italians in Congested Districts." *Charities and the Commons* 20 (April 1908): 55–57.

Teper, Lazar, and Nathan Weinberg. "Aspects of Industrial Homework in Apparel Trades." International Ladies Garment Workers Union Research Paper. July 1941.

Van Kleeck, Mary. *Artificial Flower Makers*. New York: Russell Sage Foundation, Survey Associates, 1913.

——. "Child Labor in New York City Tenements." *Charities and the Commons* 19 (18 January 1908): 1–16.

——. *Working Girls in Evening Schools*. New York: Russell Sage Foundation, Survey Associates, 1914.

Zimand, Savel. "District Health Administration in New York City." In *District Health Administration: A Study of Organization and Planning*, edited by Ira Hiscock, p. 41. New York: Milbank Memorial Fund, 1936.

Books and Articles

Anderson, Michael. *Family Structure in Nineteenth Century Lancashire*. Cambridge: Cambridge University Press, 1971.

Banfield, Edward. *The Moral Basis of a Backward Society*. Glencoe, Ill.: Free Press, 1958.

Barton, Josef. *Peasants and Strangers: Italians, Rumanians, and Slovaks in an American City, 1890–1950*. Cambridge: Harvard University Press, 1975.

Baum, Charlotte, Paula Hyman, and Sonya Michel. *The Jewish Woman in America*. New York: Dial Press, 1976.

Becker, Gary. "A Theory of the Allocation of Time." *Economic Journal* 75 (September 1965): 493–517.

Bell, Rudolf. "Emigration from Four Italian Villages: Strategy and Decision." In *The Urban Experience of Italian-Americans*, ed. Pat Gallo, pp. 9–35. Staten Island, N.Y.: American Italian Historical Association, 1977.

——. *Fate and Honor, Family and Village*. Chicago: University of Chicago Press, 1979.

Benson, Susan. *Counter Cultures: Saleswomen, Managers, and Customers in American Department Stores, 1890–1940*. Urbana: University of Illinois Press, 1986.

Bernstein, Irving. *The Lean Years*. Boston: Houghton Mifflin, 1960.

Blok, Anton. *The Mafia of a Sicilian Village, 1860–1960*. New York: Harper and Row, 1975.

Bodnar, John. "Immigration and Modernization: The Case of Slavic Peasants in Industrial America." *Journal of Social History* 10 (Fall 1976): 47–71.

——. "Immigration, Kinship and the Rise of Working Class Realism in Industrial America." *Journal of Social History* 14 (Fall 1980): 45–65.

——. "Materialism and Morality: Slavic-American Immigrants and Education, 1890–1940." *Journal of Ethnic Studies* 3 (Winter 1976): 1–19.

——. *The Transplanted: A History of Immigration in Urban America*. Bloomington: Indiana University Press, 1985.

Boris, Eileen, and Cynthia Daniels, eds. *Homework: Historical and Contemporary Perspectives on Paid Labor at Home*. Urbana: University of Illinois Press, 1987.

Bott, Elizabeth. *Family and Social Networks: Roles, Norms, and External Relationships in Ordinary Urban Families*. London: Tavistock, 1957.

Bowles, Samuel, and Herbert Gintis. *Schooling in Capitalist America*. New York: Basic Books, 1976.

Briggs, John. "Fertility and Cultural Change among Families in Italy and America." *American Historical Review* 91 (December 1986): 1129–45.

——. *An Italian Passage: Immigrants to Three American Cities, 1890–1930*. New Haven: Yale University Press, 1978.

Cades, Hazel. *Jobs for Girls*. New York: Harcourt Brace, 1930.

Callahan, Raymond. *Education and the Cult of Efficiency*. Chicago: University of Chicago Press, 1962.

Cameron, Ardis. "Women's Culture and Working-Class Activism." In Ruth Milkman, ed., *Women, Work and Protest: A Century of U.S. Women's Labor History*. Boston: Routledge and Kegan Paul, 1985.

Campisi, Paul. "Ethnic Family Patterns: The Italian Family in the United States." *American Journal of Sociology* 53 (May 1948): 443–47.

Caroli, Betty Boyd. *Italian Repatriation from the United States, 1900–1914*. New York: Center for Migration Studies, 1973.

Chafe, William. *The American Woman: Her Changing Social, Economic, and Political Roles, 1920–1930*. New York: Oxford University Press, 1972.

Chapman, Charlotte Gower. *Milocca: A Sicilian Village*. London: Schenkman, 1971.

Child, Irwin. *Italian or American? The Second Generation in Conflict*. New Haven: Yale University Press, 1943.

Cinel, Dino. *From Italy to San Francisco: The Immigrant Experience*. Stanford, Calif.: Stanford University Press, 1982.

Cohen, Miriam. "Changing Education Strategies among Immigrant Generations: New York Italians in Comparative Perspective." *Journal of Social History* 15 (Spring 1982): 443–66.

——. "Italian American Women in New York City, 1900–1950: Work and School." In *Class, Sex and the Woman Worker*, ed. Milton Cantor and Bruce Laurie, pp. 120–43. Westport, Conn.: Greenwood Press, 1977.

Cohen, Miriam, and Michael P. Hanagan. "The Politics of Gender and the Making of the Welfare State in England, France and the United States." *Journal of Social History* 24 (Spring 1991): 469–84.

Cooper, Patricia. *Once a Cigarmaker: Men, Women and Work Culture in American Cigar Factories, 1900–1919*. Urbana: University of Illinois Press, 1987.

Cordasco, Francesco, ed. *Italians in the City: Health and Related Social Problems*. New York: Arno Press, 1975.

Cordasco, Francesco, and Eugene Buccioni. *The Italians: Social Background of an American Group*. Clifton, N.J.: Augustus M. Kelley, 1974.

Cornelisen, Ann. *Women of the Shadows: The Wives and Mothers of Southern Italy*. New York: Vintage Books, 1976.

Cott, Nancy F. *The Grounding of Modern Feminism*. New Haven: Yale University Press, 1987.

Covello, Leonard. *The Heart Is the Teacher*. New York: McGraw-Hill, 1958.
——. *The Social Background of the Italo-American School Child*. Totowa, N.J.: Rowman and Littlefield, 1972 [Ph.D. diss., 1944].

Cremin, Laurence. *The Transformation of the School: Progressivism in American Education, 1876–1957*. New York: Alfred Knopf, 1961.

Cronin, Constance. *The Sting of Change: Sicilians in Italy and Australia*. Chicago: University of Chicago Press, 1970.

Daniels, Harriet. *The Girl and Her Chance: A Study of the Conditions Surrounding the Young Girl Between Fourteen and Eighteen Years in New York City*. New York: Fleming H. Revell, 1914.

Davies, Margery. *Woman's Place Is at the Typewriter: Office Work and Office Workers, 1870–1930*. Philadelphia: Temple University Press, 1982.

Davis, J. K. *Land and Family in Pisticci*. New York: Humanities Press, 1973.

De Conde, Alex. *Half Bitter, Half Sweet: An Excursion into Italian-American History*. New York: Charles Scribners' Sons, 1971.

Demarco, Domenico. *La Calabria: Economia e Societa*. Naples: Edizione Scientifiche Italiane, 1966.

DeVault, Ileen A. *Sons and Daughters of Labor: Class and Clerical Work in Turn-of-the-Century Pittsburgh*. Ithaca, N.Y.: Cornell University Press, 1990.

DiDonato, Pietro. *Christ in Concrete*. New York: Bobbs-Merrill, 1937.

di Leonardo, Micaela. *The Varieties of Ethnic Experience: Kinship, Class and Gender among California Italian-Americans*. Ithaca, N.Y.: Cornell University Press, 1984.

Diner, Hasia. *Erin's Daughters in America*. Baltimore, Md.: Johns Hopkins University Press, 1983.

Dore, Grazia. *La Democrazia Italiana et L'emigrazione in America*. Brescia: Morcelliana, 1964.

Douglass, William. "The South Italian Family: A Critique." *Journal of Family History* 5 (Winter 1980): 338–59.

Draschler, Julius. *A Statistical Study of the Amalgamation of European Peoples*. New York: Columbia University, 1921.

Dublin, Thomas. *Women and Work: The Transformation of Work and Community in Lowell, Massachusetts, 1826–1860*. New York: Columbia University Press, 1979.

DuBois, Ellen, Mary Jo Buhle, Temma Kaplan, Gerda Lerner, and Carroll Smith-Rosenberg. "Politics and Culture in Women's History: A Symposium." *Feminist Studies* 6 (Spring 1980): 28–64.

Dubovsky, Melvyn. *When Workers Organize: New York City in the Progressive Era*. Amherst: University of Massachusetts Press, 1968.

Dye, Nancy Schrom. *As Equals and as Sisters: Feminism, the Labor Movement and the Women's Trade Union League of New York*. Columbia: University of Missouri Press, 1980.

Easterlin, Richard. "An Economic Framework for Fertility Analysis." *Studies in Family Planning* 6 (1975): 54–63.

Eisenstadt, S. N. *The Adaptation of Immigrants*. London: Routledge and Kegan Paul, 1954.

Ets, Marie Hall. *Rosa, the Life of an Italian Immigrant*. Minneapolis: University of Minnesota Press, 1970.

Ewen, Elizabeth. *Immigrant Women in the Land of Dollars: Life and Culture on the Lower East Side, 1890–1925*. New York: Monthly Review Press, 1985.

Fass, Paula S. *Outside In: Minorities and the Transformation of American Education*. New York: Oxford University Press, 1989.

Felt, Jeremy. *Hostages of Fortune: Child Labor Reform in New York State*. Syracuse, N.Y.: Syracuse University Press, 1965.

Fenton, Edwin. *Immigrants and Unions: A Case Study, Italians and American Labor, 1870–1920*. 1957; reprint, New York: Arno Press, 1975.

Foerster, Robert. *The Italian Emigration of Our Times*. Cambridge: Harvard University Press, 1919.

Fox-Genovese, Elizabeth. *Feminism without Illusions: A Critique of Individualism*. Chapel Hill: University of North Carolina Press, 1991.

Franchetti, Leopoldo, and Sidney Sonnino. *La Sicilia nel 1876*, vol. 2: *I Contadini*. Florence: Vallecchi Editore, 1921.

Fried, Marc. *World of the Urban Working Class*. Cambridge: Harvard University Press, 1973.

Friedl, Ernestine. "The Position of Women: Appearance and Reality." *Anthropological Quarterly* 40 (1967): 93–108.

Furstenberg, Frank, John Modell, and Douglas Strong. "The Timing of Marriage in the Transition to Adulthood: Continuity and Change, 1860–1975." In *Turning Points: Historical and Sociological Essays on the Family*, ed. John Demos and Sarane Spence Boocock, pp. S120–50. Chicago: University of Chicago Press, 1978.

Gabaccia, Donna. *From Sicily to Elizabeth Street: Housing and Social Change among Italian Immigrants, 1880–1930*. Albany: State University of New York Press, 1984.

——. "Immigrant Women: Nowhere at Home?" *Journal of American Ethnic History* 10 (Summer 1991): 61–87.

Gambino, Richard. *Blood of My Blood*. Garden City, N.Y.: Doubleday, 1974.

Gans, Herbert. *The Urban Villagers: Group and Class in the Life of Italian-Americans*. New York: Free Press, 1965.

Garson, Barbara. *All the Livelong Day: The Meaning and Demeaning of Routine Work*. New York: Doubleday, 1975.

Glasco, Laurence. "Life Cycles of American Ethnic Groups: Irish, Germans and Native-born Whites in Buffalo, 1865." *Journal of Urban History* 1 (May 1975): 339–64.

Glazer, Nathan, and Daniel P. Moynihan. *Beyond the Melting Pot: The Negroes, Puerto Ricans, Jews, Italians, and Irish of New York City*. 2nd ed. Cambridge, Mass.: M.I.T. Press, 1970.

Glenn, Susan. *Daughters of the Shtetl: Life and Labor in the Immigrant Genera-tion*. Ithaca, N.Y.: Cornell Univrsity Press, 1990.

Golab, Caroline. *Immigrant Destinations*. Philadelphia: Temple University Press, 1977.

Goldin, Claudia. "Family Strategies and the Family Economy in the Late Nine-teenth Century: The Role of Secondary Workers." In *Philadelphia: Work, Space, Family, and Group Experience in the Nineteenth Century*, ed. Theodore Hershberg, pp. 277-310. New York: Oxford University Press, 1981.

Gonzales, Nancy. *Black Carib Households: A Study of Migration and Moderniza-tion*. Seattle: University of Washington Press, 1970.

Goode, William. *World Revolution and Family Patterns*. New York: Free Press, 1963.

Goody, Jack. "Inheritance, Property and Women." In *Family and Inheritance*, ed. Jack Goody, Joan Thirsk, and E. P. Thompson, pp. 10-36. Cambridge: Cam-bridge University Press, 1976.

——. *Production and Reproduction*. London: Cambridge University Press, 1976.

Gordon, Linda. *Heroes of Their Own Lives: The Polticis and History of Family Violence in Boston, 1880-1960*. New York: Viking Press, 1988.

Gordon, Linda, ed. *Women, the State, and Welfare*. Madison: University of Wis-consin Press, 1990.

Gordon, Milton. *Assimilation in American Life*. New York: Free Press, 1965.

Greeley, Andrew, and William C. McCrowley. "The Transmission of Cultural Heritage: The Case of the Irish and Italians." In *Ethnicity, Theory and Experi-ence*, ed. Nathan Glazer and Daniel P. Moynihan, pp. 209-35. Cambridge: Harvard University Press, 1975.

Greenwald, Maurine Weiner. "Working Class Feminism and the Family Wage Ideal: The Seattle Debate on Married Women's Right to Work, 1914-1920." *Journal of American History* 76 (June 1989): 118-49.

Griffen, Clyde. "Occupational Mobility in Nineteenth Century America: Prob-lems and Possibilities." *Journal of Social History* 5 (Spring 1972): 310-30.

Groneman, Carol. "Working Class Women in Mid-Nineteenth Century New York: The Irish Women's Experience." In *Class, Sex, and the Woman Worker*, ed. Milton Cantor and Bruce Laurie, pp. 83-100. Westport, Conn: Greenwood Press, 1977.

Gutman, Herbert. "Work, Culture and Society in Industrializing America." *Amer-ican Historical Review* 78 (June 1973): 531-88.

Habbukuk, H. J. "Family Structure and Economic Change." *Journal of Economic History* 15 (1955): 1-12.

Hajnal, John. "Age of Marriage and Proportions Marrying." *Population Studies* (November 1953): 111-36.

Handlin, Oscar. *The Uprooted*. Boston: Little Brown, 1951.

Hansen, Marcus Lee. *The Immigrant in American History*. Cambridge: Harvard University Press, 1948.

Hannerz, Ulf. "Ethnicity and Opportunity in Urban America." In Abner Cohen, ed., *Urban Ethnicity*, pp. 37–76. London: Tavistock, 1974.

Hareven, Tamara K. "Family Time and Industrial Time: Family and Work in a Planned Corporation Town, 1900–1924." *Journal of Urban History* 1 (May 1973): 365–89.

——. "The Laborers of Manchester, New Hampshire, 1912–1925: The Role of Family and Ethnicity in Adjustment to American Life." *Labor History* 14 (1975): 249–65.

Hareven, Tamara K., and Maris A. Vinovskis. "Marital Fertility, Ethnicity and Occupations in Urban Families: An Analysis of South Boston and South End in 1880," *Journal of Social History* 8 (Spring 1975): 69–93.

Hartmann, Heidi. "The Family as the Locus of Gender, Class and Political Struggle: The Example of Housework." *Signs* 6 (Spring 1981): 366–94.

Heinze, Andrew. *Adapting to Abundance: Jewish Immigrants, Mass Consumption, and the Search for American Identity.* New York: Columbia University Press, 1990.

Hewitt, Nancy. "Beyond the Search for Sisterhood: American Women's History in the 1980's." In *Unequal Sisters: A Multicultural Reader in U.S. Women's History*, ed. Ellen Carol DuBois and Vicki Ruiz, pp. 1–14. New York: Routledge, Chapman and Hall, 1990.

Howe, Irving. *World of Our Fathers.* New York: Harcourt, Brace and Jovanovich, 1976.

Howe, Louise Kapp. *Pink Collar Workers.* New York: Putnam's Sons, 1977.

Iorizzo, Luciano, and Salvatore Mondello. *The Italian Americans.* New York: Twayne Publishers, 1971.

Jacoby, Susan. "What Do I Do for the Next Twenty Years?" *New York Times Magazine* (17 June 1973), p. 10.

Jencks, Christopher. *Inequality: A Reassessment of the Effects of Family and Schooling in America.* New York: Basic Books, 1972.

Johnson, Eleanor Hope. "Social Service and the Public Schools." *The Survey* 30 (May 3, 1913): 173–82.

Jones, Jacqueline. *Labor of Love, Labor of Sorrow: Black Women, Work and the Family from Slavery to the Present.* New York: Basic Books, 1985.

Kantor, Harvey, and David B. Tyack, eds. *Work, Youth and Schooling.* Stanford, Calif.: Stanford University Press, 1982.

Katz, Michael. *Class, Bureaucracy and the Schools.* New York: Praeger, 1971.

——. *The Irony of Early School Reform.* Cambridge: Harvard University Press, 1968.

——. "Occupational Classification in History." *Journal of Interdisciplinary History* 3 (Summer 1972): 63–68.

Katz, Michael, and Ian Davey. "Youth and Early Industrialization in a Canadian City." In John Demos and Sarane Spence Boocock, eds., *Turning Points: His-*

torical and Sociological Essays on the Family, pp. S81–119. Chicago: University of Chicago Press, 1978.

Katz, Michael, and Mark Stern. "Fertility, Class, and Industrial Capitalism: Erie County, New York, 1855–1915." *American Quarterly* 33 (Spring 1981): 63–92.

Katz, Michael B., Michael Doucet, and Mark J. Stern. *The Social Organization of Early Industrial Capitalism*. Cambridge: Harvard University Press, 1982.

Kelly-Gadol, Joan. "Family and Society." In Joan Kelly-Gadol, ed., *Women, History and Theory*, pp. 110–55. Chicago: University of Chicago Press, 1984.

Kerber, Linda. "Separate Spheres, Female Worlds, Woman's Place: The Rhetoric of Women's History." *Journal of American History* 75 (June 1988): 9–39.

Kerblay, Basile. "Chayanov and the Theory of the Peasant Economy as a Specific Type of Economy." In Theodore Shanin, ed., *Peasants and Peasant Society*, pp. 150–60. London: Penguin, 1971.

Kessler-Harris, Alice. "Equal Opportunity Employment Commission v. Sears, Roebuck and Company: A Personal Account." *Radical History Review* 35 (1986): 57–79.

——. "Organizing the Unorganizable: Three Jewish Women and Their Union." *Labor History* 17 (Winter 1976): 5–23.

——. "Where Are the Organized Women Workers?" *Feminist Studies* 3 (Fall 1975): 92–110.

Kessner, Thomas. *The Golden Door: Italian and Jewish Immigrant Mobility in New York City, 1880–1915*. New York: Oxford University Press, 1977.

Kett, Joseph F. *Rites of Passage*. New York: Basic Books, 1977.

Klaczynska, Barbara. "Why Women Work—A Comparison of Various Groups—Philadelphia, 1910–1930." *Labor History* 17 (Winter 1976): 73–87.

Klein, Herbert. "The Integration of Italian Immigrants into Argentina and the United States: A Comparative Analysis." *American Historical Review* 88 (April 1983): 306–29.

Kleinberg, Susan J. "The Systematic Study of Urban Women." In Milton Cantor and Bruce Laurie, eds., *Class, Sex, and the Woman Worker*, pp. 20–42. Westport, Conn: Greenwood Press, 1977.

——. "Technology and Women's Work: The Lives of Working Class Women in Pittsburgh, 1870–1910." *Labor History* 17 (Winter 1976): 58–72.

Klepper, Paul. *The Bureau of Attendance and Child Welfare of the New York City School System*. New York: New York Attendance Bureau, 1915. Reprinted in *Education Review*, November 1915.

Komarovsky, Mirra. *Blue Collar Marriage*. New York: Random House, 1964.

Krause, Corinne A. "Urbanization without Breakdown: Italian, Jewish and Slavic Immigrant Women in Pittsburgh, 1900–1945." *Journal of Urban History* 4 (May 1978): 291–306.

Lamphere, Louise. *From Working Daughters to Working Mothers: Immigrant*

Women in a New England Industrial Community. Ithaca, N.Y.: Cornell University Press, 1987.

——. "Strategies, Cooperation and Conflict among Women in Domestic Groups." In Michelle Rosaldo and Louise Lamphere, eds., *Woman, Culture and Society*, pp. 97–112. Stanford, Calif.: Stanford University Press, 1974.

Landes, William M., and Lewis C. Colman. "Compulsory Schooling Legislation: An Economic Analysis of Law and Social Change in the Nineteenth Century." *Journal of Economic History* 32 (March 1972): 54–91.

Langer, Elinor. "Inside the New York Telephone Company." In William O'Neill, ed., *Women at Work*. pp. 307–60. Chicago: Quadrangle Books, 1972.

Lasch, Christopher. *Haven in a Heartless World*. New York: Basic Books, 1977.

Leuchtenburg, William E. *Franklin D. Roosevelt and the New Deal*. New York: Harper and Row, 1963.

Levi, Carlo. *Christ Stopped at Eboli*. New York: Farrar, Straus, 1947.

Levine, Louis. *The Women's Garment Workers*. New York: International Ladies Garment Workers Union, B. W. Huebsch, 1924.

Lindquist, Russell, and Donald K. Smith. "Industrial Homework." *Minnesota Law Review* 29 (1944–45): 295–317.

Livi-Bacci, Massimo. *A History of Italian Fertility during the Last Two Centuries*. Princeton, N.J.: Princeton University Press, 1977.

——. *L'Immigrazione et l'Assimilazione degli Italiani negli Stati Uniti*. Milan: Dot. A. Giuffrè, 1961.

Loft, Jacob. "Jewish Workers in the New York City Men's Clothing Industry." *Jewish Social Studies* 2 (January 1940): 61–77.

Lopreato, Joseph. *Italian Americans*. New York: Random House, 1970.

MacDonald, J. S. "Some Socio-Economic Emigration Differentials in Rural Italy, 1902–1913." *Economic Development and Cultural Change* 7 (1958): 61–75.

MacDonald, John S., and Leatrice MacDonald. "Institutional Economics and Rural Development: Two Italian Types." *Human Organization* (Summer 1974): 113–18.

McLaughlin. *See* Yans-McLaughlin.

Maller, J. B. "Vital Indices and Their Relation to Psychological and Social Factors." *Human Biology* 5 (February 1933): 94–121.

Martha, Donald. "Wage, Hour and Child Labor Legislation in the Roosevelt Administration." *Lawyers Guild Review* 5:3 (1945): 185–91.

Mason, Karen Oppenheim, Maris A. Vinovskis, and Tamara K. Hareven. "Women's Work and the Life Course in Essex County, Massachusetts, 1880." In Tamara K. Hareven and Maris A. Vinovskis, eds., *Transitions: The Family and the Life Course in Historical Perspective*, pp. 187–216. New York: Academic Press, 1978.

May, Martha. "The Historical Problem of the Family Wage: The Ford Motor Company and the Five Dollar Day." *Feminist Studies* 8 (Summer 1982): 55–77.

Mendelsohn, Ezra. *Class Struggle in the Pale; The Formative Years of the Jewish*

Workers' Movement in Tsarist Russia. New York: Cambridge University Press, 1970.

Milkman, Ruth. "Women's Work and Economic Crisis: Some Lessons from the Great Depression." In Nancy F. Cott and Elizabeth H. Pleck, eds., *A Heritage of Her Own: Toward a New Social History of American Women*, pp. 507–41. New York: Simon and Schuster, 1979.

Milkman, Ruth, ed. *Women, Work and Protest: A Century of U.S. Women's Labor History*. Boston: Routledge and Kegan Paul, 1985.

Model, Suzanne W. "The Effects of Ethnicity in the Work Place on Blacks, Italians, and Jews in New York." Center for Studies of Social Change, New School for Social Research, Working Papers Series no. 7. March 1985.

——. "Work and Family: Blacks and Immigrants from South and East Europe." In Virginia Yans-McLaughlin, ed., *Immigration Reconsidered: History, Sociology, and Politics*, pp. 130–59. New York: Oxford University Press, 1990.

Modell, John. "Patterns of Consumption, Acculturation and Family Income Strategies in Late Nineteenth-Century America." In Tamara K. Hareven and Maris Vinovskis, eds., *Family and Population in Nineteenth-Century America*, pp. 206–240. Princeton, N.J.: Princeton University Press, 1978.

Modell, John, Furstenberg, Frank, and Theodore Hershberg. "Social Change and Transitions to Adulthood in Historical Perspective." In *Philadelphia: Work, Space, Family and Group Experience in a Nineteenth-Century City*, ed. Theodore Hershberg, pp. 311–41. New York: Oxford University Press, 1981.

Modell, John, and Tamara K. Hareven. "Urbanization and the Malleable Household: An Enumeration of Boarding and Lodging in American Families." *Journal of Marriage and the Family* 35 (August 1973): 467–79.

More, Louise Bolard. *Wage Earners' Budgets: A Study of Standards and Cost of Living in New York City*. New York: Henry Holt, 1907.

Mormino, Gary Ross. *Immigrants on the Hill: Italian-Americans in St. Louis, 1882–1982*. Urbana: University of Illinois Press, 1986.

Moss, Leonard W., and Walter H. Thompson. "The South Italian Family: Literature and Observation." *Human Organization* 18 (Spring 1957): 35–41.

Murdoch, Katharine. "A Study of Race Differences in New York City." *School and Society* 11 (31 January 1920): 147–50.

Musmanno, Michael. *The Story of the Italians in America*. Garden City, N.Y.: Doubleday, 1965.

Nelli, Humbert. *Italians in Chicago, 1880–1914*. New York: Oxford University Press, 1970.

Nerlove, Marc. "Toward a New Theory of Population and Economic Growth." In Theodore Schultz, ed., *Economics of the Family, Marriage, Children, and Human Capital*, pp. 527–45. Chicago: University of Chicago Press, 1974.

Olneck, Michael, and Marvin Lazerson. "The School Achievement of Immigrant Children, 1900–1930." *History of Education Quarterly* 14 (Winter 1974): 454–82.

Oppenheimer, Valerie Kincaid. "Demographic Influence on Female Employment and the Status of Women." *American Journal of Sociology* 78 (1973): 946–61.
———. *The Female Labor Force in the United States*. Population Monograph Series no. 5. Westport, Conn.: Greenwood Press, 1970.
Orsi, Robert. *The Madonna of 115th Street: Faith and Community in Italian Harlem, 1880–1950*. New Haven: Yale University Press, 1985.
Panunzio, Constantine. *The Soul of an Immigrant*. 1921; reprint, New York: Arno Press, 1969.
Park, Robert. "The City: Suggestions for the Investigation of Human Behavior in the Urban Environment." In Richard Sennett, ed., *Classic Essays on the Culture of the Cities*, pp. 91–130. New York: Appleton Century Crofts, 1969.
Park, Robert, and Herbert Miller. *Old World Traits Transplanted*. New York: Harper and Brothers, 1921.
Peiss, Kathy. *Cheap Amusements: Working Women and Leisure in Turn-of-the-Century New York*. Philadelphia: Temple University Press, 1986.
Perceroni, Albert. "The Italians in the United States." *Forum* 45 (January 1911): 15–59. Reprinted in Francesco Cordasco and Eugene Bucchioni, eds., *The Italians: Social Background of an American Group*. Clifton, N.J.: Augustus M. Kelley, 1974.
Perlmann, Joel. "After Leaving School: The Jobs of Young People in Providence, R.I., 1880–1915." In Richard K. Goodenow and Diane Ravitch, eds., *Schools in Cities: Consensus and Conflict in American Educational History*, pp. 1–14. New York: Holmes and Meier, 1983.
Peters, Iva, and Lorine Pruette. *Women Workers through the Depression*. New York: Macmillan, 1934.
Pisani, Laurence. *The Italians in America*. New York: Exposition Press, 1957.
Pitkin, Donald. "Land Tenure and Family Organization in an Italian Village." *Human Organization* 18 (Winter 1958–59): 169–73.
Pleck, Elizabeth. "A Mother's Wages: A Comparison of Income-Earning Among Urban Black and Italian Married Women, 1896–1911." In Michael Gordon, ed., *The American Family in Socio-Historical Perspective*, pp. 490–510. 2d ed. New York: St. Martin's Press, 1978.
———. "Two Worlds in One: Work and Family." *Journal of Social History* 10 (Winter 1976): 178–95.
Puzo, Mario. *The Fortunate Pilgrim*. New York: Atheneum, 1965.
Redfield, Robert. "The Folk Society." In Richard Sennett, ed., *Classic Essays on the Culture of Cities*, pp. 180–205. New York: Appleton Century Crofts, 1969.
Reed, Dorothy. *The Leisure Time of Girls in a Little Italy*. Portland, Ore.: privately published, 1911.
Rischin, Moses. *The Promised Land: New York's Jews, 1870–1914*. Cambridge: Harvard University Press, 1962.
Rogers, Susan. "Female Forms of Power and the Myth of Male Dominance: A Model of Female/Male Interaction in Peasant Society." *American Ethnologist* 2 (1975): 727–56.

Rosaldo, Michelle. "The Use and Abuse of Anthropology: Reflections on Feminism and Cross-Cultural Understanding." *Signs* 5 (Spring 1980): 389–417.

——. "Women, Culture and Society: A Theoretical Overview." In Michelle Rosaldo and Louise Lamphere, eds. *Woman, Culture and Society*, pp. 17–42. Stanford, Calif.: Stanford University Press, 1974.

Rosenwaike, Ira. *Population History of New York City.* Syracuse, N.Y.: Syracuse University Press, 1972.

——. "Two Generations of Italians in America: Their Fertility Experience." *International Migration Review* 7 (Fall 1973): 271–80.

Rozensweig, Roy. *Eight Hours for What We Will: Workers and Leisure in an Industrial City, 1870–1920.* New York: Cambridge University Press, 1983.

Ryan, Joseph A., ed. *White Ethnics.* Englewood Cliffs, N.J.: Prentice-Hall, 1973.

Ryan, Mary. *Cradle of the Middle Class: The Family in Oneida County, NY, 1790–1865.* New York: Cambridge University Press, 1981.

Schlesinger, Arthur, Jr. *The Age of Roosevelt*, vol. 3: *The Politics of Upheaval.* Boston: Houghton Mifflin, 1960.

Schneider, Jane. "Of Vigilance and Virgins: Honor, Shame and Access to Resources in Mediterranean Societies." *Ethnology* 10 (January 1971): 1–24.

Schneider, Jane, and Peter Schneider. *Culture and Political Economy in Western Sicily.* New York: Academic Press, 1976.

Schultz, Theodore, ed. *Economics of the Family, Marriage, Children and Human Capital.* Chicago: University of Chicago Press, 1974.

Scott, Joan, and Louise Tilly. "Women's Work and the Family in Nineteenth Century Europe." *Comparative Studies in Society and History* 17 (January 1975): 36–64.

Seago, Dorothy Wilson, and Theresa Shulkin Kolden. "A Comparative Study of the Mental Capacity of Sixth Grade Jewish and Italian Children." *School and Society* 22 (31 October 1925): 564–68.

Seidman, Joel. *The Needle Trades.* New York: Farrar and Rineharts, 1942.

Sen, Amartya. "Economics and the Family." *Asian Development Review* 1 (1983): 14–26.

Sergeant, Elizabeth Shipley. "Toilers of the Tenements: Where the Beautiful Things of the Great Shops Are Made." *McClure's* 35 (July 1910): 231–48.

Shaw, Adele Marie. "The True Character of New York Public Schools." *World's Work* 7 (December 1903): 4215–17.

Silverman, Sydel F. "Agricultural Organization, Social Structure and Values in Italy: Amoral Familism Reconsidered." *American Anthropologist* 70 (1968): 1–20.

——. "Life Crisis as a Clue to Social Functions." *Anthropological Quarterly* 40 (1967): 127–38.

Simmel, George. "The Metropolis and Mental Life." In Richard Sennett, ed., *Classic Essays on the Culture of the Cities*, pp. 47–60. New York: Appleton Century Crofts, 1969.

Smith, Judith. *Family Connections: A History of Italian and Jewish Immigrant Lives in Providence, Rhode Island, 1900–1940.* Albany: State University of New York Press, 1985.

——. "Our Own Kind: Family and Community Networks in Providence." In Nancy F. Cott and Elizabeth H. Pleck, eds., *A Heritage of Her Own: Toward a New Social History of American Women*, pp. 393–411. New York: Simon and Schuster, 1979.

Spadoni, Adriani. "The Italian Working Woman in New York." *Collier's* 49 (March 1912): 14–16.

Spring, Joel. *Education and the Rise of the Corporate State.* Boston: Beacon Press, 1972.

Stack, Carol B. *All Our Kin: Strategies for Survival in a Black Community.* New York: Harper and Row, 1974.

Stambler, Moses. "The Effect of Compulsory Education and Child Labor Laws on High School Attendance in New York City, 1898–1917." *History of Education Quarterly* 8 (Summer 1968): 189–214.

Steinberg, Stephen. *The Ethnic Myth: Race, Ethnicity and Class in America.* New York: Atheneum, 1981.

Stinchcombe, Arthur I. *Rebellion in a High School.* Chicago: Quadrangle Books, 1964.

Stone, Elizabeth. "It's Still Hard to Grow Up Italian." *New York Times Magazine,* 17 December 1978, p. 42.

Tentler, Leslie Woodcock. *Wage-Earning Women: Industrial Work and Family Life in the United States, 1900–1930.* New York: Oxford University Press, 1979.

Thernstrom, Stephan. *The Other Bostonians: Poverty and Progress in the American Metropolis, 1880–1970.* Cambridge: Harvard University Press, 1973.

Thompson, Edward P. "Happy Families." *New Society* 8 (September 1977): 499–501.

Tilly, Charles. "Did the Cake of Custom Break?" In John Merriman, ed., *Consciousness and Class Experience in Nineteenth-Century Europe*, pp. 17–44. London: Holmes and Meier, 1979.

——. "Population and Pedagogy in France." *History of Education Quarterly* 13 (1973): 113–28.

Tilly, Charles, and C. Harold Brown. "On Uprooting Kinship and the Auspices of Migration." *Journal of Contemporary Migration* 8 (September 1967): 139–64.

Tilly, Louise A. "Comments on the Yans-McLaughlin and Davidoff Papers." *Journal of Social History* 7 (Summer 1974): 452–59.

——. "Individual Lives and Family Strategies in the French Proletariat." *Journal of Family History* 4 (Summer 1979): 137–52.

——. "Urban Growth, Industrialization and Women's Employment in Milan, Italy, 1881–1911." *Journal of Urban History* 3 (August 1977): 467–84.

Tilly, Louise, and Miriam Cohen. "Does the Family Have a History?" *Social Science History* 6 (Spring 1982): 131–79.

Tilly, Louise, and Joan Scott. *Women, Work and Family.* New York: Holt Rinehart and Winston, 1978.

Tilly, Louise, Joan Scott, and Miriam Cohen. "Women's Work and European Fertility Patterns." *Journal of Interdisciplinary History* 6 (Winter 1976): 447–76.

Tomasi, Lydio. *The Italian-American Family: The Southern Italian Family's Process of Adjustment to Urban America.* Staten Island, N.Y.: Center for Migration Studies, 1973.

Trattner, Walter J. *Crusade for the Children.* Chicago: Quadrangle Books, 1970.

Turbin, Carole. "And We are Nothing but Women: Irish Working Women in Troy." In Carole Berkin and Mary Beth Norton, eds., *Women of America: A History,* pp. 202–20. Boston: Houghton Mifflin, 1979.

——. "Beyond Dichotomies: Interdependence in Mid-Nineteenth Century Working-Class Families in the United States." *Gender and History* 1 (Autumn 1989): 293–312.

Vecoli, Rudolph. "Contadini in Chicago: A Critique of The Uprooted." *Journal of American History* 51 (December 1964): 404–17.

——. "Le fonti americane per lo studio dell'immigrazione italiana." In Symposium de Studi Americani 3rd 1969, Florence [Rudolph Vecoli, ed.], *Gli Italiani negli Stati Uniti,* pp. 1–24. Florence: Istituto di studi americani, Università degli studi, 1972.

——. "Prelates and Peasants: Italian Immigrants and the Catholic Church." *Journal of Social History* 2 (Spring 1969): 217–68.

Ware, Caroline. *Greenwich Village, 1920–1930.* Boston: Houghton Mifflin, 1935.

Ware, Susan. *Holding Their Own: American Women in the 1930's.* Boston: Twayne Publishers, 1982.

Warner, W. Lloyd, and Leo Srole. *Social Systems of American Ethnic Groups, Yankee City,* vol. 3. New Haven: Yale University Press, 1943.

Weber, Max. *The City,* trans. Don Martindale and Gertrud Neuwirth. New York: Free Press, 1958.

Webster, Janice Reiff. "Domestication and Americanization: Scandinavian Women in Seattle, 1888–1900." *Journal of Urban History* 4 (May 1978): 275–90.

Weinberg, Sydney Stahl. *World of Our Mothers: The Lives of Jewish Immigrant Women.* Chapel Hill: University of North Carolina Press, 1988.

Weld, Ralph Foster. *Brooklyn Is America.* New York: Columbia University Press, 1950.

Welfare and Health Council of New York, Research Bureau. *Characteristics of the Population by Health Areas, New York City, 1950.* New York: Research Bureau, 1953.

Westwood, Sallie. *All Day , Every Day: Factory and Family in the Making of Women's Lives.* Urbana: University of Illinois Press, 1985.

White, Henry. "Perils of the Home Factory." *Harper's Weekly* 55 (February 11, 1911): 10.

Whyte, William. *Street Corner Society.* Chicago: University of Chicago Press, 1943.

Wiehl, Dorothy. "The Diets of Low Income Families in New York City." *Milbank*

Memorial Fund Quarterly 11 (October 1933): 308–24.

Williams, Phyliss. *South Italian Folkways in Europe and America: A Handbook for Social Workers, Visiting Nurses, School Teachers and Physicians*. New Haven: Yale University Press, 1938.

Williams, Raymond. "Base and Superstructure in Marxist Cultural Theory." *New Left Review* 82 (November–December 1973): 3–16.

Wilson, William Julius. *The Truly Disadvantaged: The Inner City, the Underclass, and Public Policy*. Chicago: University of Chicago Press, 1987.

Winsey, Rossilli Valentine. "The Italian-American Woman Worker in the United States before World War I." In Francesco Cordasco, ed., *Studies in Honor of Leonard Covello*, pp. 199–210. Trenton, N.J.: Rowman and Littlefield, 1975.

Wirth, Louis. "Urbanism as a Way of Life." In Richard Sennett, ed., *Classic Essays on the Culture of Cities*, pp. 143–79. New York: Appleton Century Crofts, 1969.

Wolf, Eric. *Peasants*. New York: Prentice-Hall, 1966.

——. "Types of Latin American Peasantry: A Preliminary Discussion." *American Anthropologist* 57 (1955): 452–71.

Wrigley, E. A. "Fertility Strategy for the Individual and the Group." In Charles Tilly, ed., *Historical Studies of Changing Fertility*, pp. 135–54. Princeton, N.J.: Princeton University Press, 1978.

——. *Population and History*. New York: McGraw-Hill, 1969.

Yans-McLaughlin, Virginia. *Family and Community: Italian Immigrants in Buffalo 1880–1930*. Ithaca, N.Y.: Cornell University Press, 1977.

——. "A Flexible Tradition: Southern Italian Immigrants Confront a New York Experience." *Journal of Social History* 10 (Summer 1974): 429–45.

——. "Patterns of Work and Family Organization: Buffalo's Italians." *Journal of Interdisciplinary History* 2 (Autumn 1971): 299–314.

——. ed. *Immigration Reconsidered: History, Sociology, and Politics*. New York: Oxford University Press, 1990.

Young, Michael, and Peter Wilmott. *Family and Kinship in East London*. London: Routledge and Kegan Paul, 1957.

Zimmerman, Joan G. "The Jurisprudence of Equality: The Women's Minimum Wage, the First Equal Rights Amendment, and Adkins v. Children's Hospital, 1905–1923." *Journal of American History* 78 (June 1991): 188–215.

Unpublished Papers, Dissertations

Berrol, Selma. "Immigrants at School." Ph.D. dissertation, City University of New York, 1967.

Concistre, Marie J. "Adult Education in a Local Area: A Study of a Decade in the Life and Education of the Adult Italian Immigrant in East Harlem, New York City." Ph.D. dissertation, New York University, 1943.

Davey, Ian. "The Rhythm of Work and Rhythm of School, Hamilton, Ontario in the Nineteenth Century." Unpublished paper, 1977(?).

Gabaccia, Donna R. "Houses and People: Sicilians in Sicily and New York, 1890–1930." Ph.D. dissertation, University of Michigan, 1979.

Maynes, Mary Jo. "Boys and Girls Together: Family and Education in Early Modern France and Germany." Unpublished paper, Ann Arbor, Mich., 1976.

Strom, Sharon Hartman. "Italian American Women and Their Daughters in Rhode Island: The Adolescents of Two Generations, 1900–1950." Unpublished paper, Providence, 1977.

Valles, Anne. "Miss America Takes Shorthand: Job Manuals and the Changing World of Women and Work, 1900–55." Senior thesis, Vassar College, 1979.

Woods, Theresa. "Family and Community, Kingston, New York." Term paper, Vassar College, 1978.

INDEX